The History
of the Reign
# of King Henry
the Seventh

Francis Bacon

THE EUROPEAN HISTORIOGRAPHY SERIES
F. J. Levy, General Editor

The History of the Reign of King Henry the Seventh

Francis Bacon

Edited by
F. J. Levy

THE BOBBS-MERRILL COMPANY, INC.
INDIANAPOLIS · NEW YORK

Copyright © 1972 by The Bobbs-Merrill Company, Inc.
Printed in the United States of America
Library of Congress Catalog Card Number 70-177471
First Printing
Designed by Anita Duncan

Foreword

Historians, at their best, are problem-solvers. Sometimes the problems appear simple: "What happened?" At other times, they may be much more difficult: "Why did it happen this way and not another? Why did it happen this year and not earlier or later?" Or, at the highest level of abstraction, a historian may ask: "Is there a pattern in human events? Are there laws of history?" Sometimes a historian's answers to problems are accepted by all, or almost all of his successors. More commonly, later generations, while rejecting their predecessors' answers to specific questions, nonetheless adopt (or adapt) the method used to seek out such answers.

The student of historiography, therefore, is interested primarily in the methods previous historians have used to attain their results. To conduct his own investigation, he needs to remember that any historian is influenced by his predecessors as well as by his contemporaries; that is, there is a tradition of historical writing to which historians are heir while, at the same time, the intellectual life of their own day plays its part in forming their outlook. Gibbon was the product of seventeenth-century erudition as well as of eighteenth-century rationalism. In one sense, the study of historiography is part of the more general study of intellectual history; in another, it is the study of a tradition of historical writing which, while not independent of more general currents of ideas, may nonetheless be isolated for a detailed examination.

Thus, the study of historiography serves to remind us to accept our predecessors only after due criticism. We must ask: "Why was that problem investigated? Why was that method chosen?" before we decide if the results are correct or incorrect, stimulating or barren. Similarly, the study of historiography reminds us as historians that we are part of the subject we profess, just as our predecessors have always been. There is no way a western historian can escape from the tradition of European historiography. Finally, if there is a distinctly historical mode of thought—as I am convinced there is—then it can do us only good to examine how that mode grew and developed, how it may be used and misused.

"Historical thinking is more than historical knowledge." Lord Acton's dictum might serve as our motto. The European Historiography Series has been designed to make texts available for those whose primary interest is in historical thought. The purpose of each volume is to present an historian in as much detail as is necessary to understand how he undertakes to solve historical problems. Where they exist, the historian's own pronouncements concerning his historical method will be printed; but practice will always be tested against theory, and narrative will not be ignored. Where possible, texts will be printed in their entirety; where a text proves too long, it will be abbreviated in such a way as to present to the reader the most accurate possible portrait of the historian.

The portrait of Francis Bacon which follows must, inevitably, be colored by the fact that Bacon came to history only after he had already developed a philosophy that encompassed the whole of creation. Bacon, more than most, could see men and their activities *sub specie aeternitatis;* yet Bacon was a politician as ardently as he was a scientist, and he attempted to combine the two points of view in his *History of Henry the Seventh.* In so doing, Bacon abandoned the providential view of the past which had characterized most of his immediate predecessors and had led them to see all human activity as a reflection of God's will. He replaced this by a new political history based on the work of Machiavelli and Guicciardini, the historians of Renaissance Florence; and, like them, he saw man's past actions as the raw materials for a science of politics. But Bacon was more than an English follower of the Italians: he insisted that the method of a political science based on historical examples was similar to the method of the natural sciences, and so produced a theoretical framework that linked politics and history and science together in one great scheme. In so doing he provided a justification for the new way of writing history similar to his justification for the new science: both would lead to the same result, man's greater understanding of himself and his world as a first step toward control, and amelioration. Thus Bacon went beyond his Italian masters by delineating a theory to justify the practice; and thereby he abandoned the cynicism so evident especially in Guicciardini and replaced it with a new optimism. History, properly thought through, would enable man to plan a better future. That was Bacon's vision, and in his *History of Henry the Seventh* he took the first steps toward showing how the vision might be attained.

Because of Bacon's great reputation, his account was accepted as the standard history of the reign for more than two centuries. Then, in the nineteenth century, Bacon was subjected to the new German source criticism, and it was discovered that his work was not a primary source for any factual information about Henry or his reign. The immediate result was a tendency to dismiss the *History* as worthless. That judgment entirely ignored the fact that Bacon's interpretation of Henry, and of Henry's reign, is still plausible even today, when much more information is available. And it ignored as well the fact that the *History* is an important document not only for our understanding of the history of historiography but also for our knowledge of the temper of Jacobean England.

F. J. Levy

Acknowledgments

The editor is grateful to his friends Professors Michael Kammen of Cornell University and Thomas Hankins of the University of Washington for their kindness in commenting on the introduction. Professor William Stoebuck of the Law School of the University of Washington clarified some points of legal history. Much of the material on which the introduction is based was accumulated during a summer in London for which thanks are due the Graduate School of the University of Washington and the Boies Penrose Fund of the American Philosophical Society.

Contents

Introduction

The young men who were born in the decades just preceding and just following the accession of Queen Elizabeth grew up in a world constantly balanced on the edge of calamity. Their fathers had persisted through a quarter-century of rapid and unpredictable change, years which had seen England become first non-Roman Catholic, then Protestant, then Roman Catholic, and finally Protestant once more. And, since politics was a function of religion, these years had seen the growth of monarchical power at home, at least in part as an answer to a constant threat of interference from abroad. The accession of the twenty-five-year-old Elizabeth in 1558 marked the triumph of Protestantism in England—but, of course, no one knew that at the time. Contemporaries—if they were Protestants—rejoiced at the new Queen's coming, but they were apprehensive as well. Elizabeth was young, unmarried, inexperienced—and a woman. A young woman could be dominated by the arrogant and powerful men who would throng to her court; she could marry unadvisedly (as her sister Mary Tudor had done); she could die, leaving Mary Stuart—a Catholic with strong pro-French sentiments—as heir.

The events of 1558 gave occasion for hope and for prayer; they did not augur certainty.

The men chosen by the young Queen as her advisors always felt the chill wind of change blowing down their spines. Most of them were not aristocrats and thus had neither established position nor inherited land to cushion any fall from the political heights. What lands they possessed had come to them as royal gifts, a part of the royal profits derived from the Reformation confiscations. Without their appointive positions, they were nonentities. If the Queen fell, they fell with her. Naturally, they were ambitious men, anxious, even greedy for themselves and their families. But they were also competent and well-trained servants, and their education had taught them that service to the crown was not merely profitable but was a duty as well. Sir Nicholas Bacon, Lord Keeper of the Great Seal, principal judicial officer of England, and father of Francis, was one of them.

Most of the Queen's servants had been exposed to the newly-imported concepts which we call humanism. Of the various strands making up that complex of ideas, only one concerns us: political humanism.[1] The new emphasis on the study of the

---

[1] I am introducing the term "political humanism" to call attention to a phenomenon similar to that called "civic humanism" by Professor Hans Baron in *The Crisis of the Early Italian Renaissance*, 2nd ed. (Princeton, 1966). Professor Baron, however, describes civic humanism in such a way as to make it appear appropriate only in the context of a republic. But even in Italy, there was something related to what Baron calls civic humanism, something that might be called the humanism of princely courts, and it was this humanism that came to England through books such as Castiglione's *Courtier*. Erasmus introduced somewhat similar ideas, and these were adapted by men like John Colet and worked into the very foundations of the revived English grammar school system. Because of its Erasmian component, the political humanism of sixteenth-century England had a strong moral, Christian tone; the aim of the educational system based on it was to produce a Christian statesman, that is, the Christian servant of a Christian prince. To call this "courtier humanism" would be a little misleading; I prefer the somewhat more neutral "political humanism."

ancient, and especially the Latin, classics had encouraged men to mold their lives on the pattern of the noble Romans. St. Augustine, who had rejected the active life of the typical Roman patrician for the contemplation of the Christian, and St. Bernard, who had rejected a life in the world for one in the cloister, no longer served as models. Instead, men looked to Cicero or Seneca, who had combined worldly activity in politics with a contemplative retirement devoted to philosophy. No longer was the active life considered a second-best, to be resorted to by those unable or unwilling to seek retirement from mundane cares. Indeed, the active life supplied the materials for the contemplative. Philosophy became more and more a discussion of how men were to act when they came into contact with other men. Metaphysics was abandoned to the theologians; humanist philosophers concerned themselves with ethics and with politics.

Thus a young man such as Francis Bacon was early exposed to an ideal of political service:

> I ever bare a mind . . . to serve her Majesty; not as a man born under Sol, that loveth honour; nor under Jupiter, that loveth business (for the contemplative planet carrieth me away wholly); but as a man born under an excellent Sovereign, that deserveth the dedication of all men's abilities.[2]

For him, contemplation and withdrawal had a personal appeal, but it was an appeal which duty told him ought to be resisted. And the Puritanism of the Bacon family, especially that of his mother, merely underlined the same point. The Puritan ethic of love of God expressed through activity in this world, activity profitable for all men (instead of profitable only for the withdrawn saint), joined with the ethic of political humanism to force the young Bacon to try to make a career in the service of the Queen. The example of a much-admired father, the expectation that men had of this son of Sir Nicholas Bacon (whom the

[2] James Spedding, *The Letters and the Life of Francis Bacon*, 7 vols. (London: Longman, Green, Longman, and Roberts, 1861–1874), I, 108.

Queen had from his childhood called her little Lord Keeper), reinforced the teachings absorbed from his earliest youth.

Bacon was not the only one affected by this pattern of thought. A whole generation of Elizabethans—Sir Philip Sidney, Sir Walter Ralegh, Sir Fulke Greville—had been raised to believe that it was their duty to serve their Queen. Nor was this, in most cases, only a question of a theoretical teaching. Young Sidney had been sent on the Grand Tour, and then on diplomatic missions, to prepare him for his career; the young Ralegh had trained himself as a soldier on land and sea for much the same purpose; Greville served his apprenticeship in minor duties at court; and Francis Bacon, like the others, passed from the university to a kind of professional training suitable for a courtier. Since the family tradition was a legal one, Trinity College, Cambridge, was followed by a spell at the Inns of Court, and this in turn was succeeded by "apprenticeship" to Sir Amyas Paulet, ambassador at Paris.

During the stay in Paris young Francis's luck changed. Suddenly and unexpectedly, Lord Keeper Bacon died. He had been a wealthy man, but he had married twice: the eldest son of the first marriage inherited the family estates, other sons had been provided for, only Francis was not supplied with the means for continuing the career he had begun. Sir Nicholas had been about to make arrangements for his youngest—and favorite—son. Death intervened. Francis had to consider how he would earn a living. The high hopes, the expectations that he had and others had for him, would have to be deferred—unless, perhaps, his uncle would assume that burden of support. Francis's mother —Sir Nicholas' second wife—was sister to the wife of Lord Treasurer Burghley. But Burghley limited himself to giving sage advice. He was too busy making a place for his own younger son, Robert Cecil, and had no desire to encourage competition. Francis Bacon returned to the study of law.

Even without this setback, Bacon's career might not have been as smooth as he had hoped. The avenues toward advancement were gradually being blocked. When the first generation of humanist courtiers sought office, they had little difficulty in achieving it: their numbers were few and their services were much in demand. But the supply of well-trained men increased rapidly; and one result of this training was that they insisted on being allowed to serve the crown. Moreover, it had become clear that the road to wealth and position lay through governmental service, and that even relatively minor officials had been able to accumulate enough land to establish themselves as country gentlemen. Competition for court office thus was increasing rapidly, and was to continue to increase all through Francis Bacon's life and beyond. But by the time young Bacon himself first sought to enter the magic circle in the 1580s, a further complication had been introduced. As Queen Elizabeth grew older, she grew more and more conservative: she preferred to see the old faces around her Council board, she was unwilling to trust any young man with real responsibility. The Queen had no objection to having these eager youths about her—indeed she positively basked in the light of their admiration; but the employment she found for them was trivial. And when some of them went off on their own, they returned to find that the Queen, on whose favor everything depended, now frowned on them.

Thus the milieu in which Bacon had to make his way was acutely frustrating. Once it became clear that the Cecils (Lord Burghley and his son) would give him no assistance, Bacon sought a new patron. He found him in Robert Devereux, Earl of Essex, a man a few years younger even than himself, but a man whose ability and good looks had enabled him to succeed his stepfather, the Earl of Leicester, in the role of the Queen's favorite. An Elizabethan favorite, if he were to survive the intrigues at court, needed more than active intelligence and charm. He required a staff to feed him information, to sort out the play of personalities around the Queen, to perform the devious maneuverings through which everything was accomplished. And the favorite needed to establish working relationships with as many men in official positions as possible: he helped them by representing them at court, and they helped him by giving him access to the patronage on which any faction depended. Essex managed to recruit most of the young men who had once formed the circle

of Sir Philip Sidney before that paragon of Elizabethan virtues
had been killed in action against the Spanish in 1586. Essex himself had been bequeathed Sidney's sword; he married Sidney's
widow; and he thought of himself as the heir to Sidney's martial,
anti-Spanish views.

It is difficult to say just how disillusioned Sidney had become before his early death, but there is no doubt that in the
years after 1586, some of his friends, like Fulke Greville, were
beginning to have serious qualms about their chances of advancement, and were setting about transforming this personal
view into a more general analysis of society. What had once
seemed an open society was rapidly taking on the aspect of a
closed one. Or, to look at it in terms of appropriate classical
models—and such analogies were a favorite Elizabethan form of
argument—the relevant comparison was not that between England and Republican Rome but between England and the Rome
of the Emperors. The historian who proved most illuminating, in
terms of his convertibility into the contemporary idiom, was
Tacitus, the recorder of empire and the struggle against it, not
Livy, the encomiast of republican virtue. Or, if one preferred to
read modern historians for the light they could throw on the situation faced by these late Elizabethans, then Machiavelli and
Guicciardini were the obvious choices. These were the historians
who wrote about the realities of power politics, who rejected the
argument that history taught morality or illustrated ideals, but
used history instead to teach men how to advance themselves.
Sidney himself had read deeply in these men and, though he did
not adopt their ideas completely, nevertheless he placed the illus-
tration of ethical teaching firmly in the fictive realm of poetry,
rather than in that of history. About the value remaining to
history, Sidney was less sure, at least in his theoretical work; in
his practice, he made use of Machiavelli's model.

Francis Bacon had not been one of the followers of Sidney,
but on his entry into Essex's service, he soon found himself in
constant communication with men who had been in the Sidney
circle. For a time, he and Fulke Greville, Sidney's friend and
biographer, both lived in Essex House; he communicated with
Sir Henry Savile, the translator of Tacitus; he had occasion

enough to see Henry Cuffe, once professor of Greek at Oxford and center of a group of men reading Tacitus, now one of Essex's secretaries. At the same time, Bacon became one of the Earl's principal advisors, and thus could compare the theory with the practice of politics. One result was the publication of Bacon's first work, the *Essays,* in 1597. Essays with titles such as "Suitors," "Of Faction," "Of Negociating," testify to Bacon's interest in the mechanics of politics; and, like most of his works, the essays were didactic, the subject taught being the very practical one of how to get ahead in this world.

Yet one wonders whether Bacon was quite the right teacher of the subtle art of self-advancement. His association with Essex had not done for him what he had hoped. Partly, it was his own fault: by opposing the government on the question of the collection of extraordinary taxes, he had alienated the Queen. Even Essex was unable to advance Bacon for some years after that contretemps, though he tried to obtain for his friend the positions first of Attorney-General, then of Solicitor-General. By the time the Queen was prepared once more to have Bacon around the court, Essex's own behavior had become so irrationally arrogant that an association with him did more harm than good. At the time of Elizabeth's death, Bacon's fortune consisted of an appointment as Queen's counsel (without pay) and a reversion to the lucrative post of clerk of the Privy Council (worthless until the present clerk died, which he obstinately refused to do). Bacon had access to the Queen but was altogether unable to turn that privilege to account. The Cecils always stood in his path; his own high estimate of his virtues was a little too obvious and thus unpalatable; and Essex somehow managed to do his friends little real good.

For Essex, the interminable struggle at court grew too intense. The Earl had always suffered from inner confusion: he had been uncertain whether his career lay at court or in retirement, and whenever matters did not go his way, he was inclined to withdraw into solitude, an attitude which infuriated the Queen and left his enemies in victorious possession of the field of battle. Moreover, the Earl saw himself as a great military leader. Even if his estimate of himself had been correct (which is doubtful), a general could function only on the battlefield, which meant prolonged absences from Court. Bacon and Greville and others of the Earl's associates tried to convince him that the real battlefield, for one seeking to achieve political dominance, was at Court and in the Privy Council. The Earl refused to believe them, and his frustrations grew as, time after time, while he was away at the wars, the Cecils accomplished their ends at home.

Eventually, Essex forced his own appointment as Lord Lieutenant in Ireland where the Earl of Tyrone, with Spanish help, had held a series of Elizabeth's commanders at bay. Bacon had warned him against any involvement in Ireland: too many reputations had been lost there already. Essex went ahead and, like his predecessors, failed miserably. His return home, against the Queen's explicit orders, led to an investigation before the Privy Council. Bacon did what little he could to help, advised the Earl on how to regain favor, pleaded for him until his own credit with the Queen was in danger. Nothing helped. When Essex lost his monopoly of the sale of sweet wines—his major source of income—he turned desperate. Plans were laid for a *coup d'état* in which the Cecilians would be replaced by his own followers. But Bacon had nothing to do with these hopeless measures. He had always made it clear

> that I aspire to the conscience and commendation first of *bonus civis*, which with us is a good and true servant to the Queen, and next of *bonus vir*, that is an honest man. I desire your Lordship also to think that though I confess I love some things much better than I love your Lordship, as the Queen's service, her quiet and contentment, her honour, her favour, the good of my country, and the like, yet I love few persons better than yourself, both for gratitude's sake, and for your own virtues . . .[3]

Others of the Earl's followers shared this view. Fulke Greville and Robert Sidney (Sir Philip's younger brother) were among those who seized the rebellious Essex at his house; Bacon took a prominent part in the trial which ensued.

---

[3] Spedding, *Letters and Life*, II, 191

Bacon's actions at the time of Essex's downfall, because they exceeded the limits of mere formality, led even his contemporaries to level charges of ingratitude against him.[4] Essex had done his best for Bacon, sought offices for him, given him gifts; and in the end Bacon had turned against him. What else Bacon could have done is unclear; what is certain is that James, King of Scotland and heir to the throne of England, in whose interest the Essex conspirators claimed to be acting, shed his favor on the survivors of the revolt, and was not overly well-inclined to a man who owed much to Essex and repaid him by seeming treachery. Bacon's role in the Essex affair did little to improve his credit with the old Queen and it did him less good still in the eyes of the new King. And Robert Cecil, who became James's principal servant after 1603, was unlikely to do anything for his cousin. Those of the discontented who had hoped that a new monarch would give them a chance were to be disappointed as long as Cecil retained power. For a decade, Robert Cecil prolonged the atmosphere of the last years of Elizabeth. With all hope of political office gone, at least for the foreseeable future, Bacon turned once more to writing.

Up to 1603, Bacon had published only his *Essays;* he had also helped to compose some masques and entertainments. But in the intervals left him by his duties as lawyer and as advisor to Essex, he had not been idle. As long as public office was closed to him, Bacon was free to seek his other great goal of service to mankind, the reform of philosophy. Ever since his early youth he had known what was wrong with contemporary philosophy:

Whilst he was commorant [resident] in the university, about sixteen years of age, (as his lordship hath been pleased to impart unto

[4] Bacon's biographers, especially Macaulay, have made much of his ingratitude. The importance of the problem is questionable. My own opinion—without here rehearsing the debate, and without going into the background of the behavior expected of courtiers—is that the only way Bacon could have avoided attacking Essex would have been to succumb to a diplomatic illness.

myself), he first fell into the dislike of the philosophy of Aristotle; not for the worthlessness of the author, to whom he would ever ascribe all high attributes, but for the unfruitfulness of the way; being a philosophy (as his lordship used to say) only strong for disputations and contentions, but barren of the production of works for the benefit of the life of man; in which mind he continued to his dying day.[5]

Thus, Bacon needed to do two things to complete his program of reform: destroy the authority of Aristotle and those who thought like him—which meant most of the learned men of Europe; and establish a new and more fruitful philosophy to take the place of the discredited Aristotelianism. But Bacon realized that this dual task was too much for a single man; and one of his justifications for seeking political influence was that a position of power would enable him to bring others into the work. The search for office, though, took much of his time, leaving less for philosophy. From that dilemma he was never able to escape; and the fact that he opened his mind to others, including his uncle, Lord Burghley, made it still more difficult for him to find the employment he sought, for who would trust a government servant who planned to use his office to advance philosophy?

I confess that I have as vast contemplative ends, as I have moderate civil ends: for I have taken all knowledge to be my province; and if I could purge it of two sorts of rovers, whereof the one with frivolous disputations, confutations, and verbosities, the other with blind experiments and auricular traditions and impostures, hath committed so many spoils, I hope I should bring in industrious observations, grounded conclusions, and profitable inventions and discoveries; the best state of that province. This, whether it be curiosity, or vain glory, or nature, or (if one take it favourably) *philanthropia*, is so fixed in my mind as it cannot be removed. And I do easily see, that place of any reasonable countenance doth bring commandment of more wits than of a man's own; which is the thing I greatly affect.

[5] William Rawley, *Life of . . . Francis Bacon*, 1657, in James Spedding, R. E. Ellis, and D. D. Heath, *Works of Francis Bacon*, 7 vols. (London: Longman and Co., 1857–1859), I, 4. [Hereafter referred to as *Works*.]

And then, having said so much, he went on to threaten Burghley that if no office were forthcoming

> I will sell the inheritance that I have, and purchase some lease of quick revenue, or some office of gain that shall be executed by deputy, and so give over all care of service, and become some sorry bookmaker, or a true pioner [sic] in that mine of truth . . .[6]

In practice, Bacon resolved his dilemma by alternating the pursuit of office with the pursuit of knowledge and using each to give him an advantage in the other. For publication reminded the King of his existence, and experience was the substance from which his theories were spun. The result was the *Advancement of Learning*, which appeared in 1605 with a fulsome dedication to His Majesty King James I.

At this stage, the mood of the disinterested scholar was still upon Bacon. In a letter written to Sir Thomas Bodley, founder of the university library at Oxford, sent together with a copy of the *Advancement*, Bacon repeated

> I think no man may more truly say with the Psalm *Multum incola fuit anima mea*, than myself. For I do confess, since I was of any understanding, my mind hath in effect been absent from that I have done; and in absence are many errors which I do willingly acknowledge; and amongst the rest this great one that led the rest; that knowing myself by inward calling to be fitter to hold a book than to play a part, I have led my life in civil causes; for which I was not very fit by nature, and more unfit by the preoccupation of my mind. Therefore calling myself home, I have now for a time enjoyed myself; whereof likewise I desire to make the world partaker.[7]

But the old insatiable quest was soon with him once more. He used all means to call himself to the attention of the King; he behaved in the House of Commons with admirable discretion; he

[6] Spedding, *Letters and Life,* I, 109.[Also, see below, pp. 292–293 *(On the Interpretation of Nature).*]

[7] Spedding, *Letters and Life*, III, 253.

conducted himself soberly. In 1607, his reward finally came: the post of Solicitor-General was his. Fifteen years earlier, he had scorned it as unworthy of him; the intervening drought made the post welcome enough now. The Solicitor had no particular influence; the Attorney-General was his superior in legal affairs, and Robert Cecil (now Earl of Salisbury) continued to block any attempt by Bacon to advise the King. Not until 1613 did Bacon reach the next rung on the ladder; and by that time Salisbury was not only dead but discredited.

For a time James decided to act as his own Principal Secretary, aided only by his Scottish favorite, the Earl of Somerset. The experiment was notably unsuccessful. The Parliament of 1614 was so abysmal a failure that it has been known ever since as "Addled," and poor preparation was a major reason for the fiasco. Bacon had made some suggestions as to how the business should have been managed, but he was ignored—which was a pity, since he saw the problems more clearly than those whose advice was heeded. It is possible that the failure of others helped promote Bacon. It is certainly true that by 1615, Somerset's hold over the King was slackening, and that a new favorite, George Villiers, soon to be Duke of Buckingham, was being thrust forward by a group among whom Bacon could be found. At the same time, James's perennial lack of money—the principal cause of most of his woes—was becoming worse. Bacon made suggestions on how to economize. He worked with Lionel Cranfield in cutting royal expenses and rationalizing procedures. By 1617, Bacon had been placed on the Privy Council; the same year, he achieved the rank of Lord Keeper and thus finally held the post that had once been his father's; the year following, he was advanced in dignity by being made Lord Chancellor (the office of Lord Keeper with a grander title) and Baron Verulam. The long quest was over.

The new Lord Keeper began his regime with a tremendous burst of energy. He cleared up the backlog of cases which had disgraced the Court of Chancery; he wrote out a series of instructions for the operation of the court (instructions which were still being used centuries later); he defended his court from the attacks of competing jurisdictions; besides all this he continued to advise the King from his seat on the Privy Council, and to dream of remaking the hodge-podge of statutes, customs, and judicial decisions that was the law of England into a neatly-organized and structured code based on rational principles. There was less time for other things. Bacon did not supervise his under-lings, at the Chancery or at home, with very much care, and the opportunities for graft open to those surrounding one of the Crown's great officers were numerous and tempting. He did not take the risk of arguing with the favorite, Buckingham, who attempted to interfere with judicial decisions; he did not dispute with the King over the issuance of patents of monopolies, though as a good Parliament-man Bacon knew how unpopular the mo-nopolies were. And he found neither the time nor the energy to use his high office in the service of knowledge, though that had all along been the pretext for his driving ambition. In brief, Bacon acted the part of the accomplished courtier, deferential to those with greater power, arrogant to those with less. He made no friends and many enemies, and he provided weapons to men who were determined to ruin him.

The occasion was the Parliament of 1621. Ironically, only a few days before it met, Bacon had been promoted to the title of Viscount St. Albans. Then the storm broke. The immediate oc-casion was an attack on the royal grants of monopolies. Monop-olies might perhaps have been defended on grounds of offering protection to inventors and allowing a necessary regulation of the economy; in fact, the grants had been used as a means of rewarding courtiers at the expense of the population at large rather than that of the royal treasury. The monopolies were thus a constant source of grievance: Queen Elizabeth had been forced to back down on this issue, and more than one of James's parlia-ments had been embittered with debates concerning the grants. Bacon, always in favor of royal consultation with Parliament, had recommended calling a Parliament in 1621, but had pru-dently suggested that some of the most obnoxious grants be cancelled first. Nothing had been done. The session opened with the predicted attack. Mitchell and Mompesson, two of the worst offenders among the rapacious monopolists, were the first victims: one of them fled into exile, the other was imprisoned in the Tower. But these were small fry. The Commons sought bigger game. The King was untouchable; Buckingham wisely ranged himself on the side of the Commons and developed a sudden desire to put down abuses in the grants of patents of monopoly. The Commons perforce turned to the commission of referees who supervised the grants.

Bacon had been among the referees and his conduct had been less than exemplary. On the one hand, he had certainly suggested that some monopolies be cancelled; on the other, he had gone along with Buckingham whenever the latter requested favors—and that was all too often. But Bacon in his capacity of a referee was saved by the King's insistence that an attack on his agents was an attack on the royal prerogative; and the Commons did not yet feel strong enough to make an issue of ministerial responsibility. Instead, they turned to a personal attack on Bacon himself. Two old enemies were prepared to act as leaders: Edward Coke, once Chief Justice, a man whose career had fluctuated in time with Bacon's own, who had become Elizabeth's Attorney-General when Bacon sought the post, who had been compulsorily retired from the bench of judges when Bacon's advance was most rapid; and Lionel Cranfield, once a merchant, now chief architect of financial reform, who disliked Bacon for his sycophancy and who resented Bacon's sneers at his base origins. Their opportunity came when a number of litigants in the Court of Chancery accused the Chancellor of taking bribes: they were infuriated because they had thought their bribes would lead to favorable decisions and were disappointed when the court decided against them. An attempt to excuse the whole business by blaming the Chancellor for lax control over his servants failed: he had all too clearly been involved in it himself. The impeachment—the first in well over a century—went ahead.

Bacon made no attempt to defend himself. When the Commons presented the charges to the House of Lords, the Lord

Chancellor took to his bed. His responses were in writing, and constituted a grudging but complete confession. Insofar as any excuse was offered, it was merely that the money received in no way affected the eventual decision (which was, of course, what those who had been mulcted were complaining about). The King did the only thing possible: Bacon was dismissed from his post. The Lords did what was expected of them: with only one vote dissenting—Buckingham's—they sentenced the former Lord Chancellor to a fine of £40,000 and imprisonment during the King's pleasure, as well as disabling him from ever again holding public office, sitting in Parliament, or coming within the verge of the Court. Bacon's career was over. Though he might delude himself that all would be pardoned—as the fine was pardoned and the prison sentence reduced to a few days—the King had acquiesced too thoroughly in the proceedings to take the risk of ever again employing Bacon in the royal service. Guilty though he undoubtedly was, Bacon had been made a scapegoat for others more guilty still, and once the crown had agreed to sacrifice him to the anger of the Commons, there was no going back. His accusers gained little. Coke never again held office. Cranfield was promoted for a time, then himself became the victim of an irate House and suffered the second of the Jacobean impeachments. As for bribery, that was too much a part of the way of life at James's court for one successful prosecution to snuff it out.

The formal part of the punishment was not too grievous. No one expected James to keep Bacon imprisoned for long; nor did he. The fine was remitted, and the remission was handled in such a way as to leave Bacon, for the moment, free from the pressure of his creditors. Relief from that part of his sentence prohibiting him from coming within a dozen miles of the Court was more difficult, and it was in this matter that James and Buckingham showed how much they had valued Bacon's services. No pardon could go through without Buckingham's recommendation; and Buckingham would agree to nothing until Bacon made over his old family residence, York House, to the favorite. With his family pride under attack, Bacon for once resisted. The uneven tug-of-war continued for almost a year; but London contained the libraries Bacon needed for his work, the friends he relied on if he were to be reinstated in favor; at last, he gave in.

That Bacon was both shocked and disappointed at the sudden collapse of his hopes would be an understatement. His first reaction, nonetheless, was not one of resigned submission. He had faced adversity before. Thus, when he turned his mind once more to literary projects, it was not to the program outlined in the *Advancement of Learning* (1605), nor to the completion of the logic adumbrated in the *Novum Organum* (1620) that he set himself. Instead, he offered once again to codify the laws of England; and when that suggestion met with little response, he recollected that once, many years before, King James had expressed a desire for a good history of England. Perhaps favor could be regained by lifting up the historian's pen.

The idea of writing history was not new to Bacon. In a letter to Lord Keeper Ellesmere, written in 1605 in response to King James's request for a new history of England [see below, p. 254], he had sketched out a few of what he considered to be the leading ideas that ought to be covered. A little while later, he expanded the treatment slightly in a fragment called "The History of the reigns of K. Henry the VIII, K. Edward, Q. Mary, and part of Q. Elizabeth," [see below, p. 258] which he loaned to John Speed for use in the enormous *History of Great Britaine* which appeared in 1611. The very fact that Bacon was willing to part with so undeveloped a fragment suggests strongly that he had then no plans for expanding it. Nor was the panegyric of the late Queen, "In felicem memoriae Elizabethae" [see below, p. 266] in any sense a history of the reign, though historical matters entered into it. However, it is clear that Bacon had begun to think about the writing of history long before he actually sat down to it in 1621, and the rapidity with which he worked then indicates that he had already made some notes. Thus the *History of King Henry the Seventh*, the first volume of what was intended to be a series extending from the union of the two houses of Lancaster and York in 1485 to the union of the two crowns of Scotland and England in 1603, culminating in a history of James's own reign, was written very rapidly in a few months in the middle of 1621. A fair copy was ready on the 8th of October and was sent at once to the King:

> It may please your most excellent Majesty,
>   I do very humbly thank your Majesty for your gracious remission of my fine. I can now (I thank God and you) die, and make a will.
>   I desire to do, for the little time God shall send me life, like the merchants of London, which when they give over trade, lay out their money upon land. So being freed from civil business, I lay forth my poor talent upon those things which may be perpetual, still having relation to do you honour with those powers I have left.
>   I have therefore chosen to write the Reign of Henry the 7th, who was in a sort your forerunner, and whose spirit, as well as his blood, is doubled upon your Majesty.
>   I durst not have presumed to intreat your Majesty to look over the book and correct it, or at least to signify what you would have amended. But since you are pleased to send for the book, I will hope for it.[8]

By the end of the year, the King had read the manuscript, had made a few corrections (mostly verbal), and had passed it on, with commendations, to Lord Brooke (Bacon's old friend Fulke Greville) for a further check. For some unknown reason, the Bishop of London, official censor of the publishers, delayed the printing for a short while, but the volume nevertheless appeared before the end of March 1622. John Chamberlain, who had an opinion about everything, commented at once that

> The late Lord Chauncellor hath set out the life or raign of Henry the seventh. Yt is pitie he shold have any other employment. I have not read much of yt, but yf the rest of our historie were aunswerable to yt, I thincke we shold not need to envie any other nation in that kind.[9]

[8] Spedding, *Letters and Life*, VII, 303.
[9] *The Letters of John Chamberlain*, ed. N. E. McClure, 2 vols. (Philadelphia: The American Philosophical Society, 1939), II, 430.

But of course, as always happened with Bacon's work, this
one remained incomplete. The reign of Henry VIII was never
written, though Bacon had promised it to Prince Charles. Other
projects supervened; and, though the keeper of the records in
the Tower was ordered to open his archives to Bacon's inspec-
tion, the great private collector, Sir Robert Cotton, who had
helped Bacon with Henry VII, refused to do so again. And the
writing of the history had done Bacon's career no real good. The
King was certainly sympathetic, perhaps even impressed, but
that was insufficient reason to reinstate a discredited servant.
Bacon was now sixty-three; if office were really no longer open
to him, he would spend his remaining years on the works he was
sure would yield him immortality:

[I am confirmed] to spend my time wholly in writing; and to
put forth that poor talent, or half talent, or what it is, that God hath
given me, not as heretofore to particular exchanges, but to banks or
mounts of perpetuity, which will not break. Therefore having not
long since set forth a part of my *Instauration*; which is the work that
in mine own judgment (*si nunquam fallit imago*) I do most esteem;
I think to proceed in some new parts thereof . . . . And again, for
that my book of *Advancement of Learning* may be some preparative,
or key, for the better opening of the *Instauration*; because it exhibits
a mixture of new conceits and old; whereas the *Instauration* gives the
new unmixed, otherwise than with some little aspersion of the old for
taste's sake; I have thought good to procure a translation of that book
into the general language, not without great and ample additions, and
enrichment thereof; especially in the second book, which handleth the
Partition of Sciences; in such sort, as I hold it may serve in lieu of the
first part of the *Instauration*, and acquit my promise in that part.
Again, because I cannot altogether desert the civil person that I have
borne, which if I should forget, enough would remember; I have also
entered into a work touching *Laws*, . . . Now having in the work of
my *Instauration* had in contemplation the general good of men in their
very being, and the dowries of nature; and in my work of laws, the
general good of men likewise in society, and the dowries of government; I thought in duty I owed somewhat unto mine own country,
which I ever loved; insomuch as although my place hath been far
above my desert, yet my thoughts and cares concerning the good

thereof were beyond, and over, and above my place: so now being (as I am) no more able to do my country service, it remained unto me to do it honour: which I have endeavoured to do in my work of *The Reign of King Henry the Seventh*. As for my *Essays*, and some other particulars of that nature, I count them but as the recreations of my other studies, and in that sort purpose to continue them . . .[10]

The few years remaining were devoted primarily to filling out the sketch of the "Great Instauration." Since the publication of the *Advancement* had done nothing for science in England, Bacon hoped for better results from the rest of Europe. The *Advancement* was translated into Latin, the universal scholarly language, and was much expanded in the process. The scientific instances on which the induction outlined in the *Novum Organum* was to operate had not yet been summed up in appropriate lists: the work was begun in the "Historia Ventis" (Natural History of Winds); "Historia Vitae et Mortis" (Natural History of Life and Death); "Historia Densi et Rari" (Of Density and Sparsity); and in the very miscellaneous "Sylva Sylvarum" (Forest of Forests, i.e., Collection of Collections). None was as careful or as analytical as Bacon would have liked, but at least they showed how the new science should begin. And Bacon revised and expanded his *Essays*. The list is appalling in its length and diversity, the more so as Bacon was by this time far from well. He continued working until the last illness, a chill contracted while he was conducting an experiment on the preservative qualities of snow.

Bacon's works, his *History* among them, were in part the products of a series of unresolved tensions. Ambition and training alike drove him to seek public office—as it did numbers of his contemporaries—not only because that road led to wealth and position but because there was no alternative. Contemplation was excluded from consideration because its good was essentially private, and the public good was preferable. "Men must know, that in this theatre of man's life it is reserved only for

[10] Spedding, *Letters and Life*, VII, 372–374.

God and Angels to be lookers on."[11] Unfortunately, it soon became evident that Bacon was much more eager to give service than the Queen was to receive it. The group that eventually collected around Essex shared the disillusioned conviction that political influence had replaced merit as the chief criterion for advancement. By the end of the century, Bacon was beginning to question his priorities: contemplation was still somehow a lesser good than activity—but was his way of thinking necessarily contemplative in the old sense? His philosophy of utility offered a way out by defining a kind of contemplation that was public rather than private in its usefulness. But this raised a new question. If contemplation was justifiable, then the search for office became irrelevant. For Bacon, however, seeking political power had become a reflex action, and he ended by using the "advancement of learning" as an excuse for seeking office: the projected program was so enormous in its scope that only someone with access to public funds could hope to achieve it.

The disillusionment with politics, which had sparked the revaluation of philosophy, survived Bacon's restructuring of priorities. Political humanism had been converted to scientific philosophy; or, at least, the arena in which the citizen might perform his civic duty had been extended beyond politics. And indeed, politics gradually ceased to have anything to do with humanism; the humanists had, after all, been moral philosophers, and it became more and more evident that practical politics had been cut off from morality. Bacon's own experiences proved that to him. So politics became merely one type of activity among many others requiring a handbook based on the analysis of what actually happened, not a manual deduced from some immutable laws. By the time Bacon achieved his political success, "success" had altered its meaning for him. The personal success remained —his father would have been proud; but Bacon himself had labored to convince the world that there were other roads to success for the active citizen than to become Lord Chancellor.

[11] *Works*, III, 421. *Advancement of Learning*.

Bacon's philosophy embraced the whole universe of knowledge: it included not only the entire perceivable world but also the way in which we should perceive it. He drew no distinction between the known and the still-to-be-discovered—except insofar as he gave directions for making the discoveries; he included the "is" and the "ought." A concise summary of the whole scheme would run to a greater length than this essay: we can only indicate here the place of historical writing in the greater universal plan. Nor will it be possible to discuss the growth and development of Bacon's world view. As it happens, his views concerning history changed very little.[12]

The Great Instauration, the sum total of all of Bacon's scientific theorizing and fact-collecting, remains a fragment. Of the six parts, only the first, the division of the sciences, was left in a state not far from perfection. Here Bacon attempted a summary of all knowledge with the purpose of pointing out what needed to be done to fill the lacunae in the fabric, and what could be improved in those areas of knowledge where work had already begun. That had, in fact, been the task he had set himself in the *Advancement of Learning* and, when it came to filling in the framework of the *Great Instauration,* Bacon adopted Book I of the *Advancement* in its entirety and then rewrote Book II in an expanded form as *De Augmentis Scientiarum* [see below, p. 295]. The second part of the scheme was to have been an elaboration of the new logic on which so much depended: half of this had been published as the *Novum Organum* in 1620, but the full analysis of Bacon's method of induction was never finished, though enough survives to indicate some of what its author had in mind. Induction depended on a large number of examples; the third part of the *Great Instauration* was to be a carefully sifted and ordered collection of them. The fourth part was to consist of the logic of the *Novum Organum* applied to the examples; of this, Bacon gave

[12] The discussion of Bacon's philosophy is drawn primarily from the *Advancement of Learning,* modified where appropriate by references to the *De Augmentis Scientiarum.*

no more than a hint in the second section of his volume on logic. At this stage in his thinking Bacon had begun to realize that he had projected too much for anyone, even himself, to accomplish; and the fifth part of his scheme consisted of anticipations of the new philosophy, a collection of provisional observations, to be abandoned when necessary. It was to this section that the post-humously published *Sylva Sylvarum* belonged; Bacon spent much of his time on these matters during the last years of his life. Finally, at the apex of the pyramid, was to be the new science, the generalizations about the world that would be developed from all the material so laboriously collected and analyzed. Since the groundwork was only just being laid, the superstructure could not yet be built, and even Bacon admitted that he was unable to predict precisely what the outcome would be. Of one thing only was he certain, that "the matter in hand is no mere felicity of speculation, but the real business and fortunes of the human race."[13]

Most of Bacon's thinking in the *Great Instauration* concerned the realm of nature, and the part played in all this by man considered as a historical creature was small. This is a partial explanation of certain characteristics in Bacon's thought, such as his distrust of the past. Time and again, he makes it clear that the philosophers of ancient times are not worth the veneration they have received, that the past should in no way be allowed to control the present. In an allusion to the question of the "Ancients and Moderns," Bacon sidesteps the usual answers by asserting that the terms of the question have been ill put; we are the ancients, for are we not older than those who lived nearly two millenia earlier, during the youth of the world? There is here a glimmering of the idea of progress, not yet fully worked out; and part of the reason for Bacon's failure to develop the idea is his insistence that true progress could not begin until mankind adopted his way of thinking, or something like it.

[13] *The New Organon and Related Writings*, ed. Fulton H. Anderson (Indianapolis: The Bobbs-Merrill Co., 1960), 29. Plan of the *Great Instauration*.

Again, he was given to frequent use of an image describing time as a river that carried with it only the light and superficial, leaving behind the weighty achievements of the past, as a rushing stream abandons the stones over which it hurtles. With such a dislike for the past, Bacon nonetheless admired the works of certain historians and wrote history himself. The reason for this would appear to be the same as that lying behind the fifth part of the *Great Instauration:* we should not accept the theories spun out by ancient thinkers, but their observations are worth sifting and recording. The experiences of men, as recorded by historians, are artifacts that might be used in constructing theories of psychology and politics in the same way that the works of nature, observed by scientists, are artifacts to be used for the new science.

There is, in all of Bacon's writing, this emphasis on use. Knowledge was worth nothing for its own sake; it was worth less than nothing if it was used merely to spin idle theories. Certainly, Bacon had nothing against theorizing; it was idleness that he opposed. He drew a distinction between "experiments of light" and "experiments of fruit,"[14] and preferred the former, but this did not prevent him from insisting that theories should be tested by the positive achievements that could be drawn from them. Gunpowder, the compass, and the printing press were the

[11] The distinction is made in *The New Organon*, ed. Anderson, 96. Book One, Aphorism xcix: "then only will there be good ground of hope for the further advance of knowledge when there shall be received and gathered together into natural history a variety of experiments which are of no use in themselves but simply serve to discover causes and axioms, which I call *Experimenta lucifera,* experiments of *light,* to distinguish them from those which I call *fructifera,* experiments of *fruit.*

"Now experiments of this kind [of light] have one admirable property and condition: they never miss or fail. For since they are applied, not for the purpose of producing any particular effect, but only of discovering the natural cause of some effect, they answer the end equally well whichever way they turn out; for they settle the question."

great discoveries that had been made by modern man; it was these that set the moderns above the ancients; yet none of the three was directly ascribable to scientific theorizing. Instead, they were the result of the labors of artisans, not of scholars; and it was to harness these labors that Bacon worked out his system. That work was for him an act of charity, and charity, in the Baconian vocabulary, was a crucial term. It was the motive that made a man look about him to seek out the needs of others, not necessarily those of the individual needy, but of mankind, and impelled him to alleviate them. This charity did not (necessarily) relieve a single poor neighbor but it could, ultimately, abolish poverty. The disinterested scientist in his laboratory is derived from this aspect of Bacon's thought.

Not only had the scientist to be a disinterested seeker after a truth the eventual value of which would be measured by its usefulness, but he had to submit himself totally to his materials. "For man is but the servant and interpreter of nature: what he does and what he knows is only what he has observed of nature's order in fact or in thought; beyond this he knows nothing and can do nothing. For the chain of causes cannot by any force be loosed or broken, nor can nature be commanded except by being obeyed."[15] But man, by submitting, becomes the victor: the end result is a restoration of his ability to control nature, an ability lost when Adam fell from Paradise, and never since regained. But it could be regained. For Bacon saw man as moving in the direction of utopia, a utopia described once by God in Genesis—and again by Bacon in the *New Atlantis*. Charity, as the greatest of virtues, would lead once more to paradise, but now to a paradise on earth.

The key to all this was in thinking rightly. The old method of logic had to be abandoned and the new substituted for it.

There are and can be only two ways of searching into and discovering truth. The one flies from the senses and particulars to the most general axioms, and from these principles, the truth of which it takes for settled and immovable, proceeds to judgment and to the dis-

[15] *New Organon*, ed. Anderson, 29. Plan of the *Great Instauration*.

covery of middle axioms. And this way is now in fashion. The other derives axioms from the senses and particulars, rising by a gradual and unbroken ascent, so that it arrives at the most general axioms last of all. This is the true way, but as yet untried.[16]

The new logic depended on the collection of instances and, above all, on their careful arrangement. Bacon never suggested that it was desirable or possible to list every instance; instead, he laid down rules for determining which were important. Apparent exceptions were crucial. In the end, the investigators would reach an axiom (an hypothesis), which would be tested further, for it would suggest fresh lines of investigation. That a single negative instance, among thousands of positive ones, could disrupt the entire logical chain, was a fact of which Bacon was perfectly aware. But what else could be done? The old method might be more satisfying from the point of view of an abstract logic, but it did not work. Philosophical scepticism had no appeal because it led nowhere. The only way to settle the question of whether anything can be known was to try; argument settled nothing.

The logical question was settled by a process of elimination. Induction had to be the answer because deduction did not work, and pure scepticism was pointless. But there was a further problem. The very raw materials upon which induction was to work might be tainted. It was possible that the senses and the mind of man, through which observations had to be filtered, might distort both the observations and the reasoning process. The only solution was to identify those aberrations of the mind that produced distortions. The metaphors of the Idols served just this admonitory purpose. Man's judgment might be warped by the Idols of the Tribe—the peculiarities inherent in the nature of man—and these included a propensity for seeing more regularity in nature than really existed, as well as a habit of over-generalizing from too few instances, and of over-ready abstraction. Moreover, Bacon realized that the senses themselves could easily be deceived by just such propensities. Not only did men suffer from these generic difficulties, they suffered as well from

[16] *New Organon*, ed. Anderson, 43. Book One, Aphorism xix.

individual differences, the Idols of the Cave. Some men were given to seeking out differences, others sought similarities; some loved antiquity, others chased novelty. And the words themselves, through which knowledge had to be imparted, could be dangerous. For men worshipped the Idols of the Marketplace and allowed words to rule their understanding. As for the Idols of the Theatre, the fine-spun theories of the philosophers, Bacon could only issue a warning: there was no hope of defeating the philosophers, since there was no agreement even on first principles. Only a reminder of the past uselessness of theorizing would serve. If these limits of the mind—and hence of the senses —could be remembered, then there was hope for the new logic; if the limits of man's abilities were forgotten, then he could expect no more than to plod on as he had before.

As for the remaining question, Bacon both asks and answers it:

It may also be asked (in the way of doubt rather than objection) whether I speak of natural philosophy only, or whether I mean that the other sciences, logic, ethics, and politics, should be carried on by this method. Now I certainly mean what I have said to be understood of them all; and as the common logic, which governs by the syllogism, extends not only to natural but to all sciences, so does mine also, which proceeds by induction, embrace everything. For I form a history and table of discovery for anger, fear, shame, and the like; for matters political; and again for the mental operations of memory, composition and division, judgment, and the rest; not less than for heat and cold, or light, or vegetation, or the like. But, nevertheless, since my method of interpretation, after the history has been prepared and duly arranged, regards not the working and discourse of the mind only (as the common logic does) but the nature of things also, I supply the mind such rules and guidance that it may in every case apply itself aptly to the nature of things. And therefore I deliver many and diverse precepts in the doctrine of interpretation, which in some measure modify the method of invention according to the quality and condition of the subject of the inquiry.[17]

[17] *New Organon*, ed. Anderson, 115–116. Book One, Aphorism cxxvii.

Unfortunately, the method was never demonstrated for anything other than heat and cold.

The only places where Bacon does discuss history and politics in a theoretical way are the *Advancement of Learning* and its expansion, *De Augmentis Scientiarum* [see below, p. 295], where these subjects, along with a great many others, are fitted into Bacon's total scheme. Bacon divided the functions of the mind into three parts: Reason, Imagination, and Memory; the subjects pertaining to each are Philosophy, Poesy, and History. History, taken in its broad sense, included the sub-divisions of Natural History and Civil History, with Literary History and Ecclesiastical History included in the latter. Natural History does not concern us. Civil History itself was sub-divided into Memorials, Perfect Histories, and Antiquities; that is, history unfinished, perfected, and defaced. By Memorials, Bacon had in mind lists of happenings, collections of public acts, and the like: essentially, raw materials. Antiquities were the physical remnants of the past. Perfect Histories were of several sorts: they could be of a time (that is, chronicles); of a person (lives); or of a single action (relations, narrations). Narrations had the advantage that they were most likely to be based on observation, though their scope was frequently too narrow. Chronicles were unquestionably more complete, but they tended to concentrate on the superficial pomp of events, and their authors, in order to give the full story, were inclined to fill in the gaps with conjectures or inventions. Lives were altogether more satisfactory, as they avoided the superficiality of chronicles as well as extending the narrow range of narrations. Finally, Bacon acknowledged the existence of a ruminative history, a commentary on the historical facts, but decided that this would more logically fit into the realm of Reason.

Like all his contemporaries, Bacon insisted that history had to be useful. Due to the fact that the *Advancement of Learning* concentrated on describing those arts and sciences that were deficient, Bacon has little to say about the uses of Civil History, which, despite some large gaps, was well-represented on the world's bookshelves. However, Literary History, that is, the history of all sorts of learning, had never been written, and as a result Bacon expatiated on the subject, telling us that "the use and end of which work I do not so much design for curiosity, or satisfaction of those that are the lovers of learning; but chiefly for a more serious and grave purpose, . . . that it will make learned men wise in the use and administration of learning."[18] Again, there is the insistence on practical use; and it is notable that Bacon all but rejects the common view of his contemporaries that history could serve to teach morality. It is likely that he was influenced by the views of Sir Philip Sidney. Sidney had recognized that a candid look at history did anything but demonstrate the penalties of vice and the rewards of virtue. On the contrary, evil men not uncommonly flourished while good men died unremembered and unmourned. If one's purpose was to teach morality, it was better to write poetry, where the actions could demonstrate whatever was appropriate. By defining poesy as feigned history, Bacon took much the same view:

> Because the acts or events of true history have not that magnitude which satisfieth the mind of man, poesy feigneth acts and events greater and more heroical; because true history propoundeth the successes and issues of action not so agreeable to the merits of virtue and vice, therefore poesy feigns them more just in retribution, and more according to revealed providence; because true history representeth actions and events more ordinary and less interchanged, therefore poesy endueth them with more rareness, and more unexpected and alternative variations. So as it appeareth that poesy serveth and conferreth to magnanimity, morality, and to delectation.[19]

If history were to teach at all, then its lessons had to be looked at coldly, without prejudice, and the realm wherein it taught was that of practical behavior. That had little to do with memory and much with reason: "For it is the true office of history to represent the events themselves together with the counsels, and to

[18] *Works*, III, 330. *Advancement of Learning.*
[19] *Works*, III, 343. *Advancement of Learning.*

leave the observations and conclusions thereupon to the liberty and faculty of every man's judgment."[20]

Human Philosophy was but one branch of philosophy taken more generally (the others were Divine Philosophy and Natural Philosophy), and it was itself sub-divided into knowledge of individual men and knowledge of men in society (though Bacon also spoke of an over-arching Human Philosophy that analyzed Human Nature, that is, the concordances between mind and body). Moreover, Bacon extended this division of private and public man to his discussion of good and evil. Not only did a private good exist but so did a public good, and this last consisted not only of the common duty of every man as a member of the state but also of the special duty of each man in regard to his profession, vocation, and place. Here, interestingly, Bacon found one of those gaps in knowledge that he was at such pains to point out. Absolute definitions of good and evil could be found readily enough in Scripture. But there was no equivalent source for the particular good and evil associated with each profession and vocation, and such information would be invaluable. For a knowledge of evil arts, "we are much beholden to Machiavel and others, that write what men do and not what they ought to do."[21] And for a knowledge of the nature of men, it is necessary to turn to history, poesy, and common experience. All of this, Bacon thought, still required elaboration.

As for civil knowledge, the knowledge of man in society, that is entirely a matter of external rather than internal goodness. As a result, no a priori moral rules apply: but another result is that generalizations about civil knowledge are hard to make, for this of all subjects is most immersed in "matter," the quagmire of the mundane. Difficulty is no excuse for not trying, and Bacon proceeds in his usual fashion to divide and sub-divide. Civil knowledge, then, consists of three parts, Conversation, Negotiation, and Government, that is, wisdom of behavior, of business,

[20] *Works*, III, 339. *Advancement of Learning.*
[21] *Works*, III, 430. *Advancement of Learning.*

and of state. Behavior, which has been handled adequately by others, is simply the outward art of appearing a courtier. Negotiation, the lowly but practical art of conducting one's own affairs in society, has never been properly studied, for wise men have preferred to spend their time on the more alluring (if intractable) problem of the theory of government. Plenty of material exists from which axioms of negotiation could be distilled; and Bacon analyzed some of Solomon's aphorisms to prove his point. However, "the form of writing which of all others is fittest for this variable argument of negotiation and occasions is that which Machiavel chose wisely and aptly for government; namely, *discourse upon histories or examples.*"[22] Works such as Machiavelli's *Discourses on the First Ten Books of Titus Livius* have the especial advantage that the examples are not drawn out of context to illustrate a point of view adopted beforehand, but instead give each historical act with all its attendant circumstances.

Discourses on histories are best of all for government, though they are also of use for business; lives, the other subdivision of perfect history, form the best source for knowledge of business (together with discourses on letters, such as those of Cicero to Atticus). However, a careful reading of all this discloses some ambiguity—and there is a good chance that it was purposeful. Government, as Bacon used the term, applied especially to princes. Since King James prided himself on his kingcraft—he had himself written a book on the subject—Bacon felt it unwise to offer advice on the subject in a volume dedicated to the King. Hence, the portion concerning discourses on histories (which were useful for government) was slipped into a section dealing with negotiation. As for negotiation itself, that had a double meaning: it denoted a man's own business in the context of society as well as his business as a servant of society. A discourse on lives would help him in the latter situation but would be quite irrelevant in the former.

This sub-division of negotiation was expressed by Bacon in

[22] *Works*, III, 453. *Advancement of Learning.*

a slightly different way. "For there is a wisdom of counsel, and again there is a wisdom of pressing a man's own fortune; and they do sometimes meet, and often sever. For many are wise in their own ways that are weak for government or counsel; like ants, which is a wise creature for itself, but very hurtful for the garden."[23] There is nothing to be gained by ignoring Fortune: the man who takes all credit to himself will soon fail for over-confidence. Nonetheless, *Faber quisque fortunae suae*, man can be the maker of his own fortune (or, "the mould of a man's fortune is in himself"). And the art of making one's fortune is an-other of the lacunae that Bacon was determined should be filled. That such matters should be considered in a serious work re-quired some defense, and Bacon came fully armed. Good fortune is as difficult to achieve as virtue and deserves equally to be studied. Moreover, the method of study is much the same for this art as for others and is not inherently inferior (and has, besides, the advantage of showing that the learning could be practical). Certainly the pursuit of virtue was preferable to the pursuit of fortune; nevertheless, fortune deserved consideration. Whereupon Bacon proceeded to lay down some suggestions, carefully illustrated by historical examples. These amount to ways of discovering the thoughts of others ("But the soundest disclosing and expounding of men is by their natures and ends; wherein the weakest sort of men are best interpreted by their natures, and the wisest by their ends."[24]); the ways of finding out about ourselves; the methods by which one advanced oneself (pliancy is recommended: it had worked for Bacon); and so on. That all of this could easily appear to be not so much an accept-ance of Machiavellian doctrine as an extension of it was clear enough. Machiavelli was sufficiently hated for Bacon to feel that he had to cover himself: these are good arts, he insisted, and then quoted by contrast some of Machiavelli's evil principles, such as that the appearance of virtue was more important than its attain-ment. Such evil principles are, if anything, even more numerous

---

[23] *Works*, III, 454. *Advancement of Learning.*
[24] *Works*, III, 459. *Advancement of Learning.*

than the good: "But it is in life as it is in ways; the shortest way is commonly the foulest, and surely the fairer way is not much about."[25] A few words about Providence do little to convince us. Bacon's advice is not immoral, nor is it moral: considerations of morality are merely an afterthought. Here, as elsewhere in his writings, the human and the divine were kept clearly separated; if one wished to know God's demands, one read Scripture; if one wished to learn the art of self-advancement, one read Bacon. The ensuing and final section on divine learning, which should have capped the structure, comes almost as an anticlimax, a bow to public opinion.

A careful consideration of the whole argument indicates that in Civil History, as in Natural History, Bacon separated the functions of the compiler from those of the theorist. Because civil history was pre-eminent among human writings for its dignity and authority, the historian was no negligible figure. His task was as difficult as it was important:

> For to carry the mind in writing back into the past, and bring it into sympathy with antiquity; diligently to examine, freely and faithfully to report, and by the light of words to place as it were before the eyes, the revolutions of times, the characters of persons, the fluctuations of counsels, the courses and currents of actions, the bottoms of pretences, and the secrets of governments; is a task of great labour and judgment—the rather because in ancient transactions the truth is difficult to ascertain, and in modern it is dangerous to tell.[26]

Nor was Bacon unaware of the problems involved in the sifting of documentary evidence. But however important the compiler of histories, he still took second place in Bacon's mind to the thinker who commented on histories. For Bacon, the absolute separation of the two functions of compilation and comment was possible, and his concentration on the second of these may help to explain why he did not try to apply the metaphors of the idols to the question of historical research, why he was unable to see

[25] *Works*, III, 472. *Advancement of Learning.*
[26] *Works*, IV, 302. *De Augmentis.*

that preconceived ideas could blind the compiler of histories quite as much as they might blind the scientific researcher. Bacon's commentator on histories was inclined to accept without further checking what he was given by his subordinate, the compiler. That might lead to gross inaccuracy. As a theory of the actual practice of historical writing, Bacon's separation of functions was worse than useless: it verged on the catastrophic.

Whatever our view of this separation of functions, Bacon did try to adhere to it. The original edition of the *Essays* was a series of aphorisms on whatever subjects happened to interest Bacon at the moment; but the essays newly added to the editions of 1612 and 1625 were related to specific functions outlined in the *Advancement of Learning*. It has been shown that the essays can be divided among the varying branches of moral and civil knowledge, so that "Of Boldness" and "Of Simulation and Dissimulation," for example, are parallel to the *Faber quisque fortunae suae* section of the *Advancement;* others, such as "Of Empire," and "Of the True Greatness of Kingdoms and Estates," might have fitted into the section on the art of government that Bacon felt it inexpedient to include in his book, and they are related to certain papers of advice that he submitted to James privately.[27] Histories were intended to supply materials for the art of government, as in this comment on the proper treatment of the nobility by rulers:

For their nobles; to keep them at a distance, it is not amiss; but to depress them, may make a king more absolute, but less safe; and less able to perform any thing that he desires. I have noted it in my History of King Henry the Seventh of England, who depressed his nobility; whereupon it came to pass that his times were full of difficulties and troubles; for the nobility, though they continued loyal unto him, yet did they not co-operate with him in his business. So that in effect he was fain to do all things himself.[28]

[27] R. S. Crane, "The Relation of Bacon's *Essays* to his Program for the Advancement of Learning," in *Schelling Anniversary Papers,* ed. A. H. Quinn (New York: The Century Co., 1923), 87–105.

[28] *Works*, VI, 422. *Essays:* "Of Empire."

And Bacon, in accordance with his prescription in the *Advancement*, multiplied such examples in the later editions of the *Essays*.

Thus, if one wishes to discover Bacon's ideas concerning the object of historical writing, his *History of Henry the Seventh* is not the place to seek them. Instead, one should turn to his philosophical writings, which shed a great deal of light on his historical work. The point that comes through most clearly is that the separation of natural and divine knowledge, which is so much a part of his scientific work, applies equally to his ideas about man and his past.

For it was not that pure and uncorrupted natural knowledge whereby Adam gave names to the creatures according to their propriety, which gave occasion to the fall. It was the ambitious and proud desire of moral knowledge to judge of good and evil, to the end that man may revolt from God and give laws to himself, which was the form and manner of the temptation.[29]

And further,

The prejudice hath been infinite that both divine and human knowledge hath received by the intermingling and tempering of the one with the other; as that which hath filled the one full of heresies, and the other full of speculative fictions and vanities.[30]

In short, history was transferred from the realm of moral philosophy to that of civil knowledge. The lessons it taught were those of politics. The politician, and the historian, might be (indeed they ought to be) religious in the conventional sense; but for man to interpret the past in moral terms was trespassing on God's preserves. The ultimate meaning of human history was above man's understanding; what was within reach had to do with lessons of human behavior, practical lessons that aided a man in making the best of himself, a prince in raising his country

[29] *New Organon*, ed. Anderson, 15. Preface to the *Great Instauration*.

[30] *Works*, III, 219. *Valerius Terminus*.

to greatness. For Bacon, history was past politics and present politics as well.

Before we turn our attention to Bacon's actual historical writing, it is necessary to say something about the state of the art in his day. A quick glance at the historians actually in circulation gives point to Bacon's feeling that "the greater part [are] beneath mediocrity."[31] Too many still suffered from the great vice of the chronicle tradition, over-inclusiveness. The chronicler was certain that historiography had a purpose, but was afraid to choose one of the several possible alternatives. Medieval writers were usually given to a form of providentialism, which meant that they spent little time on discovering possible human causes for events, but concentrated on finding God's pattern for man's history. To that they added the idea that history could preach morality, or that it might serve in lieu of experience as an educative force, but they ignored the question of whether anything might be learned from a descriptive history that omitted human causation. At the same time, chroniclers were prone to write for several sorts of audiences simultaneously. These might include London merchants, courtiers, even apprentices, but each wanted a different sort of material included. Hence a chronicler saw nothing amiss in printing lists of the mayors and aldermen of London, in publishing treaties and other state papers verbatim, in furnishing long and lavish descriptions of royal and city pageants. Most of these habits persisted throughout the sixteenth century; about all that was omitted was the aspect of universal history. The *Polychronicon* and similar volumes began with the Creation and made at least an attempt to cover everything that had occurred since—naturally with an emphasis on matters English. That proved too burdensome and too superficial; the only attempt at such a book in the Elizabethan period—the original plan for what afterwards came to be known as Holinshed's Chronicles—failed because of the magnitude of the task.

[31] *Works*, III, 336. *Advancement of Learning.*

Some cracks had begun to appear in this structure during the first half of the sixteenth century. Under the pounding of new ideas deriving either from Italian humanism or from the controversies of the Reformation, some aspects of the traditional chronicle gradually began to alter. Italians such as Lorenzo Valla had begun to make men aware of the concept of anachronism, of the idea that each period is a separate entity in its own right, and that institutions and manners could not be transferred from one to another. Dressing Alexander the Great as a knight (were not all warriors knights?) would no longer do. Valla's method of applying the concept of anachronism proved a potent weapon in the discovery of spurious or falsely-dated documents; and the Reformation provided compelling reasons for using it. Controversies were frequently fought over historical ground— when were bishops introduced? when did transubstantiation become dogma?—and each side had a stake in attacking the massed erudition of the other. Since religion, and theological controversy, was the most important subject of the day, historians could hardly help but be influenced. And some of them began to apply these methods to purely historical documents.

Imported humanism had become a staple of the newly re-organized English grammar schools just at the time when more and more men attended them: as we have seen, the humanist courtier is a sixteenth-century phenomenon. The education was primarily classical and although there was no particular emphasis on the classical historians, still it was difficult to avoid considerable exposure to them. Most educated men knew something of Livy and Plutarch, they had probably read Caesar and Sallust; a few had read the Greeks or Tacitus. For those unwilling or unable to read them in the original, translations soon became available—this was the great age of translation. It would be impossible to weigh all the effects of this sort of reading, but it is safe to say that the Roman idea of civic virtue was implanted in a good many heads; and new histories were written to do the same thing. Moreover, classical histories were anything but providential (in the religious sense; fortune certainly played a part), and the rational analyses that they contained were soon being imitated. The best example of all this is Sir Thomas More's *History of Richard III,* which was much influenced by the author's reading of Suetonius and Tacitus, and which gave a hard, psychological analysis of its leading character. More, however, had relatively little influence although his work was constantly reprinted: the reprintings usually contained additions that tried to make his brief and subtle study over into the pattern of a typical chronicle. In a real sense, though, More's *Richard III* is the true ancestor of Bacon's *Henry the Seventh:* separated though they are by almost a century, the two books are very much alike.

Much more influential was the infinitely less subtle Italian Polydore Vergil. Asked originally by Henry VII to produce a history of England in the new mode, Vergil was encouraged by Henry VIII to continue the project. The result was a massive Latin tome which was pillaged by every later writer (including Bacon). Polydore's achievement was two-fold: he challenged a number of much-cherished legends (such as that concerning King Arthur), using the common-sense analysis pioneered by his countrymen, and he organized his work by reigns. A regnal division was nothing unusual—most medieval chroniclers had used some such device—but Polydore tried to give the reigns a degree of internal unity by concentrating on one or two important issues. In his discussion of the fifteenth century, he pushed this even further and worked out a causal scheme linking the reigns from Richard II to Henry VIII—but the linkage was essentially providential rather than political. Nonetheless, Polydore (and his friend and contemporary Thomas More) pioneered a historiography based on something other than a massive accumulation of material.

One other development may be attributed to the humanist influence on English historiography: the rise of antiquarianism. Where historians concerned themselves with the chronological ordering of their evidence, the antiquaries were more interested in arranging it by subjects. Originally, this idea derived from the feeling of most humanists that the ancients had written so much about their own history, and had done it so well, that it was foolish to attempt to improve on them; but it was possible to try to answer questions that classical historians had never asked. Thus there appeared long essays on ancient coinage, on ancient institutions, on Roman provinces, and so on. When antiquarianism first appeared in England, it was in the attempt to write a history of the Roman province of Britain—a task that was not to be completed until William Camden published his *Britannia* in 1586, nearly half a century after John Leland had first projected such a work. Antiquarianism began as an attempt to explicate the classical authors, but as the subject developed, two changes took place: the antiquaries began to investigate a wide field of ancient life, and thus broadened the scope of the study of the past; and other men took up the idea and applied it to the history of post-Roman England. Even before Camden published his book, William Lambarde had been studying the institutions of the Anglo-Saxons through their surviving law codes (he had to learn Old English, a virtually unknown tongue, to do it). The antiquaries were sufficiently well-known to Bacon for him to include a section on antiquities in his three categories of civil history; and it is likely that legal antiquarianism influenced his own insistence on the value of discussing statutes when writing history.

The new ideas, which are here associated with humanism, rapidly exerted an influence on Tudor chronicling. Edward Hall's *Union of the Two Noble and Illustre Houses of York and Lancaster* was an extension of Polydore Vergil—where it was not simply a translation—adopting Polydore's scheme for uniting the history of the fifteenth century, but making of it an independent book. For the first part of the period of Richard III, Hall simply copied More. In all cases, however, Hall's additions—and they were numerous, especially as he approached his own day—were cumulative: more descriptions of pageants, details of treaties, information of interest to London merchants, etc. Richard Grafton's unsuccessful *A Chronicle at Large* tried to cover all English history; the best things in it were taken from Hall, though Grafton did occasionally feel impelled to question some of the details he lifted from his medieval predecessors. His younger contemporary and competitor, John Stow, was vastly more careful in his use of evidence and went to great trouble to turn up new materials; but his arrangement of his discoveries was simply annalistic. The first real attempt to rewrite history in the modern vein was that of the publisher Rayner Wolf: the plan was to have volumes covering most of the world, thus combining the advantages of universal history with those of more detailed scholarship. Wolf died before much was accomplished, and his successors limited the project to Great Britain. The principal author was Raphael Holinshed, by whose name the chronicle is usually called. Holinshed was a little uncertain of his ground: he tried humanist source-criticism, he inserted occasional causal explanation (some of it political), but he also believed in the providential theory of history and was convinced that much of value in life and morals could be learned from the study of the past. The result was a vast book—two folio volumes in the first edition, three in the second—that crammed in everything. By the time the second edition appeared, Holinshed was dead, and his continuators were still less discriminating in their inclusiveness; it was to this edition that Shakespeare applied his talent for finding the essentials in the events of the past. Not until John Speed's *History of Great Britaine* appeared in 1611 was there a volume employing all the lessons that might have been learned from the humanists: and Speed was dependent, at least to some extent, on Bacon.

More detailed comments on Bacon's actual sources will concern us below; but it is appropriate here to examine what sorts of materials and ideas he would have found had he examined past writers on Henry VII. Robert Fabyan, an early sixteenth century chronicler, simply provided a few pages of miscellaneous information, though the Great Chronicle of London, a work emanating from the city merchants and possibly from Fabyan himself, contained much more. Most of this, however, was of purely local interest, though there are records of complaints about Henry's taxes; there are as well descriptions of the panoply occasioned by the marriage of Henry's son Arthur to Catherine of Aragon. Polydore Vergil's account was more satisfactory, though he was given to writing about portents, and his

attempts at political explanation were a little simple: he preferred
to point a moral, and his emphasis on the King's avarice may be
partially attributable to this trait. Hall merely translated and
expanded Polydore: the added material was rarely of substance.
Stow's *Annals* could be described as an up-to-date version of a
London chronicle. The editors of Holinshed's second edition—
the one that Bacon was most likely to have seen—took the
original text (itself deriving from Polydore) and emphasized the
morals implicit in the story: much was made of the King's clemency, of his promptness in repaying debts, and so on; and they
added bits of Guicciardini's *History of Italy* to supply some of
the missing continental background for the story of Henry's foreign affairs. Only in Speed was there a real unity: the emphasis
was on the relation between fortune and ability (but this almost
certainly came from Bacon's early draft of Tudor history, which
Speed quotes). And Speed was not only very assiduous in locat-
ing sources for his history but also was not averse to making
some necessary conjectures. His own opinions on causation, on
those occasions when he was not quoting Bacon, tended to be
moralistic. Only in Speed could Bacon have found a coherent
story, though he could have found additional information in the
others.

While Speed incorporated the techniques derived from the
earlier generations of Italian and English humanists, new trends
were already visible by the time his book appeared. Florentine
humanism had undergone a change that can be attributed in part
to the loss of freedom that was an aftermath of the French invasion of 1494. The new history, as represented by Machiavelli
and Guicciardini, was much more purely political in its outlook
and eschewed moral stances altogether. Both men, each in his
own way, preached the doctrine that any participant in politics
had to make a choice: he could be moral at the risk of failure, or
he could succeed at the risk of his soul. The older idealistic tradition, which hoped to train magistrates to be moral, was abandoned in favor of a separation between personal and political
morality. Since Machiavelli's name rapidly became a byword for

immorality and atheism, men usually referred to Guicciardini or even to Tacitus (who was seen as propounding similar ideas and who, as an ancient Roman, was perforce respectable). One group of English Taciteans eventually coalesced around the Earl of Essex and Bacon thereby came into contact with them. He certainly knew everyone who has been placed in the category of "politic historian." John Hayward, who attached himself to Essex (somewhat to the Earl's embarrassment), was the author of a history of Henry IV which in fact dealt almost entirely with the deposition of Richard II. The dedication of the book to Essex, the emphasis on deposition, the attack on Richard for favoritism (which Queen Elizabeth read as an attack on herself), led to a long sojourn in the Tower for Hayward, and only Bacon's intervention saved him from worse. Bacon tells the story himself:

> The book of deposing Richard the second . . . had much incensed queen Elizabeth. And she asked Mr. Bacon, being then of her learned counsel; *Whether there were no treason contained in it?* Mr. Bacon intending to do him a pleasure, and to take off the Queen's bitterness with a jest, answered; *No, madam, for treason I cannot deliver opinion that there is any, but very much felony.* The Queen, apprehending it gladly, asked; *How, and wherein?* Mr. Bacon answered; *Because he had stolen many of his sentences and conceits out of Cornelius Tacitus.*[32]

The joke aside, Hayward's book, with its purely political explanations and its advice for political action, represented the first (in England) of a new kind of history. And the changes in the political situation at the end of Elizabeth's reign account for the book's popularity and for the number of men who imitated it—Bacon, for his own reasons, among them.

Other "politic historians" included Sir Robert Cotton, whose vast library Bacon used for his own work, and who later wrote a book on Henry III with little concern for chronology or the niceties of historical research but full of precepts containing

[32] *Works*, VII, 133. *Apophthegms, New and Old.*

political wisdom. The most successful venture along these lines was the *Annals* of the reign of Queen Elizabeth by that same William Camden who had earlier made his mark as an antiquary. Camden's book was carefully researched, and he did his utmost to render it as complete as possible. However, Camden was not content to produce a compilation, nor did he go to the extreme of Cotton and abandon history for the sake of aphorism. Instead, though he divided his book into regnal years, he linked the years by introducing problems and then showing how they were solved. Little was attributed to divine intervention; moralistic comments were suppressed; causation was entirely political. Camden described a situation, talked about the men who had to make decisions, and tried to show how they went about making them; and in a succeeding year, the results of their actions would become evident. The *Annals* offered lessons in political behavior, but they were much more subtle—and probably more useful— than Cotton's.

As the letter to Lord Chancellor Ellesmere makes clear [see below, p. 254], as early as 1605 Bacon had already given some thought to a history of the Tudor reigns. Similar arguments in favor of studying that period were advanced in the brief introduction entitled "A History of the Reigns of K. Henry the Eighth, K. Edward, Q. Mary, and part of the Reign of Q. Elizabeth" [see below, p. 258], which was probably written not much later. From these two pieces, it is evident that Bacon had considered the problem of what gives unity to a period of time and had rejected Polydore Vergil's and Hall's explanatory scheme, based as it was on biblical providentialism. The notion that history proceeded as a series of divine rewards and punishments (inflicted up to the third generation) was repugnant to his own political view-point; that some of his contemporaries still thought it relevant may be seen in Sir Walter Ralegh's introduction to his *History of the World*, where the old scheme is extended through the sixteenth century and up to the reign of James. Bacon's reasons for choosing a time to write about were of a different order: the age should have a variety of events, it should be noted for policies and industries; in other words, it ought to offer grist for the mill of the political commentator. Because he took that view, he was inclined to feel that even the relatively lowly historian needed some qualifications for his task:

> It is not to monks or closet penmen that we are to look for guidance in such a case; for men of that order, being keen in style, poor in judgment, and partial in feeling, are no faithful witnesses as to the real passages of business. It is for ministers and great officers to judge of these things, and those who have handled the helm of government, and been acquainted with the difficulties and mysteries of state business.[33]

The day of the cloistered chronicler was done; Bacon had before him a vision of historians such as Machiavelli and Guicciardini.

With the general subject chosen, Bacon had still to decide what kind of history he planned to write. That the projected work would come under the heading of "perfect histories" was inevitable; but even here there was a choice. About the history of times and about relations he had strong doubts. "But Lives, if they be well written, propounding to themselves a person to represent in whom actions both greater and smaller, public and private, have a commixture, must of necessity contain a more true, native, and lively representation."[34] The remark, however, seems to apply primarily to the lives of private men; those of public men, of kings, combine the advantages of the two categories of lives and histories and are the most apt for commentary. Even so, there remained the question of which Tudor to write about. For different reasons, both Henry VIII and Elizabeth had advantages as subjects. But there was another consideration:

> The true marshalling of the degrees of sovereign honour are these. In the first place are *conditores imperiorum*, founders of states and commonwealths; . . . In the second place are *legislatores*, lawgivers; which are also called *second founders*, or *perpetui principes*,

[33] *Works*, VI, 305. "On the Fortunate Memory of Elizabeth, Queen of England." Also p. 266 of this book.
[34] *Works*, III, 334. *Advancement of Learning*.

because they govern by their ordinances after they are gone; . . . In the third place are *liberatores,* or *salvatores,* such as compound the long miseries of civil wars, or deliver their countries from servitude of strangers or tyrants; as Augustus Caesar, Vespasianus, Aurelianus, Theodoricus, King Henry the Seventh of England, King Henry the Fourth of France. In the fourth place are *propagatores* or *propugnatores imperii;* such as in honourable wars enlarge their territories, or make noble defence against invaders. And in the last place are *patres patriae,* which reign justly, and make the times good wherein they live.[35]

The only Tudor monarch to appear anywhere on the list was Henry VII; and since one purpose of the book was to teach statecraft by showing how a king learned his trade, what better choice than the most eminent member of the Tudor line?

The history of Henry VII's reign was one of struggle. Much of it was that outward battle with which we are all familiar: the fighting at Bosworth Field, the distrust of the nobility, the pretenders set up by foreign enemies. Bacon tells all those stories, some of them in great detail. But they were the setting, or the external manifestations, of an inward struggle that was the historian's principal subject. To read the book aright, one must take note of certain words that recur constantly: wisdom, fortune, policy. Henry began with an advantage, a gift of fortune, which he shared with his granddaughter Elizabeth: he had lived both as a private citizen and as a possible heir to a throne, and thus had escaped the indulgence granted an heir certain of his succession in his youth, replacing it instead with a sense of wonder and gratitude at what he had gained. But a prince who gained a throne by the grace of fortune needed to learn wisdom to retain it, and Henry began by "being in his nature and constitution of mind not very apprehensive or forecasting of future events afar off, but an entertainer of fortune by the day."[36] He had to learn to understand his own nature and overcome its weaknesses;

[35] *Works,* VI, 505–506. *Essays:* "Of Honour and Reputation."

[36] *Works,* VI, 31. *History of King Henry the Seventh.* Also p. 70 of this book.

he had to learn that no man can rely on fortune forever but must instead comprehend the pattern of events and the minds of others. This was wisdom. Thus Henry had to weigh his chances of a successful war against France and act accordingly. Since he understood the minds and desires of Ferdinand of Aragon, of the Emperor Maximilian, of James IV of Scotland, as well as of his enemy the King of France, since he saw the precise manner in which battle would be waged, he negotiated a profitable peace: "These things he did wisely foresee, and did as artificially conduct, whereby all things fell into his lap as he desired."[37] "Artificially" is used here in the sense of "with artifice," and "artifice" is one of the possible synonyms for "policy." Policy, in Bacon's usage, is the political projection of wisdom. Henry learned this slowly and perhaps a little inadequately. But he learned it better than most men.

The possession or acquisition of wisdom was the principal virtue of a king. There were others: mercy (when cruelty was unnecessary), as in Henry's treatment of rebels; the ability to make good laws of permanent validity; nobility of mind. Even the art of keeping one's distance and one's own counsel could be thought of as a virtue. But absolute standards of good and evil did not apply to rulers as they might to private men. To save money and fill the treasury might be good, but avarice was bad because it alienated citizens. Keeping a distance from the commoners added to the dignity and even to the power of a king, but at the expense of alienating a nobility that might have helped him. Caution was needful, excess suspicion bred the very trouble it strained to avoid. A balance was essential, and it was wisdom that held the scales.

The wisdom needed for kingship, and the means of acquiring it, form the *leitmotiv* of the reign of Henry as Bacon saw it. Although that vision alone would have been sufficient to distinguish Bacon's work from that of most of his contemporaries, he did more than apply a single dominant idea to a body of

[37] *Works*, VI, 120. *History of King Henry the Seventh*. Also p. 141 of this book.

otherwise familiar material. He tried to find solutions to the ordinary problems that plague historians, such as how causation works, or how to construct a narrative. Under ordinary circumstances, Bacon avoided any reference to providence; he believed in God, certainly, as he believed that ultimately God controlled the universe and the men in it. Rarely was it given to men to see the workings of providence, let alone understand them; on those few occasions where it was possible—the marriage of Henry's daughter to the King of Scots, which eventually led to the accession of James and brought peace to the country, or the marriage of Prince Henry to Catherine of Aragon, which was to lead to the Reformation—Bacon reported what he saw without any feeling that it was somehow inappropriate. Normally, however, it was all that a historian could do to discover the second causes, man's activities. And these were the most interesting, for some understanding of politics and psychology was ultimately possible, whereas man could never attain an understanding of the workings of God. Psychology, which for Bacon was the study of how certain types of men behave in given situations as well as the study of individual behavior, could be learned from books (such as his own) and from experience. That was why a life in politics helped a man explain political behavior. To know that the Queen Dowager, Henry's mother-in-law, was "a busy negotiating woman"[38] who had engaged in conspiracies on several occasions gave Bacon confidence to put forward the conjecture that she was involved in the imposture of Lambert Simnell. Similarly a malcontent like the Earl of Suffolk could be explained as "a man of a light and rash spirit," who "thought every vapour would be a tempest,"[39] which accounted for his flight to the Low Countries in hope of raising rebellion.

But Bacon relied on political analysis even more than he did on psychology. It was impossible to understand the trouble with

[38] *Works*, VI, 46. *History of King Henry the Seventh*. Also p. 83 of this book.
[39] *Works*, VI, 221. *History of King Henry the Seventh*. Also p. 225 of this book.

France over Brittany without carefully considering why that province was so important to the French King. Henry saw through the deceits of the French denials of any intention of seizing the duchy, but he had to consider his own position too:

A fame of a war he liked well, but not an achievement; for the one he thought would make him richer, and the other poorer; and he was possessed with many secret fears touching his own people; which he was therefore loth to arm, and put weapons into their hands . . .[40]

Occasionally, Henry judged wrongly, but then "his error was not so much facility of belief, as an ill-measuring of the forces of the other party,"[41] and Bacon was constrained to show not only what the king thought but what the case really was. The number of such bits of analysis is large, and a listing of them would gain us little. Instead, look at one case—the peace made with France— and compare Bacon's treatment of it with those of his predecessors. Polydore Vergil certainly tried to analyze the matter politically:

These tidings [the report that the Emperor Maximilian would be unable to move] filled Henry with both fear and despair. He knew that to wage so great a war alone would be most dangerous; but he was well aware that to abandon it would lead to charges of cowardice, and foresaw that above all his English subjects would be wrathful since they would have reason to suspect him of resorting to the elaborate trappings of a war in order deceitfully to extort money from them; he was in no doubt that such statements would be made throughout the populace, and would be readily believed by all. It was for these reasons that he was fearful and bewailed that he would be cheated out of the war-alliance by Maximilian, its instigator . . . [so he moved slowly, and eventually came to an agreement with the French]

[40] *Works*, VI, 67–68. *History of King Henry the Seventh.* Also p. 102 of this book.
[41] *Works*, VI, 73. *History of King Henry the Seventh.* Also p. 106 of this book.

There were besides many who believed him to have come to an understanding with Charles before he crossed the sea, partly through fear and partly through a desire to acquire money, and a lasting report of this charge so penetrated into the minds of the public that even today many hold this opinion. Nevertheless (as some argue) it was neither greed nor fear. Henry, a man in general of the most prudent disposition, did not fear the enemy, to whose forces his own were not unequal; nor did he aim to secure cash, but was rather actuated by a desire for honour and for his own safety.[42]

Hall merely translated Polydore; Stow says nothing of all this. Speed, however, had his own view of what transpired:

His wisdome therefore saw, that in giving over the invasion of *France;* he should sloathfully abandon a goodly occasion of making himselfe universally acceptable to his people. His resolutions therefore are by him at leastwise pretended to continue, and for that cause he sufficiently encreaseth his numbers, that he might seeme able to goe through with that enterprize alone; and though the time of yeere were too farre spent (for he landed not at *Calais,* till the sixth day of October) yet marcheth he with his whole forces towards *Boloigne,* being wel assured that with this Trowell he should at once plaister two wals, that is, humor his *English* subjects, and for a peace draw himselfe store of Crownes from the *French.*[43]

Bacon was convinced that Henry never intended to go through with the war, for

He knew well that France was now entire and at unity with itself, and never so mighty many years before. He saw by the taste he had of his forces sent into Brittaine [Brittany] that the French knew well enough how to make war with the English; by not putting things to the hazard of a battle, but wearying them by long sieges of towns, and strong fortified encampings. James the Third of Scotland, his true

---

[42] Polydore Vergil, *Anglica Historia,* ed. Denys Hay, Camden Series, vol. LXXIV (London: The Royal Historical Society, 1950), 53, 57.

[43] John Speed, *The History of Great Britaine* (London: Iohn Sudbury and Georg Humble, 1611), 736.

friend and confederate, gone; and James the Fourth (that had succeeded) wholly at the devotion of France, and ill-affected towards him.
As for the conjunctions of Ferdinando of Spain and Maximilian, he
could make no foundation upon them. For the one had power and not
will; and the other had will and not power . . . Neither was he out of
fear of the discontents and ill blood within the realm; which having
used always to repress and appease in person, he was loth they should
find him at a distance beyond sea, and engaged in war. Finding therefore the inconveniencies and difficulties in the prosecution of a war, he
cast with himself how to compass two things. The one, how by the
declaration and inchoation of war to make his profit. The other, how to
come off from the war with saving of his honour. For profit, it was to
be made two ways; upon his subjects for the war, and upon his
enemies for the peace; like a good merchant that maketh his gain
both upon the commodities exported and imported back again. For
the point of honour, wherein he might suffer for giving over the war,
he considered well, that as he could not trust upon the aids of Ferdinando and Maximilian for supports of war, so the impuissance of
the one, and the double proceeding of the other, lay fair for him for
occasions [pretexts] to accept of peace.[44]

Bacon's debts are evident; so is the increased complexity of his
analysis; and it is typical that where Polydore strove to exculpate
the king, Bacon could find nothing wrong with his actions.

In constructing his book, Bacon relied for his scaffolding
upon the theme of wisdom and fortune. Certain large issues
could be treated as the major building-blocks: foreign policy was
one, the revolts against Henry were another, the king's avarice
provided a third, and his abilities as a law-maker the fourth. The
first three were familiar fare; and Speed had already shown the
advantages of treating such events as blocks, out of chronological
order. The emphasis on law was original with Bacon. In his own
legal writings, Bacon had always insisted that laws should be
seen in their historical context: that was the only way in which
a sensible law-code might be constructed. Moreover, he had
argued that Henry VII was comparable to Edward I as one of the

[44] *Works*, VI, 119–120. *History of King Henry the Seventh*. Also
pp. 140–141 of this book.

greatest of English legislators, and that to omit the king's chief virtue was tantamount to falsifying the history of the reign. And here, too, was an opportunity for a lawyer to teach laymen an important lesson, for although the laws could be found readily enough in the law books, "yet that informeth not the judgment of kings and counsellors and persons of estate so well as to see them described and entered in the table and portrait of the times."[45]

Like most historians of his time, Bacon followed the classical model in refusing to indulge himself in too many lengthy explanatory passages. Instead, he put the explanations into the mouths of the characters of his history. Almost all the speeches in the *History* are the invention of its author; frequently he had no more to go on than the information that someone had actually spoken; sometimes he did not have even so much. If records existed giving the contents of a political oration, Bacon of course had no objection to using them; but his aim here was verisimilitude rather than truth. Even in his day, some purists (such as the French philosopher and historian Jean Bodin, whose work Bacon had certainly read) objected to what they were inclined to feel was pure invention. But Bacon's literary conscience rebelled at the insertion of long passages that were evidently the result of the author's interposing himself between the reader and the subject. The speeches thus ought to be considered as part of the structuring of the book rather than as attempts at improving the evidence. And certainly, an author needed all the help he could find. For all Bacon's labors at producing a coherent organization, at the end his efforts failed. Partly, it was the fault of the evidence. Almost all his sources emphasized the first dozen years of the reign, in which the problems were concentrated, and treated the second half perfunctorily. With little to go on, Bacon followed the pattern. The war with France was over, Perkin Warbeck was dead; worse still, Henry's character began to show signs of degeneration. Gradually, the *History* became more and

[45] *Works*, VI, 97. *History of King Henry the Seventh*. Also p. 126 of this book.

more a chronicle, and we find increasingly the mark of the annalist: "In this year . . .," "This year also . . ." and the like.

The matter of Bacon's sources has come up on several occasions. Both Bacon's nineteenth century editor, James Spedding, and Wilhelm Busch, the German who wrote the standard account of Henry's reign, have investigated the matter in great detail.[46] From those studies, a number of facts emerge. Bacon's *History* was based on the earlier work of Polydore Vergil, as seen through Edward Hall's English rendering (on at least one occasion, Bacon followed Hall in a mistranslation). He had also read Fabyan and probably used Bernard André, though he might have gotten the André material from Speed's book. The brief comment on Cabot's voyage derived from Richard Hakluyt, the chronicler of exploration. At some time, Bacon had had access to the vast library of Sir Robert Cotton and had read Perkin's proclamation. And Bacon used the Parliament Rolls and the books of statutes. He had seen a book of financial transactions kept by Empson. Finally, we know that Bacon and Speed had helped each other at some time between 1605 and 1611, that is, after the year in which Bacon's letter to Ellesmere first announced an interest in history and the year in which Speed published his mammoth folio. Speed was only too happy to make use of Bacon's jottings; we may assume that Bacon was equally pleased to have access to Speed's researches. But further details concerning their mutual indebtedness cannot be found.

For his facts, Bacon followed his sources almost slavishly. When Polydore plunged into error over the chronology of the whole Breton war episode, Bacon did nothing to rectify matters; instead, he made Bishop Morton deliver a speech to a Parliament that had been called the year before the events that Morton was presenting. Perkin Warbeck's Scottish speech came from Speed, who concocted it from Perkin's proclamation; Bacon's notice of the proclamation came from his own earlier reading of the document, but since he did not have access to it when he was writing

[46] Wilhelm Busch, *England under the Tudors*. Vol. I: King Henry VII [all published] (London: A. D. Innes, 1895), Appendix II, 416–423.

(it was in London, and he was still an exile in the country), he simply gave its substance from memory. Other incidents were invented: Morton's fork was a story that had been attributed to a number of people; Bacon used it because it seemed appropriate. Henry's avarice was exaggerated, though there was some evidence for it. Henry's relations to his wife and mother-in-law were not as Bacon reported them: he elaborated some dubious hints without seeking positive evidence. There is no need to extend the litany. Bacon cannot be considered an original source for the reign of Henry VII, nor did he have available evidence that has since been lost. The *History* is a source only for what it reveals of the mind of its author; it is valuable for its interpretation, not for its facts.

Are there sources for the interpretation as well? There is no doubt that Bacon owed a great deal to the Italians Machiavelli and Guicciardini. Like most of his contemporaries, Bacon attacked some of Machiavelli's views, though he had grace enough to acknowledge some indebtedness. The debt appears in a few obvious citations, in Bacon's comments on the value of a non-professional army made up of yeomen (which derive from Machiavelli's *Art of War*), and in passages such as his remarks on the death of the Duke of Brittany, "an accident that the King might easily have foreseen, and ought to have reckoned upon and provided for"[47] (which is reminiscent of Machiavelli's judgment upon a similar failure of foresight of Cesare Borgia). But these are details. Bacon shared with Machiavelli the distinction between private and public morality, the insistence upon seeing history in terms of second causes rather than as the working-out of God's providence, the determination to analyze in political and psychological terms. He shared the Italian's disdain for detailed accuracy and his slight distaste for the profession of the simple historian. The distinction between history and commentary, which is so crucial in Bacon's thought, comes ultimately from Machiavelli's practice in his *Discourses*; all the rest follows

[47] *Works*, VI, 83. *History of King Henry the Seventh.* Also p. 114 in this book.

from that. From Guicciardini, Bacon learned how to make use
of the interpretive style he had adopted from Machiavelli. The
type of analysis, the attempt to penetrate into the minds of the
actors on the political stage, the attribution of cold reason to the
principals, these come from Guicciardini. But the particular in-
terplay of wisdom and fortune was Bacon's. Nor was he quite so
disillusioned or cynical as the Italians. England had no need of a
Machiavellian prince, and Bacon had no inclination to help train
one. Bacon did not hesitate to borrow whatever he needed from
the Italians, but he had no intention of making over his mind on
their pattern. His final judgment on the aims of Italian statecraft
was "surely the fairer way is not much about."

For all the debts, the *History* is a personal book, not only
because its composition was occasioned by a crisis late in Bacon's
life, but because its style and method were adopted as a part of
Bacon's answer to a conundrum that plagued him for most of his
career. This is not the book of a political humanist, not even of
one temporarily unemployed; it is, instead, the book of a man
who has rejected the active philosophy of political humanism for
the more sheltered one of science, whose arena is no longer the
court of one city or state, but the world. From that new view-
point, politics could be seen as the paltry shiftings of men whose
claim to moral superiority was best rejected, and whose activities
needed to be analyzed in the same way that a scientist looked
into the nature of heat and cold. Bacon could analyze thus dis-
passionately; at the same time, he could himself enter the whirl
of politics, realizing that he was neither better nor worse than
any of the other dancers in the court masque. He could dream of
power, of a King guided to greatness by the sage advice of a
wise Lord Chancellor—and we can see a shadow of that dream
in Cardinal Morton's speech to Henry VII's first Parliament, for
Bacon surely saw himself in Morton's robes. He could ask, as he
did so often, what was good and what was evil in this political
realm and construct a list of the virtues that made a king great.
And by "great," he meant successful, where the Erasmian, Christian humanist might have meant "holy." He could try to answer

the same question about a courtier. The *History* is, essentially, a courtier's book; like all such, its intention is practical. Bacon, one suspects, felt that it was part of the courtier's task to educate his king up to the requisite level; kingship meant a partnership (and one notes that Henry's principal error was his treatment of advisors, his suspicion of all opinions but his own). The *History* is a political book. Its author was a courtier and a politician; and it is some measure of the changes that took place over the course of his lifetime that he would have admitted to being both.

Bibliography

Editions of THE HISTORY OF THE REIGN
OF KING HENRY THE SEVENTH:

For the earlier editions, consult R. W. Gibson, *Francis Bacon. A Bibliography of his Works and of Baconiana to the Year 1750* (Oxford: The Scrivener Press, 1950).

The standard modern edition is that published by James Spedding, R. E. Ellis and D. D. Heath, *Works of Francis Bacon*, 7 vols. (London: Longman & Co., 1857–1859), VI, 23–245.

Prior to the year 1700, there were editions in English in 1622 (two editions), 1628 (one edition in two issues), 1629 (left-over sheets of 1628 with a new title-page), 1637, 1641, 1676; Bacon's work was also included in the great summary of seventeenth-century history writing, White Kennett, *Complete History of England* (London: B. Aylmer, 1706; reprinted 1719).

Latin editions appeared in 1638 (as part of *Operum Moralium* [London, two issues]), in 1642 and 1647 (two), published at Leyden; and in 1662 and 1695, published at Amsterdam. There was a French edition in 1627, and two Belgian editions, in 1673 and 1724.

There were editions in 1786 and 1790; J. Rawson Lumby edited the book in the Pitt Press series (Cambridge: Cambridge University Press, 1876; numerous reissues). The number of times the *History* has appeared in collections of Bacon's works defies count.

Secondary:

Material specifically related to the *History:*
Herschel Baker, *The Race of Time* (Toronto: University of Toronto Press, 1967).

Wilhelm Busch, *England under the Tudors*. Vol. I: Henry VII [all published] (London: A. D. Innes, 1895), Appendix II.

Leonard F. Dean, "Sir Francis Bacon's Theory of Civil History-Writing," *ELH* [English Literary History], VIII, no. 3 (Sept. 1941), 161–183.

F. Smith Fussner, *The Historical Revolution* (London: Routledge and Kegan Paul, 1962), esp. Chapter X, "Sir Francis Bacon and the Idea of History."

James J. Kirkwood, "Bacon's *Henry VII*: A Model of a Theory of Historiography," *Renaissance Papers* (1965), pp. 51–55.

F. J. Levy, *Tudor Historical Thought* (San Marino, Calif.: The Huntington Library, 1967).

George H. Nadel, "History as Psychology in Francis Bacon's Theory of History," *History and Theory*, V, no. 3 (1966), pp. 275–287.

Sister Mary Faith Schuster, "Philosophy of Life and Prose Style in Thomas More's *Richard III* and Francis Bacon's *Henry VII*," *Publications of the Modern Language Association*, LXX, no. 2 (June 1955), pp. 474–487.

Thomas Wheeler, "The Purpose of Bacon's *History of Henry the Seventh*," *Studies in Philology*, LIV, no. 1 (Jan. 1957), pp. 1–13.

Howard B. White, "The English Solomon: Francis Bacon on Henry VII," *Social Research*, XXIV, no. 4 (Winter 1957), pp. 457–481.

Selected list of materials on Bacon:

F. H. Anderson, *Francis Bacon, His Career and Thought* (Los Angeles: University of Southern California Press, 1962).

————, *The Philosophy of Francis Bacon* (Chicago: University of Chicago Press, 1948).

Edwin B. Benjamin, "Bacon and Tacitus," *Classical Philology*, LX, no. 2 (April 1965), pp. 102–110.

Catherine Drinker Bowen, *Francis Bacon, The Temper of a Man* (Boston: Little, Brown, 1963).

C. D. Broad, *The Philosophy of Francis Bacon* (Cambridge: Cambridge University Press, 1926).

G. Bullough, "Bacon and the Defence of Learning," in *Seventeenth Century Studies presented to Sir Herbert Grierson* (Oxford: The Clarendon Press, 1938), pp. 1–20.

Rexmond C. Cochrane, "Francis Bacon and the Architect of Fortune," *Studies in the Renaissance*, V (1958), pp. 176–195.

R. S. Crane, "The Relation of Bacon's *Essays* to his Program for the Advancement of Learning," in *Schelling Anniversary Papers*, ed. A. H. Quinn (New York: The Century Co., 1923), pp. 87–105.

Morris Croll, "Attic Prose: Lipsius, Montaigne, Bacon," in *Schelling Anniversary Papers*, ed. A. H. Quinn (New York: The Century Co., 1923), pp. 117–150.

J. G. Crowther, *Francis Bacon, The First Statesman of Science* (London: Cresset Press, 1960).

Walter R. Davis, "The Imagery of Bacon's Late Work," *Modern Language Quarterly*, XXVII, no. 2 (June 1966), pp. 162–173.

C. J. Ducasse, "Francis Bacon's Philosophy of Science," in *Theories of Scientific Method*, ed. R. M. Blake, C. J. Ducasse and E. H. Madden (Seattle, Wash.: University of Washington Press, 1960), pp. 50–74.

Benjamin Farrington, *Francis Bacon, Philosopher of Industrial Science* (New York: H. Schuman, 1949).

————, "On Misunderstanding the Philosophy of Francis Bacon," in *Science, Medicine and History, Essays . . . in Honour of Charles Singer*, ed. E. A. Underwood (London: Oxford University Press, 1953), I, pp. 439–450.

————, *The Philosophy of Francis Bacon* (Liverpool: Liverpool University Press, 1964).

Neal W. Gilbert, *Renaissance Concepts of Method* (New York: Columbia University Press, 1960).

W. H. Greenleaf, *Order, Empiricism and Politics* (London: Oxford University Press for the University of Hull, 1964).

Marie Boas Hall, "Bacon and Gilbert," *Journal of the History of Ideas*, XII, no. 3 (June 1951), pp. 466–467 [see also, Duane Roller, "Did Bacon know Gilbert's *De Magnete*?" *Isis*, XLIV, nos. 1–2 (June 1953), pp. 10–13].

_____, "In Defense of Bacon's Views on the Reform of Science,"
     The Personalist, XLIV, no. 4 (Oct. 1963), pp. 437–453.
John L. Harrison, "Bacon's View of Rhetoric, Poetry, and the Imagi-
     nation," *Huntington Library Quarterly*, XX, no. 2 (Feb. 1957),
     pp. 107–125.
Mary B. Hesse, "Francis Bacon," in *A Critical History of Western
     Philosophy*, ed. D. J. O'Connor (New York and London: The
     Free Press of Glencoe, 1964), pp. 141–152.
Christopher Hill, *Intellectual Origins of the English Revolution* (Ox-
     ford: The Clarendon Press, 1965).
Robert C. Johnson, "Francis Bacon and Lionel Cranfield," *Huntington
     Library Quarterly*, XXIII, no. 4 (Aug. 1960), pp. 301–320.
L. C. Knights, "Bacon and the Seventeenth-Century Dissociation of
     Sensibility," in *Explorations* (London: Chatto & Windus, 1946),
     pp. 92–111.
Paul H. Kocher, "Francis Bacon and His Father," *Huntington Library
     Quarterly*, XXI, no. 2 (Feb. 1958), pp. 133–158.
_____, "Francis Bacon on the Science of Jurisprudence," *Journal of
     the History of Ideas*, XVIII, no. 1 (Jan. 1957), pp. 3–26.
R. E. Larsen, "The Aristotelianism of Bacon's *Novum Organum*,"
     Journal of the History of Ideas, XXIII, no. 4 (Oct–Dec. 1962), pp.
     435–450.
C. W. Lemmi, *The Classic Deities in Bacon* (Baltimore: The Johns Hop-
     kins Press, 1933).
Vincent Luciani, "Bacon and Guicciardini," *Publications of the Modern
     Language Association*, LXII, no. 1 (Mar. 1947), pp. 96–113.
_____, "Bacon and Machiavelli," *Italica*, XXIV, no. 1 (March 1947),
     pp. 26–40.
Thomas Babington Macaulay, "Lord Bacon." [Appeared originally in
     the *Edinburgh Review* (July 1837); numerous reprints.]
Rudolph Metz, "Bacon's Part in the Intellectual Movement of his
     Time," in *Seventeenth-Century Studies presented to Sir Herbert
     Grierson* (Oxford: The Clarendon Press, 1938), pp. 21–32.
Napoleone Orsini, " 'Policy' or the Language of Elizabethan Machia-
     vellianism," *Journal of the Warburg and Courtauld Institutes*,
     IX (1946), pp. 122–134.
M. E. Prior, "Bacon's Man of Science," *Journal of the History of Ideas*,
     XV, no. 3 (June 1954), pp. 348–370.
T. K. Rabb, "Francis Bacon and the Reform of Society," in *Action and*

Conviction in Early Modern Europe, ed. T. K. Rabb and J. Seigel (Princeton: Princeton University Press, 1969), pp. 169–193.

Anne Righter, "Francis Bacon," in *The English Mind,* ed. H. S. Davies and G. Watson (Cambridge: Cambridge University Press, 1964), pp. 7–29.

Paolo Rossi, *Francis Bacon: From Magic to Science,* tr. Sacha Rabinovitch (London: Routledge and Kegan Paul, 1968).

Vernon F. Snow, "Francis Bacon's Advice to Fulke Greville on Research Techniques," *Huntington Library Quarterly,* XXIII, no. 4 (Aug. 1960), pp. 369–378.

James Spedding, *Letters and Life of Francis Bacon,* 7 vols. (London: Longman, Green, Longman and Roberts, 1861–1874).

Studies in the Literary Imagination, IV, no. 1 (April 1971) devotes the entire issue to "The Legacy of Francis Bacon."

Geoffrey Tillotson, "Words for Princes," in *Essays in Criticism and Research* (Cambridge: Cambridge University Press, 1942), pp. 31–40.

Brian Vickers, ed. *Essential Articles for the Study of Francis Bacon* (Hamden, Conn: Archon Books, The Shoestring Press, 1968).

———, *Francis Bacon and Renaissance Prose* (Cambridge: Cambridge University Press, 1968).

Karl R. Wallace, *Francis Bacon on Communication and Rhetoric* (Chapel Hill: University of North Carolina Press, 1943).

———, *Francis Bacon on the Nature of Man* (Urbana, Ill.: University of Illinois Press, 1967).

Sidney Warhaft, "Bacon and the Renaissance Ideal of Self-Knowledge," *The Personalist,* XLIV, no. 4 (Oct. 1963), pp. 454–471.

Virgil K. Whitaker, *Francis Bacon's Intellectual Milieu* (Los Angeles: William Andrews Clark Memorial Library, 1962).

Howard B. White, *Peace among the Willows* (The Hague: Martinus Nijhoff, 1968).

Basil Willey, *The Seventeenth Century Background* (New York: Anchor Books, 1953).

Robert Adolph, *The Rise of Modern Prose Style* (Cambridge, Mass.: M.I.T. Press, 1968).

Edward I. Berry, "History and Rhetoric in Bacon's *Henry VII,*" in *Seventeenth-Century Prose,* ed. S. E. Fish (Oxford, 1971).

Note on the Text

The text of the *History of the Reign of King Henry the Seventh* is based on that of Spedding; where I have altered Spedding, it is usually to bring this text into closer conformity with the first edition (1622). The pieces in the appendix have been printed verbatim from Spedding's text of Bacon's English or from Spedding's translations of Bacon's Latin.

The Historie
of the Raigne
# of King Henry the Seventh

Written by the Right Honourable,

Francis, Lord Verulam, Viscount St. Alban.

LONDON,
Printed by W. Stansby
for Matthew Lownes, and William Barret.
1622.

CHARLES,

Prince of Wales, Duke of Cornwall, Earl of Chester, etc.

It may please your Highness,

In part of my acknowledgment to your Highness, I have endeavoured to do honour to the memory of the last King of England that was ancestor to the King your father and yourself; and was that King to whom both Unions may in a sort refer: that of the Roses being in him consummate, and that of the Kingdoms by him begun. Besides, his times deserve it. For he was a wise man, and an excellent King; and yet the times were rough, and full of mutations and rare accidents. And it is with times, as it is with ways. Some are more up-hill and down-hill, and some are more flat and plain; and the one is better for the liver, and the other for the writer. I have not flattered him, but took him to life as well as I could, sitting so far off, and having no better light. It is true, your Highness hath a living pattern, incomparable, of [in] the King your father. But it is not amiss for you also to see one of these ancient pieces. God preserve your Highness.

Your Highness's most humble
and devoted servant,
FRANCIS ST. ALBAN.

THE HISTORY
OF THE REIGN
OF KING HENRY THE SEVENTH.

After that Richard, the third of that name, king in fact only, but tyrant both in title and regiment, and so commonly termed and reputed in all times since, was by the Divine Revenge, favouring the design of an exiled man, overthrown and slain at Bosworth Field; there succeeded in the kingdom the Earl of Richmond, thenceforth styled Henry the Seventh. The King immediately after the victory, as one that had been bred under a devout mother, and was in his nature a great observer of religious forms, caused *Te deum laudamus* to be solemnly sung in the presence of the whole army upon the place, and was himself with general applause and great cries of joy, in a kind of militar [military] election or recognition, saluted King. Meanwhile the body of Richard after many indignities and reproaches (the dirigies and obsequies of the common people towards tyrants) was obscurely buried. For though the King of his nobleness gave charge unto the friars of Leicester to see an honourable interment to be given to it, yet the religious people themselves (being not free from the humours of the vulgar) neglected it; wherein nevertheless they did not then incur any man's blame or censure.

104

No man thinking any ignominy or contumely unworthy of him, that had been the executioner of King Henry the Sixth (that innocent Prince) with his own hands; the contriver of the death of the Duke of Clarence, his brother; the murderer of his two nephews (one of them his lawful King in the present, and the other in the future, failing of him); and vehemently suspected to have been the impoisoner [poisoner] of his wife, thereby to make vacant his bed for a marriage within the degrees forbidden. And although he were a Prince in militar [military] virtue approved, jealous of the honour of the English nation, and likewise a good law-maker for the ease and solace of the common people; yet his cruelties and parricides in the opinion of all men weighed down his virtues and merits; and in the opinion of wise men, even those virtues themselves were conceived to be rather feigned and affected things to serve his ambition, than true qualities ingenerate in his judgment or nature. And therefore it was noted by men of great understanding (who seeing his after acts looked back upon his former proceedings) that even in the time of King Edward his brother, he was not without secret trains and mines to turn envy and hatred upon his brother's government; as having an expectation and a kind of divination, that the King, by reason of his many disorders, could not be of long life, but was like to leave his sons of tender years; and then he knew well how easy a step it was from the place of a Protector and first Prince of the blood to the Crown. And that out of this deep root of ambition it sprang, that as well at the treaty of peace that passed between Edward the Fourth and Lewis the Eleventh of France, concluded by interview of both Kings at Piqueny, as upon all other occasions, Richard, then Duke of Gloucester, stood ever upon the side of honour, raising his own reputation to the disadvantage of the King his brother, and drawing the eyes of all (especially of the nobles and soldiers) upon himself; as if the King by his voluptuous life and mean marriage were become effeminate and less sensible of honour, and reason of state, than was fit for a King. And as for the politic and wholesome laws which were enacted in his time, they were interpreted to be but the brocage of an usurper, thereby to woo and win the hearts of

the people, as being conscious to himself that the true obligations
of sovereignty in him failed and were wanting. But King Henry,
in the very entrance of his reign and the instant of time when
the kingdom was cast into his arms, met with a point of great
difficulty and knotty to solve, able to trouble and confound the
wisest King in the newness of his estate; and so much the more,
because it could not endure a deliberation, but must be at once
deliberated and determined. There were fallen to his lot, and con-
current in his person, three several titles to the imperial crown.
The first, the title of the Lady Elizabeth, with whom, by precedent pact with the party that brought him in, he was to marry.
The second, the ancient and long disputed title (both by plea
and arms) of the house of Lancaster, to which he was inheritor
in his own person. The third, the title of the sword or conquest,
for that he came in by victory of battle, and that the king in
possession was slain in the field. The first of these was fairest,
and most like to give contentment to the people, who by two-
and-twenty years reign of King Edward the Fourth had been
fully made capable of the clearness of the title of the White Rose
or house of York; and by the mild and plausible reign of the
same King towards his latter time, were become affectionate to
that line. But then it lay plain before his eyes, that if he relied
upon that title, he could be but a King at courtesy, and have
rather a matrimonial than a regal power; the right remaining in
his Queen, upon whose decease, either with issue or without
issue, he was to give place and be removed. And though he
should obtain by Parliament to be continued, yet he knew there
was a very great difference between a King that holdeth his
crown by a civil act of estates, and one that holdeth it originally
by the law of nature and descent of blood. Neither wanted there
even at that time secret rumours and whisperings (which afterwards gathered strength and turned to great troubles) that the
two young sons of King Edward the Fourth, or one of them,
(which were said to be destroyed in the Tower,) were not indeed
murdered but conveyed secretly away, and were yet living:
which, if it had been true, had prevented the title of the Lady
Elizabeth. On the other side, if he stood upon his own title of

the house of Lancaster, inherent in his person, he knew it was a
title condemned by Parliament, and generally prejudged in the
common opinion of the realm, and that it tended directly to the
disinherison [disinheritance] of the line of York, held then the
indubi[t]ate heirs of the crown. So that if he should have no issue
by the Lady Elizabeth, which should be descendants of the double line, then the ancient flames of discord and intestine wars,
upon the competition of both houses, would again return and
revive. 926

As for conquest, notwithstanding Sir William Stanley, after
some acclamations of the soldiers in the field, had put a crown
of ornament (which Richard wore in the battle and was found
amongst the spoils) upon King Henry's head, as if there were
his chief title; yet he remembered well upon what conditions and
agreements he was brought in, and that to claim as conqueror
was to put as well his own party as the rest into terror and fear;
as that which gave him power of disannulling of laws, and disposing of men's fortunes and estates, and the like points of absolute power, being in themselves so harsh and odious, as that
William himself, commonly called the Conqueror, howsoever he
used and exercised the power of a conqueror to reward his Nor-
mans, yet he forbare to use that claim in the beginning, but
mixed it with a titulary pretence, grounded upon the will and
designation of Edward the Confessor. But the King, out of the
greatness of his own mind, presently cast the die; and the inconveniences appearing unto him on all parts, and knowing there
could not be any interreign or suspension of title, and preferring
his affection to his own line and blood, and liking that title best
which made him independent, and being in his nature and constitution of mind not very apprehensive or forecasting of future
events afar off, but an entertainer of fortune by the day, resolved
to rest upon the title of Lancaster as the main, and to use the
other two, that of marriage and that of battle, but as supporters,
the one to appease secret discontents, and the other to beat
down open murmur and dispute; not forgetting that the same
title of Lancaster had formerly maintained a possession of three
descents in the crown, and might have proved a perpetuity, had

it not ended in the weakness and inability of the last prince.
Whereupon the King presently that very day, being the two and
twentieth of August [1485], assumed the style of King in his
own name, without mention of the Lady Elizabeth at all, or any
relation thereunto. In which course he ever after persisted: which
did spin him a thread of many seditions and troubles. The King,
full of these thoughts, before his departure from Leicester, despatched Sir Robert Willoughby to the castle of Sheriff-Hutton,
in Yorkshire, where were kept in safe custody, by King Richard's
commandment, both the Lady Elizabeth, daughter of King Edward, and Edward Plantagenet, son and heir to George Duke of
Clarence. This Edward was by the King's warrant delivered from
the constable of the castle to the hand of Sir Robert Willoughby;
and by him with all safety and diligence conveyed to the Tower
of London, where he was shut up close prisoner. Which act of
the King's (being an act merely of policy and power) proceeded
not so much from any apprehension he had of Dr. Shaw's tale
at Paul's Cross for the bastarding of Edward the Fourth's issues,
in which case this young gentleman was to succeed, (for that
fable was ever exploded,) but upon a settled disposition to depress all eminent persons of the line of York. Wherein still the
King, out of strength of will or weakness of judgment, did use
to shew [show] a little more of the party than of the king.

   For the Lady Elizabeth, she received also a direction to repair with all convenient speed to London, and there to remain
with the Queen dowager her mother; which accordingly she soon
after did, accompanied with many noblemen and ladies of honour. In the mean season the King set forwards by easy journeys
to the City of London, receiving the acclamations and applauses
of the people as he went, which indeed were true and unfeigned,
as might well appear in the very demonstrations and fullness of
the cry. For they thought generally that he was a Prince as ordained and sent down from heaven to unite and put to an end
the long dissensions of the two houses; which although they had
had, in the times of Henry the Fourth, Henry the Fifth, and a
part of Henry the Sixth on the one side, and the times of Edward
the Fourth on the other, lucid intervals and happy pauses; yet

they did ever hang over the kingdom, ready to break forth into new perturbations and calamities. And as his victory gave him the knee, so his purpose of marriage with the Lady Elizabeth gave him the heart; so that both knee and heart did truly bow before him.

He on the other side with great wisdom (not ignorant of the affections and fears of the people), to disperse the conceit and terror of a conquest, had given order that there should be nothing in his journey like unto a warlike march or manner; but rather like unto the progress of a King in full peace and assurance.

He entered the City upon a Saturday, as he had also obtained the victory upon a Saturday; which day of the week, first upon an observation, and after upon memory and fancy, he accounted and chose as a day prosperous unto him.

The mayor and companies of the City received him at Shoreditch; whence with great and honourable attendance, and troops of noblemen and persons of quality, he entered the City; himself not being on horseback, or in any open chair or throne, but in a close chariot; as one that having been sometimes an enemy to the whole state, and a proscribed person, chose rather to keep state and strike a reverence into the people than to fawn upon them.

He went first into St. Paul's Church, where, not meaning that the people should forget too soon that he came in by battle, he made offertory of his standards, and had orizons [prayers] and *Te Deum* again sung, and went to his lodging prepared in the Bishop of London's palace, where he stayed for a time.

During his abode there, he assembled his council and other principal persons, in presence of whom he did renew again his promise to marry with the Lady Elizabeth. This he did the rather, because having at his coming out of Brittaine [Brittany] given artificially for serving of his own turn some hopes, in case he obtained the kingdom, to marry Anne, inheritress to the duchy of Brittaine, whom Charles the Eighth of France soon after married, it bred some doubt and suspicion amongst divers that he was not sincere, or at least not fixed, in going on with the match of England so much desired: which conceit [idea] also, though it were but talk and discourse, did much afflict the poor Lady Elizabeth herself. But howsoever he both truly intended it, and desired also it should be so believed (the better to extinguish envy and contradiction to his other purposes), yet was he resolved in himself not to proceed to the consummation thereof till his coronation and a Parliament were past. The one, lest a joint coronation of himself and his Queen might give any countenance of participation of title; the other, lest in the entailing of the crown to himself, which he hoped to obtain by Parliament, the votes of the Parliament might any ways reflect upon her.

About this time in autumn, towards the end of September, there began and reigned in the city and other parts of the kingdom a disease then new: which by the accidents and manner thereof they called the *sweating-sickness*. This disease had a swift course, both in the sick body and in the time and period of the lasting thereof, for they that were taken with it, upon four-and-twenty hours escaping, were thought almost assured. And as to the time of the malice and reign of the disease ere it ceased: it began about the one and twentieth of September, and cleared up before the end of October; insomuch as it was no hindrance to the King's coronation, which was the last of October; nor (which was more) to the holding of the Parliament, which began but seven days after. It was a pestilent fever, but as it seemeth not seated in the veins or humours, for that there followed no carbuncle, no purple or livid spots, or the like, the mass of the body being not tainted; only a malign vapour flew to the heart, and seized the vital spirits; which stirred nature to strive to send it forth by an extreme sweat. And it appeared by experience that this disease was rather a surprise of nature, than obstinate to remedies, if it were in time looked unto. For if the patient were kept in an equal temper, both for clothes, fire, and drink moderately warm, with temperate cordials, whereby nature's work were neither irritated by heat nor turned back by cold, he commonly recovered. But infinite persons died suddenly of it, before the manner of the cure and attendance was known. It was conceived not to be an epidemic [contagious] disease, but to proceed from a malignity in the constitution of the air, gathered by the predispositions of seasons; and the speedy cessation declared as much.

On Simon and Jude's Even the King dined with Thomas Bourchier, Archbishop of Canterbury, and Cardinal: and from Lambeth went by land over the bridge to the Tower, where the morrow after he made twelve knights-bannerets. But for creations, he dispensed them with a sparing hand. For notwithstanding a field so lately fought, and a coronation so near at hand, he only created three: Jasper Earl of Pembroke (the King's uncle) was created Duke of Bedford; Thomas the Lord Stanley (the King's father-in-law) Earl of Derby; and Edward Courtney Earl of Devon; though the king had then nevertheless a purpose in himself to make more in time of Parliament; bearing a wise and decent respect to distribute his creations, some to honour his coronation, and some his Parliament.

The coronation followed two days after, upon the thirtieth day of October in the year of our Lord 1485. At which time Innocent the Eighth was Pope of Rome; Frederick the Third Emperor of Almain [Germany]; and Maximilian his son newly chosen King of the Romans; Charles the Eighth King of France; Ferdinando and Isabella Kings of Spain; and James the Third King of Scotland: with all of which kings and states the King was at that time in good peace and amity. At which day also (as if the crown upon his head had put perils into his thoughts) he did institute for the better security of his person a band of fifty archers under a captain to attend him, by the name of Yeomen-of-his-Guard: and yet that it might be thought to be rather a matter of dignity, after the imitation of that he had known abroad, than any matter of diffidence appropriate to his own case, he made it to be understood for an ordinance not temporary, but to hold in succession for ever after.

The seventh of November the King held his Parliament at Westminster, which he had summoned immediately after his coming to London. His ends in calling a Parliament (and that so speedily) were chiefly three. First, to procure the crown to be entailed upon himself. Next to have the attainders of all his party (which were in no small number) reversed, and all acts of hostility by them done in his quarrel remitted and discharged; and on

the other side, to attaint by Parliament the heads and principals
of his enemies. The third, to calm and quiet the fears of the rest
of that party by a general pardon; not being ignorant in how
great danger a King stands from his subjects, when most of his
subjects are conscious in themselves that they stand in his danger. Unto these three special motives of a Parliament was added,
that he as a prudent and moderate prince made this judgment,
that it was fit for him to hasten to let his people see that he meant
to govern by law, howsoever he came in by the sword; and fit
also to reclaim them to know him for their King, whom they had
so lately talked of as an enemy or banished man. For that which
concerned the entailing of the crown (more than that he was
true to his own will, that he would not endure any mention of the
Lady Elizabeth, no not in the nature of special entail), he carried
it otherwise with great wisdom and measure. For he did not press
to have the act penned by way of declaration or recognition of
right; as on the other side he avoided to have it by new law or ordinance; but chose rather a kind of middle way, by way of establishment, and that under covert and indifferent words; *that the
inheritance of the crown should rest, remain, and abide in the
King, etc.:* which words might equally be applied, That the crown
should continue to him; but whether as having former right to it
(which was doubtful), or having it then in fact and possession
(which no man denied), was left fair to interpretation either
way. And again for the limitation of the entail, he did not press it
to go farther than to himself and to the heirs of his body, not
speaking of his right heirs; but leaving that to the law to decide;
so as the entail might seem rather a personal favour to him and
his children, than a total disinherison to the house of York. And in
this form was the law drawn and passed. Which statute he procured to be confirmed by the Pope's Bull the year following, with
mention nevertheless (by way of recital) of his other titles both of
descent and conquest. So as now the wreath of three was made a
wreath of five, for to the three first titles, of the two houses or
lines and conquest, were added two more: the authorities Parlia-
mentary and Papal.

The King likewise in the reversal of the attainders of his partakers, and discharging them of all offences incident to his service

and succour, had his will; and acts did pass accordingly. In the passage whereof, exception was taken to divers persons in the House of Commons, for that they were attainted, and thereby not legal, nor habilitate to serve in Parliament, being disabled in the highest degree; and that it should be a great incongruity to have them to make laws who themselves were not inlawed. The truth was, that divers of those which had in the time of King Richard been strongest and most declared for the King's party, were returned Knights and Burgesses of the Parliament; whether by care or recommendation from the state, or the voluntary inclination of the people; many of which had been by Richard the Third attainted by outlawries, or otherwise. The King was somewhat troubled with this. For though it had a grave and specious show, yet it reflected upon his party. But wisely not shewing [showing] himself at all moved therewith, he would not understand it but as a case in law, and wished the judges to be advised thereupon, who for that purpose were forthwith assembled in the Exchequer-chamber (which is the counsel-chamber of the judges), and upon deliberation they gave a grave and safe opinion and advice, mixed with law and convenience, which was: that the knights and burgesses attainted by the course of law should forbear to come into the house till a law were passed for the reversal of their attainders. [But the judges left it there, and made no mention whether after such reversal there should need any new election or no, nor whether this sequestering of them from the house were generally upon their disability, or upon an incompetency that they should be judges and parties in their own cause. The point in law was, whether any disability in their natural capacity could trench to [infringe on] their politic capacity, they being but procurators of the commonwealth and representatives and fiduciaries of counties and boroughs; considering their principals stood upright and clear, and therefore were not to receive prejudice from their personal attainders.[1]]

[1] The passage within brackets is taken from the MS., where it is crossed out; and against the last sentence is written in the margin, "This to be altered, as his Matie told Mr. Mewtus."

It was at that time incidentally moved amongst the judges in their consultation, what should be done for the King himself who likewise was attainted? But it was with unanimous consent resolved, that the crown takes away all defects and stops in blood: and that from the time the King did assume the crown, the fountain was cleared, and all attainders and corruption of blood discharged. But nevertheless, for honour's sake, it was ordained by Parliament, that all records wherein there was any memory or mention of the King's attainder should be defaced, cancelled, and taken off the file.

But on the part of the King's enemies there were by parliament attainted, the late Duke of Gloucester, calling himself Richard the Third, the Duke of Norfolk, the Earl of Surrey, Viscount Lovell, the Lord Ferrers, the Lord Zouch, Richard Ratcliffe, William Catesby, and many others of degree and quality. In which bills of attainders nevertheless there were contained many just and temperate clauses, savings, and provisoes, well shewing [showing] and fore-tokening the wisdom, stay, and moderation of the King's spirit of government. And for the pardon of the rest that had stood against the King, the King upon a second advice thought it not fit it should pass by Parliament, the better (being matter of grace), to impropriate the thanks to himself: using only the opportunity of a Parliament time, the better to disperse it into the veins of the kingdom. Therefore during the Parliament he published his royal proclamation, offering pardon and grace of restitution to all such as had taken arms or been participant of any

---

Mr. Meautys, in a letter to Bacon, 7th Jan. 1621–2, says, "Mr. Murray tells me that the King hath given your book to my Lord Brooke, and enjoined him to read it, commending it much to him, and then my Lord Brooke is to return it to your Lp. and so it may go to the press when your Lp. please, with such amendments as the King hath made, which I have seen, and are very few, and these rather words, as *epidemic*, and *mild* instead of *debonnaire*, &c. Only that, of persons attainted enabled to serve in Parliament by a bare reversal of their attainders without issuing any new writs, the King by all means will have left out." [Note by Spedding. Lord Brooke is Bacon's old friend, Fulke Greville.]

attempts against him, so as they submitted themselves to his
mercy by a day, and took the oath of allegiance and fidelity to him.
Whereupon many came out of sanctuary, and many more came
out of fear, no less guilty than those that had taken sanctuary.

As for money or treasure, the King thought it not seasonable
or fit to demand any of his subjects at this Parliament; both because he had received satisfaction from them in matters of so
great importance, and because he could not remunerate them
with any general pardon (being prevented therein by the coronation pardon passed immediately before); but chiefly, for that it
was in every man's eye what great forfeitures and confiscations
he had at that present to help himself; whereby those casualties
of the crown might in reason spare the purses of the subject; especially in a time when he was in peace with all his neighbours.
Some few laws passed at that Parliament, almost for form sake:
amongst which there was one, to reduce aliens being made den-
izens[2] to pay strangers' customs; and another, to draw to himself
the seizures and compositions of Italians' goods, for not employment[3]: being points of profit to his coffers, whereof from the very
beginning he was not forgetful; and had been more happy at the
latter end, if his early providence, which kept him from all necessity of exacting upon his people, could likewise have attempered
his nature therein. He added during parliament to his former creations the ennoblement or advancement in nobility of a few others.
The Lord Chandos of Brittaine [Brittany] was made Earl of Bath;
Sir Giles Dawbigny was made Lord Dawbigny; and Sir Robert
Willoughby Lord Brooke.

The King did also with great nobleness and bounty (which
virtues at that time had their turns in his nature) restore Edward
Stafford, eldest son to Henry Duke of Buckingham, attainted in
the time of King Richard, not only to his dignities, but to his fortunes and possessions, which were great; to which he was moved
also by a kind of gratitude, for that the Duke was the man that

___

   [2] [A denizen was an alien with permission to reside in England on
a more or less permanent basis.]

   [3] [That is, for not being used to buy English goods for export
to Italy.]

moved the first stone against the tyranny of King Richard, and indeed made the King a bridge to the crown upon his own ruins. Thus the Parliament brake [broke] up.

The Parliament being dissolved, the King sent forthwith money to redeem the Marquis Dorset and Sir John Bourchier, whom he had left as his pledges at Paris for money which he had borrowed when he made his expedition for England. And thereupon he took a fit occasion to send the Lord Treasurer and Mr. Bray (whom he used as counsellor) to the Lord Mayor of London, requiring of the City a prest [loan] of six thousand marks. But after many parleys he could obtain but two thousand pounds. Which nevertheless the King took in good part, as men use to do that practise [scheme] to borrow money when they have no need. About this time the King called unto his Privy Council John Morton and Richard Foxe, the one Bishop of Ely, the other Bishop of Exeter, vigilant men and secret, and such as kept watch with him almost upon all men else. They had been both versed in his affairs before he came to the crown, and were partakers of his adverse fortune. This Morton soon after, upon the death of Bourchier, he made Archbishop of Canterbury. And for Foxe, he made him Lord Keeper of his Privy Seal; and afterwards advanced him by degrees, from Exeter to Bath and Wells, thence to Durham, and last to Winchester. For although the King loved to employ and advance bishops, because having rich bishoprics they carried their reward upon themselves; yet he did use to raise them by steps; that he might not lose the profit of the first fruits, which by that course of gradation was multiplied.[4]

At last upon the eighteenth of January was solemnised the so long expected and so much desired marriage between the King and the Lady Elizabeth; which day of marriage was celebrated with greater triumph and demonstrations (especially on the people's part) of joy and gladness, than the days either of his entry or coronation; which the King rather noted than liked. And it is true that all his life-time, while the Lady Elizabeth lived with him

---

[4] [A bishop newly appointed to a see had to pay the first year's income of the bishopric to the king; thus, the more times the king shuffled the bishops around, the more first fruits he could collect.]

(for she died before him), he shewed himself no very indulgent
husband towards her though she was beautiful, gentle and fruitful. But his aversion toward the house of York was so predominant in him, as it found place not only in his wars and counsels,
but in his chamber and bed.

Towards the middle of the spring, the King, full of confidence and assurance, as a prince that had been victorious in battle, and had prevailed with his Parliament in all that he desired,
and had the ring of acclamations fresh in his ears, thought the
rest of his reign should be but play, and the enjoying of a kingdom. Yet as a wise and watchful King, he would not neglect anything for his safety, thinking nevertheless to perform all things
now rather as an exercise than as a labour. So he being truly informed that the northern parts were not only affectionate to the
house of York, but particularly had been devoted to King Richard
the Third, thought it would be a summer well spent to visit those
parts, and by his presence and application of himself to reclaim
and rectify those humours. But the King, in his account of peace
and calms, did much over-cast [overestimate] his fortunes, which
proved for many years together full of broken seas, tides, and
tempests. For he was no sooner come to Lincoln, where he kept his
Easter, but he received news that the Lord Lovell, Humphrey
Stafford, and Thomas Stafford, who had formerly taken sanctuary
at Colchester, were departed out of sanctuary, but to what place
no man could tell. Which advertisement the King despised, and
continued his journey to York. At York there came fresh and
more certain advertisement that the Lord Lovell was at hand with
a great power of men, and that the Staffords were in arms in
Worcestershire, and had made their approaches to the city of
Worcester to assail it. The King, as a prince of great and profound
judgment, was not much moved with it; for that he thought it
was but a rag or remnant of Bosworth Field, and had nothing in it
of the main party of the house of York. But he was more doubtful
of the raising of forces to resist the rebels, than of the resistance
itself, for that he was in a core of people whose affections he suspected. But the action enduring no delay, he did speedily levy and
send against the Lord Lovell to the number of three thousand
men, ill armed but well assured (being taken some few out of his

own train, and the rest out of the tenants and followers of such as were safe to be trusted), under the conduct of the Duke of Bedford. And as his manner was to send his pardons rather before the sword than after, he gave commission to the Duke to proclaim pardon to all that would come in: which the Duke, upon his approach to the Lord Lovell's camp, did perform. And it fell out as the King expected; the heralds were the great ordnance. For the Lord Lovell, upon proclamation of pardon, mistrusting his men, fled into Lancashire, and lurking for a time with Sir Thomas Broughton, after sailed over into Flanders to the Lady Margaret. And his men, forsaken of their captain, did presently submit themselves to the Duke. The Staffords likewise, and their forces, hearing what had happened to the Lord Lovell (in whose success their chief trust was), despaired and dispersed, the two brothers taking sanctuary at Colnham, a village near Abingdon; which place, upon view of their privilege in the King's bench, being judged no sufficient sanctuary for traitors, Humphrey was executed at Tyburn, and Thomas, as being led by his elder brother, was pardoned. So this rebellion proved but a blast, and the King having by this journey purged a little the dregs and leaven of the northern people, that were before in no good affection towards him, returned to London.

In September following, the Queen was delivered of her first son, whom the King (in honour of the British race, of which himself was) named Arthur, according to the name of that ancient worthy King of the Britons[5]; in whose acts there is truth enough to make him famous, besides that which is fabulous. The child was strong and able, though he was born in the eighth month, which the physicians do prejudge.

There followed this year, being the second of the King's reign, a strange accident of state, whereof the relations which we have are so naked, as they leave it scarce credible; not for the na-

[5] [Henry Tudor was a Welshman; in his day, and in Bacon's, it was believed that the Welsh were the descendants of those ancient Britons who had, under Arthur, opposed the Saxons.]

ture of it (for it hath fallen out oft), but for the manner and circumstance of it, especially in the beginnings. Therefore we shall
make our judgment upon the things themselves, as they give light
one to another, and (as we can) dig truth out of the mine. The
King was green in his estate; and contrary to his own opinion and
desert both, was not without much hatred throughout the realm.
The root of all was the discountenancing of the house of York,
which the general body of the realm still affected. This did alienate the hearts of the subjects from him daily more and more,
especially when they saw that after his marriage, and after a son
born, the King did nevertheless not so much as proceed to the
coronation of the Queen, not vouchsafing her the honour of a
matrimonial crown; for the coronation of her was not till almost
two years after, when danger had taught him what to do. But
much more, when it was spread abroad (whether by error or the
cunning of malcontents) that the King had a purpose to put to
death Edward Plantagenet closely [secretly] in the Tower: whose
case was so nearly paralleled with that of Edward the Fourth's
children, in respect of the blood, like age, and the very place of the
Tower, as it did refresh and reflect upon the King a most odious
resemblance, as if he would be another King Richard. And all this
time it was still whispered everywhere, that at least one of the
children of Edward the Fourth was living. Which bruit [rumor]
was cunningly fomented by such as desired innovation. Neither
was the King's nature and customs greatly fit to disperse these
mists; but contrariwise he had a fashion rather to create doubts
than assurance. Thus was fuel prepared for the spark: the spark,
that afterwards kindled such a fire and combustion, was at the
first contemptible.

There was a subtile [subtle, devious] priest called Richard
Simon, that lived in Oxford, and had to his pupil a baker's son
named Lambert Simnell, of the age of some fifteen years; a comely
youth, and well favoured, not without some extraordinary dignity
and grace of aspect. It came into this priest's fancy (hearing what
men talked, and in hope to raise himself to some great bishoprick) to cause this lad to counterfeit and personate the second son
of Edward the Fourth, supposed to be murdered; and afterward

(for he changed his intention in the manage)[6] the Lord Edward Plantagenet, then prisoner in the Tower; and accordingly to frame him and instruct him in the part he was to play. This is that which (as was touched before) seemeth scarcely credible; not that a false person should be assumed to gain a kingdom, for it hath been seen in ancient and late times; nor that it should come into the mind of such an abject fellow to enterprise so great a matter; for high conceits do sometimes come streaming into the imaginations of base persons, especially when they are drunk with news and talk of the people. But here is that which hath no appearance [appears improbable]; that this priest, being utterly unacquainted with the true person according to whose pattern he should shape his counterfeit, should think it possible for him to instruct his player, either in gesture and fashions, or in recounting past matters of his life and education, or in fit answers to questions, or the like, any ways to come near the resemblance of him whom he was to represent. For this lad was not to personate one that had been long before taken out of his cradle, or conveyed away in his infancy, known to few; but a youth that till the age almost of ten years had been brought up in a court where infinite eyes had been upon him. For King Edward, touched with remorse of his brother the Duke of Clarence's death, would not indeed restore his son (of whom we speak) to be Duke of Clarence, but yet created him Earl of Warwick, reviving his honour on the mother's side, and used him honourably during his time, though Richard the Third afterwards confined him. So that it cannot be, but that some great person, that knew particularly and familiarly Edward Plantagenet, had a hand in the business, from whom the priest might take his aim. That which is most probable, out of the precedent and subsequent acts, is, that it was the Queen Dowager from whom this action had the principal source and motion. For certain it is, she was a busy negotiating woman, and in her withdrawing-chamber had the fortunate conspiracy for the King against King Richard the Third been hatched; which the King knew, and remembered perhaps but too well; and was at this time extremely discontent

[6] [in the course of events]

with the King, thinking her daughter (as the King handled the
matter) not advanced but depressed: and none could hold the
book so well to prompt and instruct this stage-play, as she could.
Nevertheless it was not her meaning, nor no more was it the
meaning of any of the better and sager sort that favoured this
enterprise and knew the secret, that this disguised idol should
possess the crown; but at his peril to make way to the overthrow
of the King; and that done, they had their several hopes and ways.
That which doth chiefly fortify this conjecture is, that as soon as
the matter brake forth in any strength, it was one of the King's
first acts to cloister the Queen Dowager in the nunnery of Bermondsey, and to take away all her lands and estate; and this by a
close council, without any legal proceeding, upon far-fetched
pretences: that she had delivered her two daughters out of sanctuary to King Richard, contrary to promise. Which proceeding
being even at that time taxed for rigorous and undue, both in matter and manner, makes it very probable there was some greater
matter against her, which the King upon reason of policy and to
avoid envy would not publish. It is likewise no small argument
that there was some secret in it and some suppressing of examinations, for that the priest Simon himself after he was taken was
never brought to execution; no not so much as to public trial (as
many clergymen were upon less treasons) but was only shut up
close in a dungeon. Add to this that after the Earl of Lincoln (a
principal person of the house of York) was slain in Stoke-field,
the King opened himself to some of his council, that he was sorry
for the Earl's death, because by him (he said) he might have
known the bottom of his danger.

But to return to the narration itself: Simon did first instruct
his scholar for the part of Richard Duke of York, second son to
King Edward the Fourth; and this was at such time as it was
voiced that the King purposed to put to death Edward Plantagenet
prisoner in the Tower, whereat there was great murmur. But hearing soon after a general bruit [rumor] that Plantagenet had escaped out of the Tower, and thereby finding him so much beloved
amongst the people, and such rejoicing at his escape, the cunning
priest changed his copy, and chose now Plantagenet to be the sub-

ject his pupil should personate, because he was more in the present speech and votes of the people; and it pieced better, and
followed more close and handsomely upon the bruit of Plantagenet's escape. But yet doubting that there would be too near
looking and too much perspective into his disguise, if he should
shew [show] it here in England; he thought good (after the manner of scenes in stageplays and masks) to shew it afar off; and
therefore sailed with his scholar into Ireland, where the affection
to the house of York was most in height. The King had been a
little improvident in the matters of Ireland, and had not removed
officers and counsellors, and put in their places, or at least inter-
mingled, persons of whom he stood assured; as he should have
done, since he knew the strong bent of that country towards the
house of York, and that it was a ticklish and unsettled state, more
easy to receive distempers and mutations than England was. But
trusting to the reputation of his victories and successes in England, he thought he should have time enough to extend his cares
afterwards to that second kingdom.

Wherefore through this neglect, upon the coming of Simon
with his pretended Plantagenet into Ireland, all things were prepared for revolt and sedition, almost as if they had been set and
plotted beforehand. Simon's first address was to the Lord Thomas
Fitz-Gerald, Earl of Kildare and Deputy of Ireland; before whose
eyes he did cast such a mist (by his own insinuation, and by the
carriage of his youth, that expressed a natural princely behavior)
as, joined perhaps with some inward vapours of ambition and
affection in the Earl's own mind, left him fully possessed that it
was the true Plantagenet. The Earl presently communicated the
matter with some of the nobles and others there, at the first secretly. But finding them of like affection to himself, he suffered it
of purpose to vent and pass abroad; because they thought it not
safe to resolve, till they had a taste of the people's inclination.
But if the great ones were in forwardness, the people were in fury,
entertaining this airy body or phantasm with incredible affection;
partly out of their great devotion to the house of York, partly out
of a proud humour in the nation to give a King to the realm of
England. Neither did the party in this heat of affection much

trouble themselves with the attainder of George Duke of Clarence; having newly learned by the King's example that attainders do not interrupt the conveying of title to the crown. And as for the daughters of King Edward the Fourth, they thought King Richard had said enough for them; and took them to be but as of the King's party, because they were in his power and at his disposing. So that with marvellous consent and applause, this counterfeit Plantagenet was brought with great solemnity to the castle of Dublin, and there saluted, served, and honoured as King; the boy becoming it well, and doing nothing that did bewray [betray] the baseness of his condition. And within a few days after he was proclaimed King in Dublin, by the name of King Edward the Sixth; there being not a sword drawn in King Henry his quarrel.[7]

The King was much moved with this unexpected accident, when it came to his ears, both because it struck upon that string which ever he most feared, as also because it was stirred in such a place, where he could not with safety transfer his own person to suppress it. For partly through natural valour and partly through an universal suspicion (not knowing whom to trust) he was ever ready to wait upon all his achievements in person. The King therefore first called his council together at the Charterhouse at Shine; which council was held with great secrecy, but the open decrees thereof, which presently came abroad, were three.

The first was, that the Queen Dowager, for that she, contrary to her pact and agreement with those that had concluded with her concerning the marriage of her daughter Elizabeth with King Henry, had nevertheless delivered her daughters out of sanctuary into King Richard's hands, should be cloistered in the nunnery of Bermondsey, and forfeit all her lands and goods.

The next was, that Edward Plantagenet, then close prisoner in the Tower, should be, in the most public and notorious manner that could be devised, shewed unto the people: in part to discharge the King of the envy of that opinion and bruit, how he had been put to death privily in the Tower; but chiefly to make the people

[7] [This is the old form of the possessive: King Henry's quarrel.]

see the levity and imposture of the proceedings of Ireland, and
that their Plantagenet was indeed but a puppet or a counterfeit.

The third was, that there should be again proclaimed a general pardon to all that would reveal their offences and submit
themselves by a day; and that this pardon should be conceived in
so ample and liberal a manner, as no high-treason (no not [not
even] against the King's own person) should be excepted. Which
though it might seem strange, yet was it not so to a wise King,
that knew his greatest dangers were not from the least treasons,
but from the greatest. These resolutions of the King and his council were immediately put in execution. And first, the Queen Dowager was put into the monastery of Bermondsey, and all her
estate seized into the King's hands; whereat there was much wondering that a weak woman, for the yielding to the menaces and
promises of a tyrant, after such a distance of time (wherein the
King had shown no displeasure nor alteration), but much more
after so happy a marriage between the King and her daughter,
blessed with issue male, should upon a sudden mutability or dis-
closure of the King's mind be so severely handled.

This lady was amongst the examples of great variety of fortune. She had first, from a distressed suitor and desolate widow,
been taken to the marriage bed of a bachelor-King, the goodliest
personage of his time; and even in his reign she had endured a
strange eclipse by the King's flight and temporary depriving from
the crown. She was also very happy in that she had by him fair
issue, and continued his nuptial love (helping herself by some
obsequious bearing and dissembling of his pleasures) to the very
end. She was much affectionate to her own kindred, even unto
faction; which did stir great envy in the lords of the King's side,
who counted her blood a disparagement to be mingled with the
King's. With which lords of the King's blood joined also the
King's favourite the Lord Hastings; who, notwithstanding the
King's great affection to him, was thought at times, through her
malice and spleen, not to be out of danger of falling. After her
husband's death she was matter of tragedy, having lived to see
her brother beheaded, and her two sons deposed from the crown,
bastarded in their blood, and cruelly murdered. All this while

nevertheless she enjoyed her liberty, state, and fortunes. But afterwards again, upon the rise of the wheel, when she had a King to her son-in-law, and was made grandmother to a grandchild of the best sex, yet was she (upon dark and unknown reasons, and no less strange pretences,) precipitated and banished the world into a nunnery; where it was almost thought dangerous to visit her or see her; and where not long after she ended her life; but was by the King's commandment buried with the King her husband at Windsor. She was foundress of Queen's College in Cambridge. For this act the King sustained great obloquy, which nevertheless (besides the reason of state) was somewhat sweetened to him by a great confiscation.

About this time also, Edward Plantagenet was upon a Sunday brought throughout all the principal streets of London, to be seen of the people. And having passed the view of the streets, was conducted to Paul's Church in solemn procession, where great store of people were assembled. And it was provided also in good fashion, that divers of the nobility and others of quality (especially of those that the King most suspected, and knew the person of Plantagenet best) had communication with the young gentleman by the way, and entertained him with speech and discourse; which did in effect mar the pageant in Ireland with the subjects here, at least with so many as out of error, and not out of malice, might be misled. Nevertheless in Ireland (where it was too late to go back) it wrought little or no effect. But contrariwise they turned the imposture upon the King, and gave out that the King, to defeat the true inheritor, and to mock the world and blind the eyes of simple men, had tricked up a boy in the likeness of Edward Plantagenet, and shewed him to the people, not sparing to profane the ceremony of a procession, the more to countenance the fable.

The general pardon likewise near the same time came forth; and the King therewithal omitted no diligence in giving straight order for the keeping of the ports, that fugitives, malcontents, or suspected persons might not pass over into Ireland and Flanders.

Meanwhile the rebels in Ireland had sent privy messengers both into England and into Flanders, who in both places had wrought effects of no small importance. For in England they won to their party John Earl of Lincoln, son of John De la Pole Duke of Suffolk, and of Elizabeth King Edward the Fourth's eldest sister. This Earl was a man of great wit and courage, and had his thoughts highly raised by hopes and expectations for a time. For Richard the Third had a resolution, out of his hatred to both his brethren, King Edward and the Duke of Clarence, and their lines (having had his hand in both their bloods), to disable their issues upon false and incompetent pretexts, the one of attainder, the other of illegitimation; and to design this gentleman (in case himself should die without children) for inheritor of the crown. Neither was this unknown to the King who had secretly an eye upon him. But the King having tasted of the envy of the people for his imprisonment of Edward Plantagenet, was doubtful to heap up any more distastes of that kind by the imprisonment of De la Pole also; the rather thinking it policy to conserve him as a corrival unto the other. The Earl of Lincoln was induced to participate with the action of Ireland, not lightly upon the strength of the proceedings there, which was but a bubble, but upon letters from the Lady Margaret of Burgundy, in whose succours and declaration for the enterprise there seemed to be a more solid foundation, both for reputation and forces. Neither did the Earl refrain the business, for that he knew the pretended Plantagenet to be but an idol. But contrariwise he was more glad it should be the false Plantagenet than the true; because the false being sure to fall away of himself, and the true to be made sure of by the King, it might open and pave a fair and prepared way to his own title. With this resolution he sailed secretly into Flanders, where was a little before arrived the Lord Lovell, leaving a correspondence here in England with Sir Thomas Broughton, a man of great power and dependencies in Lancashire. For before this time, when the pretended Plantagenet was first received in Ireland, secret messengers had been also sent to the Lady Margaret, advertising her what had passed in Ireland, imploring succours in an enterprise (as they said) so pious and just, and that God had so miraculously prospered in the beginning thereof; and making offer that all things should be guided by her will and direction, as the sovereign patroness and protectress of the enterprise. Margaret was second

sister to King Edward the Fourth, and had been second wife to
Charles surnamed the Hardy, Duke of Burgundy; by whom having no children of her own, she did with singular care and tenderness intend the education of Philip and Margaret, grandchildren
to her former husband[8]; which won her great love and authority
among the Dutch. This Princess (having the spirit of a man and
malice of a woman) abounding in treasure by the greatness of her
dower and her provident government, and being childless and
without any nearer care, made it her design and enterprise to see
the Majesty Royal of England once again replaced in her house,
and had set up King Henry as a mark at whose overthrow all her
actions should aim and shoot; insomuch as all the counsels of his
succeeding troubles came chiefly out of that quiver. And she bare
such a mortal hatred to the house of Lancaster, and personally to
the King, as she was no ways mollified by the conjunction of the
houses in her niece's marriage, but rather hated her niece, as the
means of the King's ascent to the crown and assurance therein.
Wherefore with great violence of affection she embraced this
overture. And upon counsel taken with the Earl of Lincoln and
the Lord Lovell, and some other of the party, it was resolved with
all speed, the two lords assisted with a regiment of two thousand
Almains [Germans], being choice and veteran bands, under the
command of Martin Swart (a valiant and experimented [experi-
enced] captain) should pass over into Ireland to the new King;
hoping that when the action should have the face of a received
and settled regality (with such a second person as the Earl of
Lincoln, and the conjunction and reputation of foreign succours),
the fame of it would embolden and prepare all the party of the
confederates and malcontents within the realm of England to give
them assistance when they should come over there. And for the
person of the counterfeit, it was agreed that if all things succeeded
well he should be put down, and the true Plantagenet received;
wherein nevertheless the Earl of Lincoln had his particular hopes.
After they were come into Ireland, and that the party took cour-

[8] [grandchildren to her husband by his former wife]

age by seeing themselves together in a body, they grew very confident of success, conceiving and discoursing amongst themselves, that they went in upon far better cards to overthrow King Henry, than King Henry had to overthrow King Richard: and that if there were not a sword drawn against them in Ireland, it was a sign the swords in England would be soon sheathed or beaten down.

And first, for a bravery upon this accession of power, they crowned their new King in the cathedral church of Dublin, who formerly had been but proclaimed only; and then sat in council what should further be done. At which council though it were propounded by some that it were the best way to establish themselves first in Ireland, and to make that the seat of the war, and to draw King Henry thither in person, by whose absence they thought there would be great alterations and commotions in England; yet because the kingdom there was poor, and they should not be able to keep their army together, nor pay their German soldiers; and for that also the sway of the Irishmen and generally of the men of war, which (as in such cases of popular tumults is usual) did in effect govern their leaders, was eager and in affection to make their fortunes upon England; it was concluded with all possible speed to transport their forces into England. The King in the mean time, who at the first when he heard what was done in Ireland, though it troubled him, yet thought he should be well enough able to scatter the Irish as a flight of birds, and rattle away this swarm of bees with their King; when he heard afterwards that the Earl of Lincoln was embarked in the action, and that the Lady Margaret was declared for it, he apprehended the danger in a true degree as it was, and saw plainly that his kingdom must again be put to the stake, and that he must fight for it. And first he did conceive, before he understood of the Earl of Lincoln's sailing into Ireland out of Flanders, that he should be assailed both upon the east parts of the kingdom of England by some impression from Flanders, and upon the north-west out of Ireland. And therefore having ordered musters to be made in both parts, and having provisionally designed two generals, Jasper Earl of Bedford, and John Earl of Oxford (meaning himself also to go in person where the affairs should most require it), and nevertheless not expecting any actual invasion at that time (the winter being far on), he took his journey himself towards Suffolk and Norfolk, for the confirming of those parts. And being come to St. Edmond's-bury, he understood that Thomas Marquis Dorset (who had been one of the pledges in France) was hasting towards him to purge himself of some accusations which had been made against him. But the King, though he kept an ear for him, yet was the time so doubtful, that he sent the Earl of Oxford to meet him and forthwith to carry him to the Tower; with a fair message nevertheless that he should bear that disgrace with patience, for that the King meant not his hurt, but only to preserve him from doing hurt either to the King's service or to himself; and that the King should always be able (when he had cleared himself) to make him reparation.

From St. Edmond's-bury he went to Norwich, where he kept his Christmas. And from thence he went (in a manner of pilgrimage) to Walsingham, where he visited our Lady's church, famous for miracles, and made his prayers and vows for his help and deliverance. And from thence he returned by Cambridge to London. Not long after, the rebels with their King (under the leading of the Earl of Lincoln, the Earl of Kildare, the Lord Lovell, and Colonel Swart) landed at Fouldrey in Lancashire, whither there repaired to them Sir Thomas Broughton, with some small company of English. The King by that time (knowing now the storm would not divide but fall in one place) had levied forces in good number; and in person (taking with him his two designed generals, the Duke of Bedford and the Earl of Oxford) was come on his way towards them as far as Coventry, whence he sent forth a troop of light-horsemen for discovery, and to intercept some stragglers of the enemies, by whom he might the better understand the particulars of their progress and purposes; which was accordingly done; though the King otherways was not without intelligence from espials [spies] in the camp.

The rebels took their way towards York without spoiling the country or any act of hostility, the better to put themselves into favour of the people and to personate[9] their King: who (no doubt out of a princely feeling) was sparing and compassionate towards his subjects. But their snow-ball did not gather as it went. For the people came not in to them; neither did any rise or declare themselves in other parts of the kingdom for them; which was caused partly by the good taste that the King had given his people of his government, joined with the reputation of his felicity; and partly for that it was an odious thing to the people of England to have a King brought in to them upon the shoulders of Irish and Dutch, of which their army was in substance compounded. Neither was it a thing done with any great judgment on the party of the rebels, for them to take their way towards York; considering that howsoever those parts had formerly been a nursery of their friends, yet it was there, where the Lord Lovell had so lately disbanded, and where the King's presence had a little before qualified discontents. The Earl of Lincoln, deceived of his hopes of the country's concourse unto him (in which case he would have temporised) and seeing the business past retreat, resolved to make on where the King was, and to give him battle; and thereupon marched towards Newark, thinking to have surprised the town. But the King was somewhat before this time come to Nottingham, where he called a council of war, at which was consulted whether it were best to protract time or speedily to set upon the rebels. In which council the King himself (whose continual vigilance did suck in sometimes causeless suspicions which few else knew) inclined to the accelerating a battle. But this was presently put out of doubt, by the great aids that came in to him in the instant of this consultation, partly upon missives and partly voluntaries, from many parts of the kingdom.

The principal persons that came then to the King's aid were the Earl of Shrewsbury and the Lord Strange, of the nobility, and of knights and gentlemen to the number of at least three-score and ten persons, with their companies; making in the whole at the least six thousand fighting men, besides the forces that were with

---

[9] [that is, to make the impersonation more plausible: a true king would not wish to pillage his own people]

the King before. Whereupon the King finding his army so bravely reinforced, and a great alacrity in all his men to fight, was confirmed in his former resolution, and marched speedily, so as he put himself between the enemies' camp and Newark; being loth their army should get the commodity of that town. The Earl, nothing dismayed, came forwards that day unto a little village called Stoke, and there encamped that night, upon the brow or hanging of a hill. The King the next day presented him battle upon the plain, the fields there being open and champion [flat]. The Earl courageously came down and joined battle with him. Concerning which battle the relations that are left unto us are so naked and negligent (though it be an action of so recent memory) as they rather declare the success of the day than the manner of the fight. They say that the King divided his army into three battails [battalions], whereof the vant-guard only well strengthened with wings came to fight. That the fight was fierce and obstinate, and lasted three hours before the victory inclined either way; save that judgment might be made, by that the King's vant-guard of itself maintained fight against the whole power of the enemies (the other two battails remaining out of action), what the success was like to be in the end. That Martin Swart with his Germans performed bravely, and so did those few English that were on that side; neither did the Irish fail in courage or fierceness, but being almost naked men, only armed with darts and skeins, it was rather an execution than a fight upon them; insomuch as the furious slaughter of them was a great discouragement and appalment to the rest. That there died upon the place all the chieftains; that is, the Earl of Lincoln, the Earl of Kildare, Francis Lord Lovell, Martin Swart, and Sir Thomas Broughton, all making good the fight without any ground given. Only of the Lord Lovell there went a report, that he fled, and swam over Trent on horseback, but could not recover the further side, by reason of the steepness of the bank, and so was drowned in the river. But another report leaves him not there, but that he lived long after in a cave or vault. The number that was slain in the field, was of the enemies' part four thousand at the least, and of the King's part one half of his vant-guard, besides many hurt, but none of name. There were taken prisoners amongst others the counterfeit Plantagenet, now

Lambert Symnell again, and the crafty priest his tutor. For Lambert, the King would not take his life, both out of magnanimity, taking him but as an image of wax that others had tempered and moulded; and likewise out of wisdom, thinking that if he suffered death he would be forgotten too soon; but being kept alive he would be a continual spectacle, and a kind of remedy against the enchantments of people in time to come. For which cause he was taken into service in his court to a base office in his kitchen; so that (in a kind of *mattacina* [dance] of human fortune) he turned a broach [spit] that had worn a crown. Whereas fortune commonly doth not bring in a comedy or farce after a tragedy. And afterwards he was preferred to be one of the King's falconers. As to the priest, he was committed close prisoner, and heard of no more; the King loving to seal up his own dangers.[10]

After the battle the King went to Lincoln, where he caused supplications and thanksgivings to be made for his deliverance and victory. And that his devotions might go round in circle, he sent his banner to be offered to our Lady of Walsingham, where before he made his vows. And thus delivered of this so strange an engine and new invention of fortune, he returned to his former confidence of mind, thinking now that all his misfortunes had come at once. But it fell out unto him according to the speech of the common people in the beginning of his reign, that said, *It was a token he should reign in labour, because his reign began with a sickness of sweat*. But howsoever the King thought himself now in a haven, yet such was his wisdom, as his confidence did seldom darken his foresight, especially in things near hand. And therefore, awakened by so fresh and unexpected dangers, he entered into due consideration as well how to weed out the partakers of the former rebellion, as to kill the seeds of the like in time to come: and withal to take away all shelters and harbours for discontented persons, where they might hatch and foster rebellions which afterwards might gather strength and motion.

And first he did yet again make a progress from Lincoln to the northern parts, though it were (indeed) rather an itinerary circuit of justice than a progress. For all along as he went, with

[10] [the King loving to keep his own dangers secret]

much severity and strict inquisition, partly by martial law and partly by commission, were punished the adherents and aiders of the late rebels. Not all by death (for the field had drawn much blood), but by fines and ransoms, which spared life and raised treasure. Amongst other crimes of this nature, there was a diligent inquiry made of such as had raised and dispersed a bruit and rumour (a little before the field fought), *that the rebels had the day, and that the King's army was overthrown, and the King fled.* Whereby it was supposed that many succours which otherwise would have come unto the King were cunningly put off and kept back: which charge and accusation, though it had some ground, yet it was industriously embraced and put on by divers, who having been in themselves not the best affected to the King's part, nor forward to come to his aid, were glad to apprehend this colour to cover their neglect and coldness under the pretence of such discouragements. Which cunning nevertheless the King would not understand, though he lodged it and noted it in some particulars, as his manner was.[11]

But for the extirpating of the roots and causes of the like commotions in time to come, the King began to find where his shoe did wring him; and that it was his depressing of the house of York that did rankle and fester the affections of his people. And therefore being now too wise to disdain perils any longer, and willing to give some contentment in that kind (at least in ceremony), he resolved at last to proceed to the coronation of his Queen. And therefore at his coming to London, where he entered in state, and in a kind of triumph, and celebrated his victory with two days of devotion, (for the first day he repaired to Paul's, and had the hymn of *Te Deum* sung, and the morrow after he went in procession, and heard the sermon at the Cross,) the Queen was with great solemnity crowned at Westminster, the twenty-fifth of November, in the third year of his reign, which was about two years after the marriage (like an old christening that had stayed long for godfathers); which strange and unusual distance of time made it subject to every man's note that it was an act against his

[11] [the king would not excuse such tricks, but kept the perpetrators in mind]

stomach, and put upon him by necessity and reason of state. Soon after, to shew that it was now fair weather again, and that the imprisonment of Thomas Marquis Dorset was rather upon suspicion of the time than of the man, he the said Marquis was set at liberty, without examination or other circumstance.

At that time also the King sent an ambassador unto Pope Innocent, signifying unto him this his marriage; and that now (like another Aeneas) he had passed through the floods of his former troubles and travails and was arrived unto a safe haven; and thanking his Holiness that he had honoured the celebration of his marriage with the presence of his ambassador; and offering both his person and the forces of his kingdom upon all occasions to do him service.

The ambassador making his oration to the Pope in the presence of the cardinals, did so magnify the King and Queen, as was enough to glut the hearers. But then he did again so extol and deify the Pope, as made all that he had said in praise of his master and mistress seem temperate and passable. But he was very honourably entertained and extremely much made on by the Pope, who knowing himself to be lazy and unprofitable to the Christian world, was wonderfully glad to hear that there were such echoes of him sounding in remote parts. He obtained also of the Pope a very just and honourable Bull, qualifying the privileges of sanctuary (wherewith the King had been extremely galled) in three points.

The first, that if any sanctuary-man did by night or otherwise get out of sanctuary privily and commit mischief and trespass, and then come in again, he should lose the benefit of sanctuary for ever after.

The second, that howsoever the person of the sanctuary-man was protected from his creditors, yet his goods out of sanctuary should not.

The third, that if any took sanctuary for case of treason, the King might appoint him keepers to look to him in sanctuary.[12]

The King also, for the better securing of his estate against

[12] [the king might set guards within the sanctuary to keep an eye on the traitor, thus preventing him from causing further mischief]

mutinous and malcontented subjects (whereof he saw the realm was full) who might have their refuge into Scotland, which was not under key as the ports were, for that cause rather than for any doubt of hostility from those parts, before his coming to London (when he was at Newcastle), had sent a solemn ambassage unto James the Third, King of Scotland, to treat and conclude a peace with him. The ambassadors were, Richard Foxe Bishop of Exeter, and Sir Richard Edgcombe comptroller of the King's house, who were honourably received and entertained there. But the King of Scotland labouring of the same disease that King Henry did (though more mortal as afterwards appeared), that is, discontented subjects apt to rise and raise tumult, although in his own affection he did much desire to make a peace with the King, yet finding his nobles averse and not daring to displease them, concluded only a truce for seven years; giving nevertheless promise in private, that it should be renewed from time to time during the two Kings' lives.

Hitherto the King had been exercised in settling his affairs at home. But about this time broke forth an occasion that drew him to look abroad and to hearken to foreign business. Charles the Eighth, the French King, by the virtue and good fortune of his two immediate predecessors, Charles the Seventh his grandfather and Lewis the Eleventh his father, received the kingdom of France in more flourishing and spread estate than it had been of many years before; being redintegrate[13] in those principal members which anciently had been portions of the crown of France, and were after dissevered, so as they remained only in homage and not in sovereignty (being governed by absolute princes of their own): Anjou, Normandy, Provence, and Burgundy. There remained only Brittaine to be re-united, and so the monarchy of France to be reduced to the ancient terms and bounds.

King Charles was not a little inflamed with an ambition to

[13] [Redintegrate = reintegrated. The meaning is that the provinces once lost to the Crown had been restored to the control of the French king.]

re-purchase and re-annex that duchy; which his ambition was a
wise and well-weighed ambition, not like unto the ambitions of his
succeeding enterprises of Italy. For at that time, being newly come
to the crown, he was somewhat guided by his father's counsels
(counsels not counsellors, for his father was his own counsel, and
had few able men about him). And that King (he knew well) had
ever distasted the designs of Italy, and in particular had an eye
upon Brittaine. There were many circumstances that did feed the
ambition of Charles with pregnant and apparent hopes of success.
The Duke of Brittaine old, and entered into a lethargy, and served
with mercenary counsellors, father of two only daughters, the
one sickly and not like to continue. King Charles himself in the
flower of his age, and the subjects of France at that time well
trained for war, both for leaders and soldiers (men of service being not yet worn out since the wars of Lewis against Burgundy).
He found himself also in peace with all his neighbour princes. As
for those that might oppose to his enterprise: Maximilian King of
Romans, his rival in the same desires (as well for the duchy as the
daughter), feeble in means; and King Henry of England as well
somewhat obnoxious [beholden] to him for his favours and benefits, as busied in his particular troubles at home. There was also a
fair and specious occasion offered him to hide his ambition and to
justify his warring upon Brittaine; for that the Duke had received
and succoured Lewis Duke of Orleans and others of the French
nobility, which had taken arms against their King. Wherefore
King Charles, being resolved upon that war, knew well he could
not receive any opposition so potent as if King Henry should
either upon policy of state in preventing the growing greatness of
France, or upon gratitude unto the Duke of Brittaine for his
former favours in the time of his distress, espouse that quarrel
and declare himself in aid of the Duke. Therefore he no sooner
heard that King Henry was settled by his victory, but forthwith
he sent ambassadors unto him to pray his assistance, or at the
least that he would stand neutral. Which ambassadors found the
King at Leicester, and delivered their ambassage to this effect:
They first imparted unto the King the success that their master
had had a little before against Maximilian in recovery of certain

towns from him; which was done in a kind of privacy and inward-
ness towards the King, as if the French King did not esteem him
for an outward or formal confederate, but as one that had part in
his affections and fortunes, and with whom he took pleasure to
communicate his business. After this compliment and some gratulation for the King's victory, they fell to their errand: declaring to
the King, that their master was enforced to enter into a just and
necessary war with the Duke of Brittaine, for that he had received
and succoured those that were traitors and declared enemies unto
his person and state. That they were no mean, distressed and
calamitous persons that fled to him for refuge, but of so great
quality, as it was apparent that they came not thither to pro-
tect their own fortune, but to infest and invade his; the head
of them being the Duke of Orleans, the first Prince of the blood
and the second person of France. That therefore rightly to understand it, it was rather on their master's part a defensive war than
an offensive, as that that could not be omitted or forborne if he
tendered the conservation of his own estate; and that it was not
the first blow that made the war invasive (for that no wise Prince
would stay for), but the first provocation, or at least the first
preparation; nay that this war was rather a suppression of rebels
than a war with a just enemy, where the case is, that his subjects
traitors [traitorous subjects] are received by the Duke of Brittaine
his homager. That King Henry knew well what went upon it in
example, if neighbour Princes should patronise and comfort rebels
against the law of nations and of leagues. Nevertheless that their
master was not ignorant that the King had been beholding to the
Duke of Brittaine in his adversity, as on the other side they knew
he would not forget also the readiness of their King in aiding him
when the Duke of Brittaine or his mercenary counsellors failed
him, and would have betrayed him; and that there was a great
difference between the courtesies received from their master and
the Duke of Brittaine, for that the Duke's might have ends of
utility and bargain, whereas their master's could not have proceeded but out of entire affection; for that if it had been measured
by a politic line, it had been better for his affairs that a tyrant
should have reigned in England, troubled and hated, than such a

Prince whose virtues could not fail to make him great and potent, whensoever he was come to be master of his affairs. But howsoever it stood for the point of obligation which the King might owe to the Duke of Brittaine, yet their master was well assured it would not divert King Henry of England from doing that that was just, nor ever embark him in so ill-grounded a quarrel. Therefore since this war which their master was now to make was but to deliver himself from imminent dangers, their King hoped the King would shew the like affection to the conservation of their master's estate, as their master had (when time was) shewed to the King acquisition of his kingdom. At the least that according to the inclination which the King had ever professed of peace, he would look on and stand neutral; for that their master could not with reason press him to undertake part in the war, being so newly settled and recovered from intestine seditions. But touching the mystery of re-annexing of the duchy of Brittaine to the crown of France, either by war or by marriage with the daughter of Brittaine, the ambassadors bare aloof from it as from a rock, knowing that it made most against them; and therefore by all means declined any mention thereof, but contrariwise interlaced in their conference with the King the assured purpose of their master to match with the daughter of Maximilian; and entertained the King also with some wandering discourses of their King's purpose to recover by arms his right to the kingdom of Naples, by an expedition in person; all to remove the King from all jealousy of any design in these hither parts upon Brittaine, otherwise than for quenching of the fire which he feared might be kindled in his own estate.

The King, after advice taken with his council, made answer to the ambassadors. And first returned their compliment, shewing he was right glad of the French King's reception of those towns from Maximilian. Then he familiarly related some particular passages of his own adventures and victory passed. As to the business of Brittaine, the King answered in few words. That the French King and the Duke of Brittaine were the two persons to whom he was most obliged of all men; and that he should think himself very unhappy if things should go so between them, as he should

not be able to acquit himself in gratitude towards them both; and
that there was no means for him, as a Christian King and a common friend to them, to satisfy all obligations both to God and
man, but to offer himself for a mediator of an accord and peace
between them; by which course he doubted not but their King's
estate and honour both, would be preserved with more safety and
less envy than by a war; and that he would spare no cost or pains,
no [not even] if it were to go on pilgrimage, for so good an effect;
and concluded that in this great affair, which he took so much to
heart, he would express himself more fully by an ambassage,
which he would speedily dispatch unto the French King for that
purpose. And in this sort the French ambassadors were dismissed:
the King avoiding to understand any thing touching the re-annexing of Brittaine, as the ambassadors had avoided to mention it;
save that he gave a little touch of it in the word *envy*. And so it
was, that the King was neither so shallow nor so ill advertised as
not to perceive the intention of the French for the investing himself of Brittaine. But first, he was utterly unwilling (howsoever
he gave out) to enter into a war with France. A fame of a war he
liked well, but not an achievement; for the one he thought would
make him richer, and the other poorer; and he was possessed
with many secret fears touching his own people, which he was
therefore loth to arm, and put weapons into their hands. Yet notwithstanding (as a prudent and courageous Prince) he was not so
averse from a war, but that he was resolved to choose it rather
than to have Brittaine carried by France; being so great and opulent a duchy, and situate so opportunely to annoy England either
for coast or trade. But the King's hopes were, that partly by neg-
ligence, commonly imputed to the French, (especially in the court
of a young King); and partly by the native power of Brittaine itself, which was not small; but chiefly in respect of the great party
that the Duke of Orleans had in the kingdom of France, and
thereby means to stir up civil troubles to divert the French King
from the enterprise of Brittaine; and lastly in regard of the power
of Maximilian, who was corrival to the French King in that pursuit; the enterprise would either bow to a peace or break in itself.
In all which the King measured and valued things amiss, as after-

wards appeared. He sent therefore forthwith to the French King, Christopher Urswick his chaplain, a person by him much trusted and employed; choosing him the rather because he was a churchman, as best sorting with an embassy of pacification; and giving him also a commission, that if the French King consented to treat, he should thence repair to the Duke of Brittaine and ripen the treaty on both parts. Urswick made declaration to the French King much to the purpose of the King's answer to the French ambassadors here, instilling also tenderly some overture of receiving to grace the Duke of Orleans, and some taste of conditions of accord. But the French King on the other side proceeded not sincerely, but with a great deal of art and dissimulation in this treaty; having for his end to gain time, and so put off the English succours, under hope of peace, till he had got good footing in Brittaine by force of arms. Wherefore he answered the ambassador, that he would put himself into the King's hands, and make him arbiter of the peace; and willingly consented that the ambassador should straightways pass into Brittaine to signify this his consent, and to know the Duke's mind likewise; well foreseeing that the Duke of Orleans, by whom the Duke of Brittaine was wholly led, taking himself to be upon terms irreconcilable with him, would admit of no treaty of peace. Whereby he should in one both generally abroad veil over his ambition, and win the reputation of just and moderate proceedings; and should withal endear himself in the affections of the King of England, as one that had committed all to his will; nay and (which was yet more fine) make faith in him that although he went on with the war, yet it should be but with his sword in his hand to bend the stiffness of the other party to accept of peace; and so the King should take no umbrage of his arming and prosecution, but the treaty to be kept on foot to the very last instant, till he were master of the field.

Which grounds being by the French King wisely laid, all things fell out as he expected. For when the English ambassador came to the court of Brittaine, the Duke was then scarcely perfect in his memory, and all things were directed by the Duke of Orleans; who gave audience to the chaplain Urswick, and upon his ambassage delivered, made answer in somewhat high terms: That the Duke of Brittaine having been an host and a kind of parent or foster-father to the King in his tenderness of age and weakness of fortune, did look for at this time from King Henry (the renowned King of England) rather brave troops for his succours than a vain treaty of peace. And if the King could forget the good offices of the Duke done unto him aforetime, yet he knew well he would in his wisdom consider of the future, how much it imported his own safety and reputation both in foreign parts and with his own people, not to suffer Brittaine (the old confederates of England) to be swallowed up by France, and so many good ports and strong towns upon the coast be in the command of so potent a neighbour King, and so ancient an enemy. And therefore humbly desired the King to think of this business as his own: and therewith broke off, and denied any further conference for treaty.

Urswick returned first to the French King, and related to him what had passed. Who finding things to sort to his desire, took hold of them, and said: That the ambassador might perceive now that which he for his part partly imagined before. That considering in what hands the Duke of Brittaine was, there would be no peace but by a mixed treaty of force and persuasion. And therefore he would go on with the one, and desired the King not to desist from the other. But for his own part, he did faithfully promise to be still in the King's power, to rule him in the matter of peace. This was accordingly represented unto the King by Urswick at his return, and in such a fashion as if the treaty were in no sort desperate[14], but rather stayed for a better hour, till the hammer had wrought and beat the party of Brittaine more pliant. Whereupon there passed continually packets and despatches between the two Kings, from the one out of desire, and from the other out of dissimulation, about the negotiation of peace. The French King meanwhile invaded Brittaine with great forces, and distressed the city of Nantes with a strait siege, and (as one who, though he had no great judgment, yet had that, that he could dissemble home) the more he did urge the prosecution of the war, the more he did at

[14] [to be despaired of]

the same time urge the solicitation of the peace; insomuch as during the siege of Nantes, after many letters and particular messages,
the better to maintain his dissimulation and to refresh the treaty,
he sent Bernard Daubigny, a person of good quality, to the King,
earnestly to desire him to make an end of the business howsoever.
The King was no less ready to revive and quicken the treaty; and
thereupon sent three commissioners, the Abbot of Abingdon, Sir
Richard Tunstall, and Chaplain Urswick formerly employed, to
do their utmost endeavour to manage the treaty roundly and
strongly.

About this time the Lord Woodvile (uncle to the Queen) a
valiant gentleman and desirous of honour, sued to the King that
he might raise some power of voluntaries under-hand, and without licence or passport (wherein the King might any ways appear)
go to the aid of the Duke of Brittaine. The King denied his request,
or at least seemed so to do, and laid strait commandment upon
him that he should not stir; for that the King thought his honour
would suffer therein, during a treaty to better a party. Nevertheless this lord (either being unruly, or out of conceit that the King
would not inwardly dislike that which he would not openly avow,)
sailed secretly over into the Isle of Wight whereof he was governor, and levied a fair troop of four hundred men, and with them
passed over into Brittaine, and joined himself with the Duke's
forces. The news whereof when it came to the French court, put
divers young bloods into such a fury, as the English ambassadors
were not without peril to be outraged. But the French King, both
to preserve the privilege of ambassadors, and being conscious to
himself that in the business of peace he himself was the greater
dissembler of the two, forbad all injuries of fact or word against
their persons or followers. And presently came an agent from the
King to purge himself touching the Lord Woodvile's going over,
using for a principal argument to demonstrate that it was without
his privity, for that the troops were so small, as neither had the
face of a succour by authority nor could much advance the Briton
affairs. To which message although the French King gave no full
credit, yet he made fair weather with the King and seemed satis-

fied. Soon after the English ambassadors returned, having two of them been likewise with the Duke of Brittaine and found things in no other terms than they were before.

Upon their return they informed the King of the state of the affairs, and how far the French King was from any true meaning of peace, and therefore he was now to advise of some other course. Neither was the King himself led all this while with credulity merely, as was generally supposed. But his error was not so much facility of belief, as an ill-measuring of the forces of the other party. For (as was partly touched before) the King had cast the business thus with himself. He took it for granted in his own judgment that the war of Brittaine, in respect of the strength of the towns and of the party, could not speedily come to a period. For he conceived that the counsels of a war that was undertaken by the French King (then childless) against an heir apparent of France, would be very faint and slow; and besides that it was not possible but that the state of France should be embroiled with some troubles and alterations in favour of the Duke of Orleans.[15] He conceived likewise that Maximilian King of the Romans was a Prince warlike and potent, who (he made account) would give succours to the Britons roundly. So then judging it would be a work of time, he laid his plot how he might best make use of that time for his own affairs. Wherein first he thought to make his vantage upon his Parliament, knowing that they being affectionate unto the quarrel of Brittaine would give treasure largely. Which treasure as a noise of war might draw forth, so a peace succeeding might coffer up. And because he knew his people were hot upon the business, he chose rather to seem to be deceived and lulled asleep by the French, than to be backward in himself; considering his subjects were not so fully capable of the reasons of state which made him hold back. Wherefore to all these purposes he saw no other expedient than to set and keep on foot a continual treaty of peace, laying it down and taking it up again as the occurrence required. Besides he had in consideration the point of honour, in

[15] [Charles was unmarried; and the Duke of Orleans was his heir.]

bearing the blessed person of a pacificator. He thought likewise to make use of the envy that the French King met with by occasion of this war of Brittaine, in strengthening himself with new alliances: as namely that of Ferdinando of Spain, with whom he had ever a consent (even in nature and customs); and likewise with Maximilian, who was particularly interessed. So that in substance he promised himself money, honour, friends, and peace in the end. But those things were too fine to be fortunate and succeed in all parts; for that great affairs are commonly too rough and stubborn to be wrought upon by the finer edges or points of wit. The King was likewise deceived in his two main grounds. For although he had reason to conceive that the council of France would be wary to put the King into a war against the heir apparent of France; yet he did not consider that Charles was not guided by any of the principal of the blood or nobility, but by mean men, who would make it their master-piece of credit and favour to give venturous counsels which no great or wise man durst or would. And for Maximilian, he was thought then a greater matter than he was; his unstable and necessitous courses being not then known.

After consultation with the ambassadors, who brought him no other news than he expected before (though he would not seem to know it till then), he presently summoned his Parliament, and in open Parliament propounded the cause of Brittaine to both houses by his chancellor Morton Archbishop of Canterbury, who spoke to this effect.

"My lords and masters, the King's Grace, our Sovereign Lord, hath commanded me to declare unto you the causes that have moved him at this time to summon this his Parliament; which I shall do in few words, craving pardon of his Grace and you all, if I perform it not as I would.

"His Grace doth first of all let you know that he retaineth in thankful memory the love and loyalty shewed to him by you at your last meeting, in establishment of his royalty, freeing and discharging of his partakers, and confiscation of his traitors and rebels; more than which could not come from subjects to their sovereign in one action. This he taketh so well at your hands, as he hath made it a resolution to himself to communicate with so loving and well approved subjects in all affairs that are of public nature at home or abroad.

"Two therefore are the causes of your present assembling: the one a foreign business; the other matter of government at home.

"The French King (as no doubt ye have heard) maketh at this present hot war upon the Duke of Brittaine. His army is now before Nantes, and holdeth it straitly besieged, being the principal city, if not in ceremony and preeminence, yet in strength and wealth, of that duchy. Ye may guess at his hopes, by his attempting of the hardest part of the war first. The cause of this war he knoweth best. He alledgeth the entertaining and succouring of the Duke of Orleans and some other French lords, whom the King taketh for his enemies. Others divine of other matters. Both parts have by their ambassadors divers times prayed the King's aids; the French King, aids or neutrality; the Britons, aids simply; for so their case requireth. The King, as a Christian Prince and blessed son of the holy church, hath offered himself as a mediator to treat a peace between them. The French King yieldeth to treat, but will not stay the prosecution of the war. The Britons, that desire peace most, hearken to it least; not upon confidence or stiffness, but upon distrust of true meaning, seeing the war goes on. So as the King, after as much pains and care to effect a peace as ever he took in any business, not being able to remove the prosecution on the one side nor the distrust on the other caused by that prosecution, hath let fall the treaty; not repenting of it, but despairing of it now, as not likely to succeed. Therefore by this narrative you now understand the state of the question, whereupon the King prayeth your advice: which is no other, but whether he shall enter into an auxiliary and defensive war for the Britons against France?

"And the better to open your understandings in this affair, the King hath commanded me to say somewhat to you from him of the persons that do intervene in this business; and somewhat of the consequence thereof, as it hath relation to this kingdom; and somewhat of the example of it in general; making nevertheless no conclusion or judgment of any point, until his Grace hath received your faithful and politic advices.

"First for the King our sovereign himself, who is the principal person you are to eye in this business; his Grace doth profess that he truly and constantly desireth to reign in peace: but his Grace saith he will neither buy peace with dishonour, nor take it up at interest of danger to ensue; but shall think it a good change, if it please God to change the inward troubles and seditions wherewith he hath been hitherto exercised into an honourable foreign war.

"And for the other two persons in this action, the French King and the Duke of Brittaine, his Grace doth declare unto you, that they be the men unto whom he is of all other friends and allies most bounden; the one having held over him his hand of protection from the tyrant; the other having reached forth unto him his hand of help for the recovery of his kingdom. So that his affection toward them in his natural person is upon equal terms. And whereas you may have heard that his Grace was enforced to fly out of Brittaine into France for doubts of being betrayed; his Grace would not in any sort have that reflect upon the Duke of Brittaine in defacement of his former benefits; for that he is throughly informed that it was but the practice of some corrupt persons about him, during the time of his sickness, altogether without his consent or privity.

"But howsoever these things do interest his Grace in his particular, yet he knoweth well that the higher bond that tieth him to procure by all means the safety and welfare of his loving subjects, doth disinteress him of these obligations of gratitude, otherwise than thus; that if his Grace be forced to make a war he do it without passion or ambition.

"For the consequence of this action towards this kingdom, it is much as the French King's intention is. For if it be no more but to range his subjects to reason who bear themselves stout upon the strength of the Duke of Brittaine, it is nothing to us. But if it be in the French King's purpose,—or if it should not be in his purpose, yet if it shall follow all one as if it were sought,—that the

French King shall make a province of Brittaine and join it to the crown of France; then it is worthy the consideration how this may import England, as well in the increasement of the greatness of France, by the addition of such a country that stretcheth his boughs unto our seas, as in depriving this nation and leaving it naked of so firm and assured confederates as the Britons have always been. For then it will come to pass that, whereas not long since this realm was mighty upon the continent, first in territory and after in alliance, in respect of Burgundy and Brittaine, which were confederates indeed, but dependent confederates; now the one being already cast partly into the greatness of France and partly into that of Austria, the other is like wholly to be cast into the greatness of France; and this island shall remain confined in effect within the salt waters, and grit about with the coast countries of two mighty monarchs.

"For the example, it resteth likewise upon the same question, upon the French King's intent. For if Brittaine be carried and swallowed up by France, as the world abroad (apt to impute and construe the actions of Princes to ambition) conceive it will, then it is an example very dangerous and universal, that the lesser neighbour estate should be devoured of the greater. For this may be the case of Scotland towards England; of Portugal towards Spain; of the smaller estates of Italy towards the greater; and so of Germany; or as if some of you of the commons might not live and dwell safely besides some of these great lords. And the bringing in of this example will be chiefly laid to the King's charge, as to him that was most interessed and most able to forbid it. But then on the other side there is so fair a pretext on the French King's part (and yet pretext is never wanting to power) in regard the danger imminent to his own estate is such as may make this enterprise seem rather a work of necessity than of ambition, as doth in reason correct the danger of the example. For that the example of that which is done in a man's own defence cannot be dangerous, because it is in another's power to avoid it. But in all this business, the King remits himself to your grave and mature advice, whereupon he purposeth to rely."

This was the effect of the Lord Chancellor's speech touching

the cause of Brittaine; for the King had commanded him to carry
it so as to affect the Parliament towards the business; but without
engaging the King in any express declaration.

The Chancellor went on:

"For that which may concern the government at home, the
King hath commanded me to say unto you; that he thinketh
there was never any King (for the small time that he hath reigned)
had greater and juster cause of the two contrary passions of joy
and sorrow, than his Grace hath. Joy, in respect of the rare and
visible favours of Almighty God, in girting the imperial sword
upon his side, and assisting the same his sword against all his
enemies; and likewise in blessing him with so many good and loving servants and subjects, which have never failed to give him
faithful counsel, ready obedience, and courageous defence. Sorrow, for that it hath not pleased God to suffer him to sheath his
sword (as he greatly desired, otherwise than for administration
of justice), but that he hath been forced to draw it so oft, to cut
off traitorous and disloyal subjects, whom it seems God hath left
(a few amongst many good) as the Canaanites amongst the people of Israel, to be thorns in their sides, to tempt and try them;
though the end hath been always (God's name be blessed therefore) that the destruction hath fallen upon their own heads.

"Wherefore his Grace saith that he seeth that it is not the
blood spilt in the field that will save the blood in the city; nor the
marshal's [martial?] sword that will set this kingdom in perfect
peace: but that the true way is to stop the seeds of sedition and rebellion in their beginnings, and for that purpose to devise, confirm, and quicken good and wholesome laws against riots and
unlawful assemblies of people and all combinations and confederacies of them by liveries, tokens, and other badges of factious
dependence; that the peace of the land may by these ordinances,
as by bars of iron, be soundly bound in and strengthened, and all
force both in court, country, and private houses be supprest. The
care hereof, which so much concerneth yourselves, and which the
nature of the times doth instantly call for, his Grace commends to
your wisdoms.

"And because it is the King's desire that this peace wherein he hopeth to govern and maintain you, do not bear only unto you leaves, for you to sit under the shade of them in safety, but also should bear you fruit of riches, wealth, and plenty; therefore his Grace prays you to take into consideration matter of trade, as also the manufactures of the kingdom, and to repress the bastard and barren employment of moneys to usury and unlawful exchanges, that they may be (as their natural use is) turned upon commerce, and lawful and royal trading. And likewise that our people be set on work in arts and handicrafts, that the realm may subsist more of itself, that idleness be avoided, and the draining out of our treasure for foreign manufactures stopped. But you are not to rest here only, but to provide further that whatsoever merchandise shall be brought in from beyond the seas may be employed upon the commodities of this land; whereby the kingdom's stock of treasure may be sure to be kept from being diminished by any overtrading of the foreigner.

"And lastly because the King is well assured that you would not have him poor that wishes you rich; he doubteth not but that you will have care, as well to maintain his revenews [revenues] of customs and all other natures, as also to supply him with your loving aids, if the case shall so require: the rather for that you know the King is a good husband, and but a steward in effect for the public, and that what comes from you is but as moisture drawn from the earth, which gathers into a cloud and falls back upon the earth again. And you know well how the kingdoms about you grow more and more in greatness, and the times are stirring; and therefore not fit to find the King with an empty purse. More I have not to say to you, and wish that what hath been said had been better expressed: but that your wisdom and good affections will supply. God bless your doings."

It was no hard matter to dispose and affect the Parliament in this business [of Brittany]; as well in respect of the emulation between the nations, and the envy at the late growth of the French monarchy; as in regard of the danger to suffer the French to make their approaches upon England, by obtaining so goodly a maritime province, full of sea-towns and havens, that might do mischief to the English, either by invasion or by interruption of

traffic. The Parliament was also moved with the point of oppression; for although the French seemed to speak reason, yet
arguments are ever with multitudes too weak for suspicions.
Wherefore they did advise the King roundly to embrace the
Britons' quarrel, and to send them speedy aids; and with much
alacrity and forwardness granted to the King a great rate of subsidy in contemplation of these aids. But the King, both to keep a
decency towards the French King, to whom he profest himself to
be obliged, and indeed desirous rather to show war than to make
it, sent new solemn ambassadors to intimate unto him the decree
of his estates, and to iterate his motion that the French would
desist from hostility; or if war must follow, to desire him to take
it in good part, if at the motion of his people, who were sensible
of the cause of the Britons as their ancient friends and confederates, he did send them succours; with protestation nevertheless that, to save all treaties and laws of friendship, he had limited
his force, to proceed in aid of the Britons, but in no wise to war
upon the French, otherwise than as they maintained the possession of Brittaine. But before this formal ambassage arrived, the
party of the Duke had received a great blow, and grew to manifest
declination. For near the town of St. Alban in Brittaine a battle
had been given, where the Britons were overthrown, and the
Duke of Orleans and the Prince of Orange taken prisoners, there
being slain on the Britons' part six thousand men, and amongst
them the Lord Woodvile, and almost all his soldiers, valiantly
fighting. And of the French part, one thousand two hundred, with
their leader James Galeot a great commander.

When the news of this battle came over into England, it was
time for the King (who now had no subterfuge to continue further
treaty, and saw before his eyes that Brittaine went so speedily for
lost, contrary to his hopes; knowing also that with his people and
foreigners both, he sustained no small envy and disreputation for
his former delays,) to dispatch with all possible speed his succours
into Brittaine; which he did under the conduct of Robert Lord
Brooke, to the number of eight thousand choice men, and well
armed; who having a fair wind, in few hours landed in Brittaine,
and joined themselves forthwith to those Briton forces that re-

mained after the defeat, and marched straight on to find the enemy, and encamped fast by them. The French wisely husbanding the possession of a victory, and well acquainted with the courage of the English, especially when they are fresh, kept themselves within their trenches, being strongly lodged, and resolved not to give battle. But meanwhile to harass and weary the English, they did upon all advantages set upon them with their light horse; wherein nevertheless they received commonly loss, especially by means of the English archers.

But upon these achievements Francis Duke of Brittaine deceased; an accident that the King might easily have foreseen, and ought to have reckoned upon and provided for; but that the point of reputation, when news first came of the battle lost, (that somewhat must be done), did overbear the reason of war.

After the Duke's decease, the principal persons of Brittaine, partly bought, partly through faction, put all things into confusion; so as the English not finding head or body with whom to join their forces, and being in jealousy of friends as well as in danger of enemies, and the winter begun, returned home five months after their landing. So the battle of St. Alban, the death of the Duke, and the retire of the English succours, were (after some time) the causes of the loss of that duchy; which action some accounted as a blemish of the King's judgment, but most but as the misfortune of his times.

But howsoever the temporary fruit of the Parliament in their aid and advice given for Brittaine, took not nor prospered not; yet the lasting fruit of Parliament, which is good and wholesome laws, did prosper, and doth yet continue to this day. For according to the Lord Chancellor's admonition, there were that Parliament divers excellent laws ordained, concerning the points which the King recommended.

First, the authority of the Star-chamber, which before subsisted by the ancient common laws of the realm, was confirmed in certain cases by act of Parliament. This court is one of the sagest and noblest institutions of this kingdom. For in the distribution of courts of ordinary justice, (besides the high court of Parliament,) in which distribution the King's bench holdeth the pleas of the crown; the Common-place, pleas civil; the Exchequer, pleas concerning the King's revenue; and the Chancery, the Pretorian power for mitigating the rigour of law, in case of extremity, by the conscience of a good man; there was nevertheless always reserved a high and preeminent power to the King's council in causes that might in example or consequence concern the state of the commonwealth; which if they were criminal, the council used to sit in the chamber called the Star-chamber; if civil, in the white-chamber or White-hall. And as the Chancery had the Pretorian power for equity, so the Star-chamber had the Censorian power for offences under the degree of capital. This court of Star-chamber is compounded of good elements, for it consisteth of four kinds of persons: councillors, peers, prelates, and chief judges. It discerneth also principally of four kinds of causes: forces, frauds, crimes various of stellionate [deceitful sales], and the inchoations or middle acts towards crimes capital, or heinous, not actually committed or perpetrated. But that which was principally aimed at by this act was force, and the two chief supports of force, combination of multitudes, and maintenance or headship of great persons.

From the general peace of the country the King's care went on to the peace of the King's house, and the security of his great officers and councillors. But this law was somewhat of a strange composition and temper. That if any of the King's servants under the degree of a lord, do conspire the death of any of the King's council, or lord of the realm, it is made capital. This law was thought to be procured by the Lord Chancellor, who being a stern and haughty man, and finding he had some mortal enemies in court, provided for his own safety; drowning the envy of it in a general law, by communicating the privilege with all other councillors and peers; and yet not daring to extend it further than to the King's servants in check-roll, lest it should have been too harsh to the gentlemen and other commons of the kingdom, who might have thought their ancient liberty and the clemency of the laws of England invaded, *if the will in any case of felony should be made the deed.* And yet the reason which the act yieldeth (that is to say, *that he that conspireth the death of councillors may be thought indirectly and by a mean to conspire the death of the King himself*) is indifferent to all subjects as well as to servants in court. But it seemeth this sufficed to serve the Lord Chancellor's turn at this time; but yet he lived to need a general law; for that he grew afterwards as odious to the country as he was then to the court.[16]

From the peace of the King's house the King's care extended to the peace of private houses and families; for there was an excellent moral law molded thus: The taking and carrying away of women forcibly and against their will (except female wards and bondwomen) was made capital; the Parliament wisely and justly conceiving, that the obtaining of women by force into possession (howsoever afterwards assent might follow by allurements) was but a rape drawn forth in length, because the first force drew on all the rest.

There was made also another law for peace in general, and repressing of murders and manslaughters, and was in amendment of the common laws of the realm, being this: That whereas by the common law the King's suit, in case of homicide, did expect the year and the day, allowed to the party's suit by way of appeal; and that it was found by experience that the party was many times compounded with, and many times wearied with the suit, so that in the end such suit was let fall; and by that time the matter was in a manner forgotten, and thereby prosecution at the King's suit by indictment (which is ever best *flagrante crimine*) neglected; it was ordained that the suit by indictment might be taken as well at any time within the year and the day as after; not prejudicing nevertheless the party's suit.[17]

---

[16] [The law says that conspiracy to kill councillors is to be held punishable in the same way as the actual commission of such a murder. Bacon notes several anomalies: that will is made the equivalent of deed; that the limitation of the law to the King's servants made little legal sense (and that its political sense did not last long) because the reason adduced in the statute—that conspiracy against councillors is equivalent to conspiring against the King—is plainly applicable to all men if it is applicable at all.]

[17] [The meaning of this appears to be that, under the old law, the family of a murdered man had the right to prosecute the supposed

The King began also then, as well in wisdom as in justice, to
pare a little the privilege of clergy, ordaining *that clerks convict*
[convicted clerks] *should be burned in the hand,*—both because
they might taste of some corporal punishment, and that they
might carry a brand of infamy. But for this good act's sake, the
King himself was after branded by Perkin's proclamation for an
execrable breaker of the rites of holy church.

Another law was made for the better peace of the country,
by which law the King's officers and farmers were to forfeit
their places and holds, in case of unlawful retainer or partaking
in routs and unlawful assemblies.

These were the laws that were made for repressing of force,
which those times did chiefly require; and were so prudently
framed as they are found fit for all succeeding times, and so continue to this day.

There were also made good and politic laws in that Parliament against usury, which is the bastard use of money; and
against unlawful chievances [certain financial arrangements, e.g.,
discount] and exchanges, which is bastard usury; and also for the
security of the King's customs; and for the employment of the
procedures of foreign commodities, brought in by merchant-
strangers, upon the native commodities of the realm; together
with some other laws of less importance.

But howsoever the laws made in that Parliament did bear
good and wholesome fruit; yet the subsidy granted at the same
time bare a fruit that proved harsh and bitter. All was inned at
last into the King's barn; but it was after a storm. For when the

---

murderer, but that this right had to be exercised within a year and a
day; only if the family failed to act within this time could the King
undertake a royal prosecution. Since, however, the family rarely
pushed the suit through, and since the delay of a year and day made
it difficult for the Crown to put its case together, murderers commonly
went unpunished. The new law allowed the Crown to begin its prosecution at once, but without prejudicing the family's right to bring
suit as well.]

commissioners entered into the taxation of the subsidy in Yorkshire and the bishoprick of Durham, the people upon a sudden
grew into great mutiny, and said openly that they had endured of
late years a thousand miseries, and neither could nor would pay
the subsidy. This no doubt proceeded not simply of any present
necessity, but much by reason of the old humour of those countries, where the memory of King Richard was so strong, that it
lay like lees in the bottom of men's hearts, and if the vessel was
but stirred it would come up. And no doubt it was partly also by
the instigation of some factious malcontents that bare principal
stroke [were leaders] amongst them. Hereupon the commissioners, being somewhat astonished, deferred the matter unto the
Earl of Northumberland, who was the principal man of authority
in those parts. The Earl forthwith wrote unto the court, signifying
to the King plainly enough in what flame he found the people of
those countries, and praying the King's direction. The King wrote
back peremptorily that he would not have one penny abated of
that which had been granted to him by Parliament; both because
it might encourage other countries to pray the like release or miti-
gation; and chiefly because he would never endure that the base
multitude should frustrate the authority of the Parliament,
wherein their votes and consents were concluded. Upon this dispatch from court, the Earl assembled the principal justices and
freeholders of the country; and speaking to them in that imperious
language wherein the King had written to him, which needed not
(save that an harsh business was unfortunately fallen into the
hands of a harsh man), did not only irritate the people, but make
them conceive by the stoutness and haughtiness of delivery of the
King's errand, that himself was the author or principal persuader
of that counsel. Whereupon the meaner sort routed together, and
suddenly assailing the earl in his house, slew him and divers of
his servants. And rested not there, but creating for their leader
Sir John Egremond, a factious person, and one that had of a long
time borne an ill talent towards the King, and being animated also
by a base fellow, called John a Chamber, a very *boutefeu* [fire-
brand], who bore much sway amongst the vulgar and popular,
entered into open rebellion, and gave out in flat terms that they

would go against King Henry and fight with him for the maintenance of their liberties.

When the King was advertised of this new insurrection (being almost a fever that took him every year), after his manner
little troubled therewith, he sent Thomas Earl of Surrey (whom
he had a little before not only released out of the Tower and
pardoned, but also received to special favour) with a competent
power against the rebels; who fought with the principal band of
them and defeated them, and took alive John a Chamber their
firebrand. As for Sir John Egremond, he fled into Flanders to the
Lady Margaret of Burgundy, whose palace was the sanctuary and
receptacle of all traitors against the King. John a Chamber was
executed at York in great state; for he was hanged upon a gibbet
raised a stage higher in the midst of a square gallows, as a traitor
paramount; and a number of his men that were his chief complices [accomplices] were hanged upon the lower story round
about him; and the rest were generally pardoned. Neither did the
King himself omit his custom to be first or second in all his warlike exploits, making good his word which was usual with him
when he heard of rebels, that *he desired but to see them.* For immediately after he had sent down the Earl of Surrey, he marched
towards them himself in person. And although in his journey
he heard news of the victory, yet he went on as far as York, to
pacify and settle those countries. And that done, returned to
London, leaving the Earl of Surrey for his lieutenant in the
northern parts, and Sir Richard Tunstal for his principal commissioner to levy the subsidy, whereof he did not remit a denier.[18]

About the same time that the King lost so good a servant as
the Earl of Northumberland, he lost likewise a faithful friend and
ally of James the Third King of Scotland by a miserable disaster.
For this unfortunate Prince, after a long smother of discontent and
hatred of many of his nobility and people, breaking forth at times
into seditions and alterations of court, was at last distressed by
them, having taken arms and surprised the person of Prince James
his son (partly by force, partly by threats that they would other-

[18] [that is, the king refused to abate the law in any way]

wise deliver up the kingdom to the King of England) to shadow their rebellion, and to be the titular and painted head of those arms. Whereupon the King (finding himself too weak) sought unto King Henry, as also unto the Pope and the King of France, to compose those troubles between him and his subjects. The Kings accordingly interposed their mediations in a round and princely manner, not only by way of request and persuasion, but also by way of protestation and menace, declaring that they thought it to be the common cause of all Kings, *If subjects should be suffered to give laws unto their sovereign;* and that they would accordingly resent it and revenge it. But the rebels, that had shaken off the greater yoke of obedience, had likewise cast away the lesser tie of respect. And fury prevailing above fear, made answer, That there was no talking of peace except the King would resign his crown. Whereupon (treaty of accord taking no place) it came to a battle, at Bannocksbourn by Strivelin. In which battle the King transported with wrath and just indignation, inconsiderately fighting and precipitating the charge before his whole numbers came up to him, was, notwithstanding the contrary express and strait commandment of the Prince his son, slain in the pursuit, being fled to a mill situate in the field where the battle was fought.

As for the Pope's embassy,[19] which was sent by Adrian de Castello an Italian legate, (and perhaps as those times were might have prevailed more,) it came too late for the embassy, but not for the ambassador. For passing through England and being honourably entertained and received of King Henry (who ever applied himself with much respect to the see of Rome), he fell into great grace with the King, and great familiarity and friendship with Morton the Chancellor. Insomuch as the King taking a liking to him, and finding him to his mind, preferred him to the bishoprick of Hereford, and afterwards to that of Bath and Wells, and employed him in many of his affairs of state that had relation to Rome. He was a man of great learning, wisdom, and dexterity in

[19] ["Embassy" is used here to mean "message" or "mission".]

business of state, and having not long after ascended to the degree of cardinal, paid the King large tribute of his gratitude in diligent and judicious advertisement of the occurrents of [occurrences in] Italy. Nevertheless in the end of his time he was partaker of the conspiracy which cardinal Alphonso Petrucci and some other cardinals had plotted against the life of Pope Leo. And this offence, in itself so heinous, was yet in him aggravated by the motive thereof, which was not malice or discontent, but an aspiring mind to the papacy. And in this height of impiety there wanted not an intermixture of levity and folly, for that (as was generally believed) he was animated to expect the papacy by a fatal mockery, the prediction of a sooth-sayer, which was, *That one should succeed Pope Leo, whose name should be Adrian, an aged man of mean birth and of great learning and wisdom;* by which character and figure he took himself to be described, though it were fulfilled of Adrian the Fleming, son of a Dutch brewer, cardinal of Tortosa, and preceptor unto Charles the Fifth; the same that, not changing his christen-name, was afterwards called Adrian the Sixth.

But these things happened in the year following, which was the fifth of this King. But in the end of the fourth year the King had called again his Parliament, not as it seemeth for any particular occasion of state. But the former Parliament being ended somewhat suddenly (in regard of the preparation for Brittaine), the King thought he had not remunerated his people sufficiently with good laws (which evermore was his retribution for treasure). And finding by the insurrection in the north, there was discontentment abroad in respect of the subsidy, he thought it good to give his subjects yet further contentment and comfort in that kind. Certainly his times for good commonwealth laws did excel; so as he may justly be celebrated for the best lawgiver to this nation after King Edward the First. For his laws (whoso marks them well) are deep and not vulgar; not made upon the spur of a particular occasion for the present, but out of providence of the future, to make the estate of his people still more and more happy; after the manner of the legislators in ancient and heroical times.

First therefore he made a law suitable to his own acts and times. For as himself had in his person and marriage made a final concord in the great suit and title for the crown; so by this law he settled the like peace and quiet in the private possessions of the subjects: ordaining, *That Fines thenceforth should be final to conclude all strangers rights;* and that upon fines levied, and solemnly proclaimed, the subject should have his time of watch for five years after his title accrued; which if he forepassed, his right should be bound for ever after; with some exception nevertheless of minors, married women, and such incompetent persons. This statute did in effect but restore an ancient statute of the realm, which was itself also made but in affirmance of the common law. The alteration had been by a statute commonly called the statute of *nonclaim*, made in the time of Edward the Third. And surely this law [of Henry VII] was a kind of prognostic of the good peace which since his time hath (for the most part) continued in this kingdom until this day. For statutes of *non-claim* are fit for times of war, when men's heads are troubled, that they cannot intend their estate; but statutes that quiet possessions are fittest for times of peace, to extinguish suits and contentions; which is one of the banes of peace.[20]

[20] [This sort of passage was likely to have been intelligible to a high proportion of Bacon's readers, since many country gentlemen of his day had some legal training. A "fine" is a settlement terminating an entail; that is, it is a final accord in a collusive suit whose purpose was to break a grant settling a piece of land on "A. B. and the heirs of his body forever." The "fee tail," as it is called, could come only to the lineal descendants of A. B., none of whom was allowed to alienate it for longer than his own life. The entail was used to make certain that a man's posterity could not alienate the given property; since social position was tied to the land (at least indirectly), it enabled a man to assure his family of some property henceforth. But an occasion might arise when an entail had to be broken, and then a collusive suit was instituted. Early laws had stated that "strangers"—men not party to the suit, but with an interest in the proceedings—had a year and a day to protest; the time allowed was considered insufficient, and com-

Another statute was made of singular policy; for the population apparently, and (if it be thoroughly considered) for the
soldiery and militar forces of the realm. Inclosures at that time
began to be more frequent, whereby arable land (which could not
be manured [cultivated] without people and families) was turned
into pasture, which was easily rid by a few herdsmen; and ten-
ancies for years, lives, and at will (whereupon much of the yeomanry lived), were turned into demesnes.[21] This bred a decay of
people, and (by consequence) a decay of towns, churches, tithes,
and the like. The King likewise knew full well, and in no wise
forgot, that there ensued withal upon this a decay and diminution
of subsidies and taxes; for the more gentlemen, ever the lower
books of subsidies. In remedying of this inconvenience the King's
wisdom was admirable, and the Parliament's at that time. Inclosures they would not forbid, for that had been to forbid the
improvement of the patrimony of the kingdom; nor tillage they
would not compel; for that was to strive with nature and utility.
But they took a course to take away depopulating inclosures and
depopulating pasturage, and yet not by that name, or by any imperious express prohibition, but by consequence. The ordinance
was, *That all houses of husbandry, that were used with twenty
acres of ground and upwards, should be maintained and kept up
for ever; together with a competent proportion of land to be used
and occupied with them;* and in no wise to be severed from them

plaint led to the passage of a statute of no-claim (in Edward III's time)
which stated that a fine did not bar stranger's rights at all (that is, no
claims were barred). But this turned out to be equally disadvanta-
geous, since it led to an infinity of lawsuits. Henry's statute went behind that of Edward III to the old law but modified it to the extent of
allowing a period of five years for strangers to make their complaints.
Bacon then comments that statutes of no-claim (like that of Edward
III) are appropriate in times of civil strife, when strangers' claims
might easily be delayed; in quieter times, men preferred to have such
matters settled more quickly.]

[21] ["i.e. lands kept by the lord of the manor in his own hands."—
Spedding]

(as by another statute, made afterwards in his successor's time, was more fully declared): this upon forfeiture to be taken, not by way of popular action, but by seizure of the land itself by the King and lords of the fee, as to half the profits, till the houses and lands were restored. By this means the houses being kept up did of necessity enforce a dweller; and the proportion of land for occupation being kept up, did of necessity enforce that dweller not to be a beggar or cottager, but a man of some substance, that might keep hinds and servants, and set the plough on going. This did wonderfully concern the might and mannerhood of the kingdom, to have farms as it were of a standard, sufficient to maintain an able body out of penury, and did in effect amortise a great part of the lands of the kingdom unto the hold and occupation of the yeomanry or middle people, of a condition between gentlemen and cottagers or peasants. Now how much this did advance the militar power of the kingdom, is apparent by the true principles of war and the examples of other kingdoms. For it hath been held by the general opinion of men of best judgment in the wars (howsoever some few have varied, and that it may receive some distinction of case) that the principal strength of an army consisteth in the infantry or foot. And to make good infantry, it requireth men bred not in a servile or indigent fashion, but in some free and plentiful manner. Therefore if a state run most to noblemen and gentlemen, and that the husbandmen and ploughmen be but as their workfolks and labourers, or else mere cottagers (which are but housed beggars), you may have a good cavalry, but never good stable bands of foot; like to coppice woods, that if you leave in them staddles[22] too thick, they will run to bushes and briars, and have little clean underwood. And this is to be seen in France and Italy, and some other parts abroad, where in effect all is noblesse or peasantry (I speak of people out of towns), and no middle people; and therefore no good forces of foot: insomuch as they are enforced to employ mercenary bands of Switzers and the like for their battalions of foot. Whereby also it comes to pass that those

[22][Staddle—"a young tree left standing when others are cut down"—N. E. D.]

nations have much people and few soldiers. Whereas the King saw that contrariwise it would follow, that England, though much less in territory, yet should have infinitely more soldiers of their native forces than those other nations have. Thus did the King secretly sow Hydra's teeth, whereupon (according to the poet's fiction) should rise up armed men for the service of this kingdom.

The King also (having care to make his realm potent as well by sea as by land), for the better maintenance of the navy, ordained, *That wines and woads from the parts of Gascoign and Languedoc, should not be brought but in English bottoms;* bowing the ancient policy of this estate from consideration of plenty to consideration of power. For that almost all the ancient statutes incite by all means merchant-strangers to bring in all sorts of commodities; having for end cheapness, and not looking to the point of state concerning the naval power.

The King also made a statute in that Parliament monitory and minatory towards justices of peace[23], that they should duly execute their office, inviting complaints against them, first to their fellow-justices, then to the justices of assize, then to the King or Chancellor; and that a proclamation which he had published of that tenor should be read in open session four times a year, to keep them awake. Meaning also to have his laws executed, and thereby to reap either obedience or forfeitures, (wherein towards his latter times he did decline too much to the left hand,) he did ordain remedy against the practice that was grown in use, to stop and damp informations upon penal laws, by procuring informations by collusion to be put in by the confederates of the delinquents, to be faintly prosecuted and let fall at pleasure, and pleading them in bar of the informations which were prosecuted with effect.[24]

[23] [a statute that both warned the justices of the peace and threatened them with punishment]

[24] [Henry was interested in two things: he wished to put a stop to collusive informations (that is, he wished to see the laws obeyed), and he wished to make certain that the forfeitures which resulted from

He made also laws for the correction of the mint, and counterfeiting of foreign coin current. And that no payment in gold should be made to any merchant-stranger, the better to keep treasure within the realm, for that gold was the metal that lay in least room [and was most easily smuggled out].

He made also statutes for the maintenance of drapery and the keeping of wools within the realm; and not only so, but for stinting and limiting the prices of cloth, one for the finer, and another for the coarser sort. Which I note, both because it was a rare thing to set prices by statute, especially upon our home commodities; and because of the wise model of this act, not prescribing [exact] prices, but stinting them not to exceed a rate; that the clothier might drape accordingly as he might afford.

Divers other good statutes were made that Parliament, but these were the principal. And here I do desire those into whose hands this work shall fall, that they do take in good part my long insisting upon the laws that were made in this King's reign. Whereof I have these reasons: both because it was the preeminent virtue and merit of this King, to whose memory I do honour; and because it hath some correspondence to my person; but chiefly because (in my judgment) it is some defect even in the best writers of history, that they do not often enough summarily deliver and set down the most memorable laws that passed in the times whereof they write, being indeed the principal acts of peace. For though they may be had in original books of law themselves; yet that informeth not the judgment of kings and counsellors and persons of estate so well as to see them described and entered in the table and portrait of the times.

About the same time the King had a loan from the City of four thousand pounds, which was double to that they lent before,

---

proper enforcement of the laws came to his treasury. The collusive practice under attack worked as follows: a man who had committed a felony had a confederate prosecute him, but the prosecution would be conducted so poorly that the case failed; the failure of the collusive prosecution would then be used to bar an effective prosecution, and the offender would go free.]

and was duly and orderly paid back at the day, as the former likewise had been: the King ever choosing rather to borrow too soon
than to pay too late, and so keeping up his credit.

Neither had the King yet cast off his cares and hopes touching Brittaine, but thought to master the occasion by policy, though
his arms had been unfortunate, and to bereave the French King of
the fruit of his victory. The sum of his design was to encourage
Maximilian to go on with his suit for the marriage of Anne the
heir of Brittaine, and to aid him to the consummation thereof. But
the affairs of Maximilian were at that time in great trouble and
combustion, by a rebellion of his subjects in Flanders, especially
those of Bruges and Gaunt [Ghent]; whereof the town of Bruges
(at such time as Maximilian was there in person) had suddenly
armed in tumult, and slain some of his principal officers, and
taken himself prisoner, and held him in durance till they had enforced him and some of his councillors to take a solemn oath to
pardon all their offences, and never to question and revenge the
same in time to come. Nevertheless Frederick the Emperor would
not suffer this reproach and indignity offered to his son to pass,
but made sharp wars upon Flanders to reclaim and chastise the
rebels. But the Lord Ravenstein, a principal person about Maximilian and one that had taken the oath of abolition with his
master, pretending the religion thereof, but indeed upon private
ambition, and (as it was thought) instigated and corrupted from
France, forsook the Emperor and Maximilian his lord, and made
himself a head of the popular party, and seized upon the towns of
Ipre and Sluce [Ypres and Sluys] with both the castles; and forthwith sent to the Lord Cordes [Desquerdes], governor of Picardy
under the French King, to desire aid, and to move him, that he on
the behalf of the French King would be protector of the united
towns, and by force of arms reduce the rest. The Lord Cordes was
ready to embrace the occasion, which was partly of his own setting, and sent forthwith greater forces than it had been possible
for him to raise on the sudden if he had not looked for such a
summons before, in aid of the Lord Ravenstein and the Flemings,
with instructions to invest the towns between France and Bruges.
The French forces besieged a little town called Dixmue [Dix-

mude], where part of the Flemish forces joined with them. While
they lay at this siege, the King of England, upon pretence of the
safety of the English pale about Calais, but in truth being loth
that Maximilian should become contemptible and thereby be
shaken off by the states of Brittaine about his marriage, sent over
the Lord Morley with a thousand men unto the Lord Daubigny,
then deputy of Calais, with secret instructions to aid Maximilian
and to raise the siege of Dixmue. The Lord Daubigny (giving it
out that all was for the strengthening of the English marches)
drew out of the garrisons of Calais, Hammes and Guines, to the
number of a thousand men more: so that with the fresh succours
that came under the conduct of the Lord Morley, they made up to
the number of two thousand or better. Which forces joining with
some companies of Almaynes [Germans], put themselves into
Dixmue, not perceived by the enemies; and passing through the
town (with some reinforcement from the forces that were in the
town) assailed the enemies' camp, negligently guarded as being
out of fear; where there was a bloody fight, in which the English
and their partakers obtained the victory, and slew to the number
of eight thousand men, with the loss on the English part of a hundred or thereabouts; amongst whom was the Lord Morley. They
took also their great ordnance, with much rich spoils, which they
carried to Newport; whence the Lord Daubigny returned to Calais, leaving the hurt men and some other voluntaries in Newport.
But the Lord Cordes being at Ipre with a great power of men,
thinking to recover the loss and disgrace of the fight at Dixmue,
came presently on and sat down before Newport and besieged it;
and after some days siege, he resolved to try the fortune of an assault; which he did one day, and succeeded therein so far, that he
had taken the principal tower and fort in that city, and planted
upon it the French banner; whence nevertheless they were presently beaten forth by the English, by the help of some fresh succours of archers, arriving by good fortune (at the instant) in the
haven of Newport. Whereupon the Lord Cordes, discouraged,
and measuring the new succours (which were small) by the success (which was great), left his siege. By this means matters grew
more exasperate between the two Kings of England and France,

for that in the war of Flanders the auxiliary forces of French and
English were much blooded one against another; which blood
rankled the more, by the vain words of the Lord Cordes, that declared himself an open enemy of the English, beyond that that
appertained to the present service; making it a common by-word
of his, *That he could be content to lie in hell seven years so he
might win Calais from the English.*

The King having thus upheld the reputation of Maximilian,
advised him now to press on his marriage with Brittaine to a conclusion. Which Maximilian accordingly did, and so far forth prevailed both with the young lady and with the principal persons
about her, as the marriage was consummate by proxy, with a ceremony at that time in these parts new. For she was not only pub-
licly contracted, but stated as a bride, and solemnly bedded, and
after she was laid, there came in Maximilian's ambassador with
letters of procuration, and in the presence of sundry noble personages, men and women, put his leg (stript naked to the knee)
between the espousal sheets, to the end that that ceremony might
be thought to amount to a consummation and actual knowledge.
This done, Maximilian (whose property was to leave things then
when they were almost come to perfection, and to end them by
imagination; like ill archers, that draw not their arrows up to the
head; and who might as easily have bedded the lady himself as to
have made a play and disguise of it,) thinking now all assured,
neglected for a time his further proceeding, and intended [at-
tended to?] his wars. Meanwhile the French King (consulting
with his divines, and finding that this pretended consummation
was rather an invention of court than any ways valid by the laws
of the church,) went more really to work; and by secret instruments and cunning agents, as well matrons about the young lady
as counsellors, first sought to remove the point of religion and
honour out of the mind of the lady herself; wherein there was a
double labour: for Maximilian was not only contracted unto the
lady, but Maximilian's daughter was likewise contracted to King
Charles. So as the marriage halted upon both feet, and was not
clear on either side. But for the contract with King Charles, the
exception lay plain and fair; for that Maximilian's daughter was

under years of consent, and so not bound by law, but a power of
disagreement left to either part. But for the contract made by
Maximilian with the lady herself, they were harder driven: having
nothing to allege, but that it was done without the consent of her
sovereign lord King Charles, whose ward and client she was, and
he to her in place of a father; and therefore it was void and of no
force, for want of such consent. Which defect (they said) though
it would not evacuate a marriage after cohabitation and actual
consummation, yet it was enough to make void a contract. For as
for the pretended consummation, they made sport with it, and
said: *That it was an argument that Maximilian was a widower,
and a cold wooer, that could content himself to be a bridegroom
by deputy, and would not make a little journey to put all out of
question.* So that the young lady wrought upon by these reasons,
finely instilled by such as the French King (who spared for no rewards or promises) had made on his side; and allured likewise by
the present glory and greatness of King Charles (being also a
young king and a bachelor); and loth to make her country the
seat of a long and miserable war; secretly yielded to accept of
King Charles. But during this secret treaty with the lady, the
better to save it from blasts of opposition and interruption, King
Charles resorting to his wonted arts, and thinking to carry the
marriage as he had carried the wars, by entertaining the King of
England in vain belief, sent a solemn embassage by Francis Lord
of Luxemburgh, Charles Marignian, and Robert Gagvien [Gag-
uin], General of the Order of the *bons-hommes* of the Trinity, to
treat a peace and league with the King; accoupling it with an article in the nature of a request, that the French King might with the
King's good will (according unto his right of seigniory and tute-
lage) dispose of the marriage of the young Duchess of Brittaine as
he should think good, offering by a judicial proceeding to make
void the marriage of Maximilian by proxy. Also all this while the
better to amuse the world, he did continue in his court and custody
the daughter of Maximilian, who formerly had been sent unto
him to be bred and educated in France, not dismissing or renvoy-
ing [returning, sending back] her, but contrariwise professing
and giving out strongly that he meant to proceed with that match;

and that for the Duchess of Brittaine, he desired only to preserve his right of seigniory, and to give her in marriage to some such ally as might depend upon him.

When the three commissioners came to the court of England, they delivered their embassage unto the King, who remitted them to his council; where some days after they had audience, and made their proposition by the Prior of the Trinity (who though he were third in place, yet was held the best speaker of them) to this effect:

"My lords, the King our master, the greatest and mightiest King that reigned in France since Charles the great (whose name he beareth), hath nevertheless thought it no disparagement to his greatness, at this time to propound a peace, yea and to pray a peace, with the King of England. For which purpose he hath sent us his commissioners, instructed and enabled with full and ample power to treat and conclude; giving us further in charge to open in some other business the secrets of his own intentions. These be indeed the precious love tokens between great Kings, to communicate one with another the true state of their affairs, and to pass by nice points of honour, which ought not to give law unto affection. This I do assure your lordships; it is not possible for you to imagine the true and cordial love that the King our master beareth to your sovereign, except you were near him as we are. He useth his name with so great respect, he remembereth their first acquaintance at Paris with so great contentment, nay he never speaks of him, but that presently he falls into discourse of the miseries of great Kings, in that they cannot converse with their equals, but with their servants. This affection to your King's person and virtues God hath put into the heart of our master, no doubt for the good of Christendom, and for purposes yet unknown to us all; for other root it cannot have, since it was the same to the Earl of Richmond that it is now to the King of England. This is therefore the first motive that makes our King to desire peace, and league with your sovereign; good affection, and somewhat that he finds in his own heart. This affection is also armed with reason of estate. For our King doth in all candour and frankness of dealing open himself unto you, that having an honourable, yea and a holy purpose, to make a voyage and war in remote parts, he considereth that it will be of no small effect in point of reputation to his enterprise, if it be known abroad that he is in good peace with all his neighbour princes, and specially with the King of England, whom for good causes he esteemeth most.

"But now (my lords) give me leave to use a few words, to remove all scruples and misunderstandings between your sovereign and ours, concerning some late actions; which if they be not cleared, may perhaps hinder this peace; to the end that for matters past neither King may conceive unkindness of other, nor think the other conceiveth unkindness of him. The late actions are two; that of Brittaine, and that of Flanders. In both which it is true that the subjects' swords of both Kings have encountered and stricken, and the ways and inclinations also of the two Kings, in respect of their confederates and allies, have severed.

"For that of Brittaine: the King your sovereign knoweth best what hath passed. It was a war of necessity on our master's part. And though the motives of it were sharp and piquant as could be, yet did he make that war rather with an olive-branch than a laurel-branch in his hand, more desiring peace than victory. Besides from time to time he sent as it were blank papers to your King to write the conditions of peace. For though both his honour and safety went upon it, yet he thought neither of them too precious to put into the King of England's hands. Neither doth our King on the other side make any unfriendly interpretation of your King's sending of succours to the Duke of Brittaine; for the King knoweth well that many things must be done of Kings for satisfaction of their people, and it is not hard to discern what is a King's own. But this matter of Brittaine is now (by the act of God) ended and passed; and, as the King hopeth, like the way of a ship in the sea, without leaving any impression in either of the Kings' minds; as he is sure for his part it hath not done in his.

"For the action of Flanders: as the former of Brittaine was a war of necessity, so this was a war of justice; which with a good King is of equal necessity with danger of estate, for else he should leave to be a King. The subjects of Burgundy are subjects in chief to the crown of France, and their Duke the homager and vassal of

France. They had wont to be good subjects, howsoever Maximilian hath of late distempered them. They fled to the King for
justice and deliverance from oppression. Justice he could not
deny; purchase [profit] he did not seek. This was good for Maximilian, if he could have seen it in people mutined, to arrest fury,
and prevent despair. My lords, it may be this I have said is need-
less, save that the King our master is tender in any thing that may
but glance upon the friendship of England. The amity between
the two Kings (no doubt) stands entire and inviolate. And that
their subjects' swords have clashed, it is nothing unto the public
peace of the crowns; it being a thing very usual in auxiliary forces
of the best and straitest confederates to meet and draw blood in
the field. Nay many times there be aids of the same nation on both
sides, and yet it is not (for all that) a kingdom divided in itself.

"It resteth (my lords) that I impart unto you a matter that I
know your lordships all will much rejoice to hear; as that which
importeth the Christian commonweal more than any action that
hath happened of long time. The King our master hath a purpose
and determination to make war upon the kingdom of Naples, being now in the possession of a bastard slip of Arragon, but appertaining unto his majesty by clear and undoubted right; which
if he should not by just arms seek to recover, he could neither
acquit his honour nor answer it to his people. But his noble and
Christian thoughts rest not here. For his resolution and hope is,
to make the reconquest of Naples but as a bridge to transport his
forces into Grecia, and not to spare blood or treasure (if it were to
the impawning his crown and dispeopling of France) till either he
hath overthrown the empire of the Ottomans, or taken it in his
way to paradise. The King knoweth well that this is a design that
could not arise in the mind of any King that did not steadfastly
look up unto God, whose quarrel this is, and from whom cometh
both the will and the deed. But yet it is agreeable to the person that
he beareth (though unworthy) of the Thrice Christian King, and
the eldest son of the church. Whereunto he is also invited by the
example (in more ancient time) of King Henry the Fourth of England, (the first renowned King of the House of Lancaster, ancestor though not progenitor to your King;) who had a purpose

towards the end of his time (as you know better) to make an expedition into the Holy-land; and by the example also (present before his eyes) of that honourable and religious war which the King of Spain now maketh and hath almost brought to perfection, for the recovery of the realm of Granada from the Moors. And although this enterprise may seem vast and unmeasured, for the King to attempt that by his own forces, wherein heretofore a conjunction of most of the Christian Princes hath found work enough; yet his Majesty wisely considereth, that sometimes smaller forces being united under one command are more effectual in proof (though not so promising in opinion and fame) than much greater forces variously compounded by associations and leagues, which commonly in a short time after their beginnings turn to dissociations and divisions. But my lords that which is as a voice from heaven that called the King to this enterprise, is a rent at this time in the house of the Ottomans. I do not say but there hath been brother against brother in that house before, but never any that had refuge to the arms of the Christians, as now hath Gemes [Djem] (brother unto Bajazet that reigneth,) the far braver man of the two; the other being between a monk and a philosopher; and better read in the Alcoran and Averroes, than able to wield the sceptre of so warlike an empire. This therefore is the King our master's memorable and heroical resolution for an holy war. And because he carrieth in this the person of a Christian soldier as well as of a great temporal monarch, he beginneth with humility, and is content for this cause to beg peace at the hands of other Christian Kings.

"There remaineth only rather a civil request than any essential part of our negotiation, which the King maketh to the King your sovereign. The King (as all the world knoweth) is lord in chief of the duchy of Brittaine. The marriage of the heir belongeth to him as guardian. This is a private patrimonial right, and no business of estate. Yet nevertheless (to run a fair course with your King, whom he desires to make another himself, and to be one and the same thing with him,) his request is, that with the King's favour and consent he may dispose of her marriage as he thinketh good, and make void the intruded and pretended marriage of Maximilian, according to justice.

"This (my lords) is all that I have to say, desiring your pardon for my weakness in the delivery."

Thus did the French ambassadors, with great shew of their King's affection and many sugared words, seek to adduce [sweeten, soften] all matters between the two Kings; having two things for their ends: the one to keep the King quiet till the marriage of Brittaine was past (and this was but a summer fruit, which they thought was almost ripe, and would be soon gathered). The other was more lasting; and that was to put him into such a temper, as he might be no disturbance or impediment to the voyage for Italy.

The lords of the council were silent, and said only, *That they knew the ambassadors would look for no answer till they had reported to the King.* And so they rose from council.

The King could not well tell what to think of the marriage of Brittaine. He saw plainly the ambition of the French King was to impatronise himself of the duchy; but he wondered he would bring into his house a litigious marriage, especially considering who was his successor. But weighing one thing with another, he gave Brittaine for lost; but resolved to make his profit of this business of Brittaine, as a quarrel for war; and of that of Naples, as a wrench and mean for peace; being well advertised how strongly the King was bent upon that action. Having therefore conferred divers times with his council, and keeping himself somewhat close, he gave a direction to the Chancellor for a formal answer to the ambassadors; and that he did in the presence of his council. And after calling the Chancellor to him apart, bad him speak in such language as was fit for a treaty that was to end in a breach; and gave him also a special caveat, that he should not use any words to discourage the voyage of Italy. Soon after the ambassadors were sent for to the council, and the Lord Chancellor spake to them in this sort:

"My lords ambassadors, I shall make answer by the King's commandment unto the eloquent declaration of you my lord

Prior, in a brief and plain manner. The King forgetteth not his former love and acquaintance with the King your master. But of this there needeth no repetition; for if it be between them as it was, it is well; if there be any alteration, it is not words that will make it up.

"For the business of Brittaine, the King findeth it a little strange that the French King maketh mention of it as matter of well deserving at his hand. For that deserving was no more but to make him his instrument to surprise one of his best confederates. And for the marriage, the King would not meddle in it if your master would marry by the book, and not by the sword.

"For that of Flanders, if the subjects of Burgundy had appealed to your King as their chief lord, at first, by way of supplication, it might have had a shew of justice. But it was a new form of process, for subjects to imprison their prince first, and to slay his officers, and then to be complainants. The King saith that sure he is, when the French King and himself sent to the subjects of Scotland (that had taken arms against their King), they both spake in another stile [style], and did in princely manner signify their detestation of popular attentates [assaults] upon the person or authority of Princes. But, my lords ambassadors, the King leaveth these two actions thus: That on the one side he hath not received any manner of satisfaction from you concerning them; and on the other, that he doth not apprehend them so deeply, as in respect of them to refuse to treat of peace, if other things may go hand in hand. As for the war of Naples and the design against the Turk; the King hath commanded me expressly to say, that he doth wish with all his heart to his good brother the French King, that his fortunes may succeed according to his hopes and honourable intentions. And whensoever he shall hear that he is prepared for Grecia,—as your master is pleased now to say that he beggeth a peace of the King, so the King then will beg of him a part in that war.

"But now, my lords ambassadors, I am to propound unto you somewhat on the King's part. The King your master hath taught our King what to say and demand. You say (my lord Prior) that your King is resolved to recover his right to Naples, wrongfully detained from him; and that if he should not thus do, he could not acquit his honour, nor answer it to his people. Think (my lords) that the King our master saith the same thing over again to you, touching Normandy, Guienne, Anjou, yea and the kingdom of France itself. I cannot express it better than in your own words. If therefore the French King shall consent that the King our master's title to France ([or] at least tribute for the same) be handled in the treaty, the King is content to go on with the rest, otherwise he refuseth to treat.''

The ambassadors being somewhat abashed with this demand, answered in some heat, *That they doubted not but that the King their sovereign's sword would be able to maintain his sceptre;* and they assured themselves he neither could nor would yield to any diminution of the crown of France, either in territory or regality. But howsoever, they were too great matters for them to speak of, having no commission. It was replied that the King looked for no other answer from them, but would forthwith send his own ambassadors to the French King. There was a question also asked at the table: *Whether the French King would agree to have the disposing of the marriage of Brittaine, with an exception and exclusion that he should not marry her himself?* To which the ambassadors answered, that it was so far out of their King's thoughts as they had received no instructions touching the same. Thus were the ambassadors dismissed, all save the Prior; and were followed immediately by Thomas Earl of Ormond, and Thomas Goldenston Prior of Christ-Church in Canterbury, who were presently sent over into France. In the mean space Lionel Bishop of Concordia was sent as nuncio from Pope Alexander the Sixth to both Kings, to move a peace between them. For Pope Alexander, finding himself pent and locked up by a league and association of the principal states of Italy, that he could not make his way for the advancement of his own house (which he immoderately thirsted after), was desirous to trouble the waters in Italy, that he might fish the better; casting the net not out of St. Peter's, but out of Borgia's bark. And doubting lest the fears from England might stay the French King's voyage into Italy, dispatched this bishop to compose all matters between the two Kings, if he could.

Who first repaired to the French King, and finding him well inclined (as he conceived), took on his journey towards England,
and found the English ambassadors at Calais on their way towards
the French King. After some conference with them, he was in
honourable manner transported over into England, where he had
audience of the King. But notwithstanding he had a good ominous
name to have made a peace,[25] nothing followed. For in the mean
time the purpose of the French King to marry the Duchess could
be no longer dissembled. Wherefore the English ambassadors
(finding how things went) took their leave and returned. And the
Prior also was warned from hence, to depart out of England. Who
when he turned his back (more like a pedant than an ambassador),
dispersed a bitter libel in Latin verse against the King; unto
which the King (though he had nothing of a pedant) yet was content to cause an answer to be made in like verse; and that as
speaking in his own person, but in a stile [style] of scorn and
sport.

About this time also was born the King's second son Henry,
who afterward reigned. And soon after followed the solemnisa-
tion of the marriage between Charles and Anne Duchess of Brittaine, with whom he received the duchy of Brittaine as her dowry;
the daughter of Maximilian being a little before sent home.
Which when it came to the ears of Maximilian (who would never
believe it till it was done, being ever the principal in deceiving
himself, though in this the French King did very handsomely second it) and tumbling it over and over in his thoughts, that he
should at one blow (with such a double scorn) be defeated both
of the marriage of his daughter and his own (upon both which he
had fixed high imaginations), he lost all patience; and casting off
the respects fit to be continued between great Kings (even when
their blood is hottest and most risen), fell to bitter invectives
against the person and actions of the French King. And (by how
much he was the less able to do, talking so much the more) spoke
all the injuries he could devise of Charles, saying: That he was
the most perfidious man upon the earth, and that he had made a

[25] [His name—Concordia—was a good omen for an ambassador
sent to make peace.]

marriage compounded between an advoutry [adultery] and a
rape; which was done (he said) by the just judgment of God to
the end that (the nullity thereof being so apparent to all the world)
the race of so unworthy a person might not reign in France. And
forthwith he sent ambassadors as well to the King of England as
to the King of Spain, to incite them to war and to treat a league
offensive against France, promising to concur with great forces of
his own. Hereupon the King of England (going nevertheless his
own way) called a Parliament, it being the seventh year of his
reign; and the first day of opening thereof (sitting under his cloth
of estate) spake himself unto his Lords and Commons in this
manner.

"My Lords and you the Commons; when I purposed to make
a war in Brittaine by my lieutenant, I made declaration thereof to
you by my Chancellor. But now that I mean to make a war upon
France in person, I will declare it to you myself. That war was to
defend another man's right, but this is to recover our own; and
that ended by accident, but we hope this shall end in victory.

"The French King troubles the Christian world. That which
he hath is not his own, and yet he seeketh more. He hath invested
himself of Brittaine. He maintaineth the rebels in Flanders: and
he threateneth Italy. For ourselves, he hath proceeded from dissimulation to neglect, and from neglect to contumely. He hath
assailed our confederates: he denieth our tribute: in a word, he
seeks war. So did not his father, but sought peace at our hands;
and so perhaps will he, when good counsel or time shall make
him see as much as his father did.

"Meanwhile, let us make his ambition our advantage, and
let us not stand upon a few crowns of tribute or acknowledge-
ment, but (by the favour of Almighty God) try our right for the
crown of France itself; remembering that there hath been a
French King prisoner in England, and a King of England crowned
in France. Our confederates are not diminished. Burgundy is in a
mightier hand than ever, and never more provoked. Brittaine
cannot help us, but it may hurt them. New acquests [acquisitions
plus conquests] are more burden than strength. The malcontents
of his own kingdom have not been base, popular, nor titulary impostors, but of an higher nature. The King of Spain (doubt ye

not) will join with us, not knowing where the French King's ambition will stay. Our holy father the Pope likes no Tramontanes [Ultramontanes, i.e., northerners] in Italy. But howsoever it be, this matter of confederates is rather to be thought on than reckoned on; for God forbid but England should be able to get reason of France without a second.

"At the battles of Cressy, Poictiers, Agent-Court, we were of ourselves. France hath much people, and few soldiers. They have no stable bands of foot. Some good horse they have, but those are forces which are least fit for a defensive war, where the actions are in the assailant's choice. It was our discords only that lost France; and (by the power of God) it is the good peace which we now enjoy that will recover it. God hath hitherto blessed my sword. I have in this time that I have reigned, weeded out my bad subjects, and tried my good. My people and I know one another, which breeds confidence. And if there should be any bad blood left in the kingdom, an honourable foreign war will vent it or purify it. In this great business let me have your advice and aid. If any of you were to make his son knight, you might have aid of your tenants by law. This concerns the knighthood and spurs of the kingdom, whereof I am father; and bound not only to seek to maintain it, but to advance it. But for matter of treasure let it not be taken from the poorest sort, but from those to whom the benefit of the war may redound. France is no wilderness, and I, that profess good husbandry, hope to make the war (after the beginnings) to pay itself. Go together in God's name, and lose no time, for I have called this Parliament wholly for this cause."

Thus spake the King. But for all this, though he shewed great forwardness for a war, not only to his Parliament and court, but to his privy council likewise (except the two bishops and a few more), yet nevertheless in his secret intentions he had no purpose to go through with any war upon France. But the truth was, that he did but traffic with that war, to make his return in money. He knew well that France was now entire and at unity with itself, and never so mighty many years before. He saw by the taste he had of his forces sent into Brittaine that the French knew well enough how to make war with the English; by not putting things

to the hazard of a battle, but wearing them by long sieges of
towns, and strong fortified encampings. James the Third of Scotland (his true friend and confederate) gone; and James the
Fourth (that had succeeded) wholly at the devotion of France, and
ill-affected towards him. As for the conjunctions of Ferdinando of
Spain and Maximilian, he could make no foundation upon them.
For the one had power and not will; and the other had will and
not power. Besides that Ferdinando had but newly taken breath
from the war with the Moors; and merchanded [dickered] at this
time with France for the restoring of the counties of Russignon
and Perpignian, oppignorated [pawned] to the French. Neither
was he out of fear of the discontents and ill blood within the
realm; which having used always to repress and appease in person, he was loth they should find him at a distance beyond sea,
and engaged in war. Finding therefore the inconveniencies and
difficulties in the prosecution of a war, he cast with himself how to
compass two things. The one, how by the declaration and inchoation of a war to make his profit. The other, how to come off from
the war with saving of his honour. For profit, it was to be made
two ways; upon his subjects for the war, and upon his enemies
for the peace; like a good merchant that maketh his gain both
upon the commodities exported and imported back again. For the
point of honour, wherein he might suffer for giving over the war,
he considered well, that as he could not trust upon the aids of
Ferdinando and Maximilian for supports of war, so the impuissance of the one, and the double proceeding of the other, lay fair
for him for occasions [pretexts] to accept of peace. These things
he did wisely foresee, and did as artificially conduct, whereby all
things fell into his lap as he desired.

For as for the Parliament, it presently took fire, being affectionate (of old) to the war of France, and desirous (afresh) to repair the dishonour they thought the King sustained by the loss of
Brittaine. Therefore they advised the King (with great alacrity) to
undertake the war of France. And although the Parliament consisted of the first and second nobility (together with principal
citizens and townsmen), yet worthily and justly respecting more
the people (whose deputies they were) than their own private

persons, and finding, by the Lord Chancellor's speech[26], the King's
inclination that way; they consented that commissioners should
go forth for the gathering and levying of a Benevolence from the
more able sort. This tax (called Benevolence) was devised by Edward the Fourth, for which he sustained much envy. It was abol-
ished by Richard the Third by act of Parliament, to ingratiate
himself with the people; and it was now revived by the King, but
with consent of Parliament; for so it was not in the time of King
Edward the Fourth. But by this way he raised exceeding great
sums. Insomuch as the city of London ([even] in those days) con-
tributed nine thousand pounds and better; and that chiefly levied
upon the wealthier sort. There is a tradition of a *dilemma* that
Bishop Morton the Chancellor used, to raise up the Benevolence
to higher rates; and some called it his fork, and some his crotch.
For he had couched an article in the instructions to the commissioners who were to levy the Benevolence, That if they met with
any that were sparing, they should tell them that they must
needs have, because they laid up; and if they were spenders, they
must needs have, because it was seen in their port and manner of
living. So neither kind came amiss.

This Parliament was merely a Parliament of war; for it was
in substance but a declaration of war against France and Scotland,
with some statutes conducing thereunto; as the severe punishing
of mort-pays[27] and keeping back soldiers' wages in captains;
the like severity for the departure of soldiers without licence;
strengthening of the common law in favour of protections for
those that were in the King's service; and the setting the gate
open and wide, for men to sell or mortgage their lands without
fines for alienation, to furnish themselves with money for the
war; and lastly the voiding of all Scotchmen out of England.
There was also a statute for the dispersing of the standard

[26] [A slip of Bacon's memory: the reference is to the end of the
king's own speech.]
[27] [The usual term is dead-pays. The practice worked as follows:
a captain was paid according to the number of men he brought with
him to the wars. If he could keep the name of a dead soldier on his
rolls, he was able to keep the dead man's portion of the total payment
for himself.]

of the exchequer throughout England, thereby to size weights and measures; and two or three more of less importance.

After the Parliament was broken up (which lasted not long) the King went on with his preparations for the war of France; yet neglected not in the mean time the affairs of Maximilian, for the quieting of Flanders and restoring him to his authority amongst his subjects. For at that time the Lord of Ravenstein, being not only a subject rebelled but a servant revolted (and so much the more malicious and violent), by the aid of Bruges and Gaunt had taken the town and both the castles of Sluice (as we said before); and having by the commodity of the haven gotten together certain ships and barks, fell to a kind of piratical trade; robbing and spoiling and taking prisoners the ships and vessels of all nations that passed alongst that coast towards the mart of Antwerp, or into any part of Brabant, Zealand, or Friezeland; being ever well victualled from Picardy, besides the commodity of victuals from Sluice and the country adjacent, and the avails of his own prizes. The French assisted him still under-hand; and he likewise (as all men do that have been on both sides) thought himself not safe, except he depended upon a third person.

There was a small town some two miles from Bruges towards the sea, called Dam; which was a fort and approach to Bruges, and had a relation also to Sluice. This town the King of the Romans had attempted often (not for any worth of the town in itself, but because it might choke Bruges, and cut it off from the sea); and ever failed. But therewith the Duke of Saxony came down into Flanders, taking upon him the person of an umpire, to compose things between Maximilian and his subjects; but being (indeed) fast and assured to Maximilian. Upon this pretext of neutrality and treaty, he repaired to Bruges; desiring of the states of Bruges to enter peaceably into their town, with a retinue of some number of men of arms fit for his estate, being somewhat the more (as he said) the better to guard him in a country that was up in arms; and bearing them in hand that he was to communicate with them of divers matters of great importance for their good; which having obtained of them, he sent his carriages and harbingers before him to provide his lodging; so that his men of war entered the city in good array, but in peaceable manner, and he followed.

They that went before inquired still for inns and lodgings, as if they would have rested there all night; and so went on till they came to the gate that leadeth directly towards Dam; and they of Bruges only gazed upon them, and gave them passage. The captains and inhabitants of Dam also suspected no harm from any that passed through Bruges; and discovering forces afar off, supposed they had been some succours that were come from their friends, knowing some dangers towards them: and so perceiving nothing but well till it was too late, suffered them to enter their town. By which kind of sleight, rather than strategem, the town of Dam was taken, and the town of Bruges shrewdly blocked up, whereby they took great discouragement.

The Duke of Saxony, having won the town of Dam, sent immediately to the King [Henry] to let him know that it was Sluice chiefly and the Lord Ravenstein that kept the rebellion of Flanders in life; and that if it pleased the King to besiege it by sea, he also would besiege it by land, and so cut out the core of those wars.

The King, willing to uphold the authority of Maximilian (the better to hold France in awe), and being likewise sued unto by his merchants, for that the seas were much infested by the barks of the Lord Ravenstein, sent straightways Sir Edward Poynings, a valiant man and of good service, with twelve ships, well furnished with soldiers and artillery, to clear the seas, and to besiege Sluice on that part. The Englishmen did not only coop up the Lord Ravenstein, that he stirred not, and likewise hold in strait siege the maritime part of the town, but also assailed one of the castles, and renewed the assault so for twenty days' space (issuing still out of their ships at the ebb), as they made great slaughter of them of the castle, who continually fought with them to repulse them; though of the English part also were slain a brother of the Earl of Oxford's, and some fifty more. But the siege still continuing more and more strait; and both the castles (which were the principal strength of the town) being distressed, the one by the Duke of Saxony, and the other by the English; and a bridge of boats, which the Lord Ravenstein had made between both castles, whereby succours and relief might pass from the one to the other, being on a night set on fire by the English; he despairing to hold the town, yielded (at the last) the castles to the English, and the town to the Duke of Saxony, by composition. Which done, the Duke of Saxony and Sir Edward Poynings treated with them of Bruges to submit themselves to Maximilian their lord; which after some time they did, paying (in some good part) the charge of the war, whereby the Almains and foreign succours were dismissed. The example of Bruges other of the revolted towns followed; so that Maximilian grew to be out of danger, but (as his manner was to handle matters) never out of necessity. And Sir Edward Poynings (after he had continued at Sluice some good while till all things were settled) returned unto the King, being then before Bulloigne [Boulogne].

Somewhat about this time came letters from Ferdinando and Isabella, King and Queen of Spain, signifying the final conquest of Granada from the Moors; which action, in itself so worthy, King Ferdinando (whose manner was never to lose any virtue for the shewing) had expressed and displayed in his letters at large, with all the particularities and religious punctos and ceremonies, that were observed in the reception of that city and kingdom: shewing amongst other things, that the King would not by any means in person enter the city, until he had first aloof seen the cross set up upon the greater tower of Granada, whereby it became Christian ground; that likewise before he would enter he did homage to God above, pronouncing by an herald from the height of that tower, that he did acknowledge to have recovered that kingdom by the help of God Almighty, and the glorious Virgin, and the virtuous Apostle Saint James, and the holy father Innocent the Eighth, together with the aids and services of his prelates, nobles, and commons; that yet he stirred not from his camp, till he had seen a little army of martyrs, to the number of seven hundred and more Christians (that had lived in bonds and servitude as slaves to the Moors), pass before his eyes, singing a psalm for their redemption; and that he had given tribute unto God, by alms and relief extended to them all, for his admission into the city. These things were in the letters, with many more ceremonies of a kind of holy ostentation.

The King, ever willing to put himself into the consort or quire [choir] of all religious actions, and naturally affecting much the King of Spain (as far as one King can affect another), partly for his virtues and partly for a counterpoise to France; upon the receipt of these letters sent all his nobles and prelates that were about the court, together with the mayor and aldermen of London, in great solemnity to the Church of Paul's; there to hear a declaration from the Lord Chancellor, now Cardinal. When they were assembled, the Cardinal, standing upon the uppermost step or half-pace before the quire [choir], and all the nobles, prelates, and governors of the City at the foot of the stairs, made a speech to them; letting them know, that they were assembled in that consecrated place to sing unto God a new song. For that (said he) these many years the Christians have not gained new ground or territory upon the Infidels, nor enlarged and set further the bounds of the Christian world. But this is now done by the prowess and devotion of Ferdinando and Isabella, Kings of Spain; who have to their immortal honour recovered the great and rich kingdom of Granada and the populous and mighty city of the same name from the Moors, having been in possession thereof by the space of seven hundred years and more. For which this assembly and all Christians are to render all laud and thanks unto God, and to celebrate this noble act of the King of Spain, who in this is not only victorious but apostolical, in the gaining of new provinces to the Christian faith; and the rather for that this victory and conquest is obtained without much effusion of blood. Whereby it is to be hoped that there shall be gained not only new territory, but infinite souls to the church of Christ; whom the Almighty (as it seems) would have live to be converted. Herewithal he did relate some of the most memorable particulars of the war and victory. And after his speech ended, the whole assembly went solemnly in procession, and *Te Deum* was sung.

Immediately after the solemnity, the King kept his May-day of his palace at Shine (now Richmond); where to warm the blood of his nobility and gallants against the war, he kept great triumphs of justing and tourney during all that month. In which space it so fell out, that Sir James Parker and Hugh Vaughan (one

of the King's gentlemen ushers), having had a controversy touching certain arms that the King-at-Arms had given Vaughan, were
appointed to run some courses one against another; and by accident of a faulty helmet that Parker had on, he was stricken into
the mouth at the first course, so that his tongue was borne unto
the hinder part of his head, in such sort that he died presently
upon the place; which because of the controversy precedent, and
the death that followed, was accounted amongst the vulgar as a
combat or trial of right.

The King towards the end of this summer, having put his
forces wherewith he meant to invade France in readiness (but so
as they were not yet met or mustered together), sent Urswick, now
made his almoner,[28] and Sir John Risley to Maximilian, to let him
know that he was in arms, ready to pass the seas into France, and
did but expect to hear from him when and where he did appoint
to join with him, according to his promise made unto him by
Countebalt his ambassador.

The English ambassadors having repaired to Maximilian did
find his power and promise at a very great distance; he being
utterly unprovided of men, money, and arms, for any such enterprise. For Maximilian, having neither wing to fly on, for that his
patrimony of Austria was not in his hands (his father being then
living), and on the other side his matrimonial territories of Flanders [being] partly in dower to his mother-in-law, and partly not
serviceable in respect of the late rebellions, was thereby destitute
of means to enter into war. The ambassadors saw this well, but
wisely thought fit to advertise the King thereof, rather than to return themselves, till the King's further pleasure were known: the
rather, for that Maximilian himself spake as great as ever he did
before, and entertained them with dilatory answers; so as the
formal part of their ambassage might well warrant and require
their further stay. The King hereupon (who doubted as much before, and saw through his business from the beginning), wrote
back to the ambassadors, commending their discretion in not returning, and willing them to keep the state wherein they found

---

[28] [an official who distributed the royal charity]

Maximilian as a secret, till they heard further from him; and meanwhile went on with his voyage royal for France, suppressing for a time this advertisement touching Maximilian's poverty and disability.

By this time was drawn together a great and puissant army into the City of London; in which were Thomas Marquis Dorset, Thomas Earl of Arundel, Thomas Earl of Derby, George Earl of Shrewsbury, Edmond Earl of Suffolk, Edward Earl of Devonshire, George Earl of Kent, the Earl of Essex, Thomas Earl of Ormond, with a great number of barons, knights, and principal gentlemen; and amongst them Richard Thomas, much noted for the brave troops that he brought out of Wales; the army rising in the whole to the number of five and twenty thousand foot, and sixteen hundred horse; over which the King (constant in his accustomed trust and employment) made Jasper Duke of Bedford and John Earl of Oxford generals under his own person. The ninth of September, in the eighth year of his reign, he departed from Greenwich towards the sea; all men wondering that he took that season (being so near winter) to begin the war, and some thereupon gathering it was a sign that the war would not be long. Nevertheless the King gave out the contrary, thus; *That he intending not to make a summer business of it, but a resolute war (without term prefixed) until he had recovered* France, *it skilled not much when he began it; especially having* Calais *at his back, where he might winter, if the reason of the war so required.* The sixth of October he embarked at Sandwich; and the same day took land at Calais, which was the rendezvous where all his forces were assigned to meet. But in this his journey towards the sea-side (wherein for the cause that we shall now speak of he hovered so much the longer), he had received letters from the Lord Cordes: who the hotter he was against the English in time of war had the more credit in a negotiation of peace, and besides was held a man open and of good faith. In which letters there was made an overture of peace from the French King, with such conditions as were somewhat to the King's taste; but this was carried at the first with wonderful secrecy. The King was no sooner come to Calais, but the calm winds of peace began to blow. For first the English am-

bassadors returned out of Flanders from Maximilian, and certified
the King that he was not to hope for any aid from Maximilian,
for that he was altogether unprovided. His will was good, but he
lacked money. And this was made known and spread throughout
the army. And although the English were therewithal nothing
dismayed, and that it be the manner of soldiers upon bad news to
speak the more bravely; yet nevertheless it was a kind of preparative to a peace. Instantly in the neck of this (as the King had laid
it) came news that Ferdinando and Isabella, Kings of Spain, had
concluded a peace with King Charles, and that Charles had restored unto them the counties of Ruscignon and Perpignian,
which formerly were mortgaged by John King of Arragon, Ferdinando's father, unto France, for three hundred thousand
crowns: which debt was also upon this peace by Charles clearly
released. This came also handsomely to put on the peace, both
because so potent a confederate was fallen off, and because it was
a fair example of a peace bought; so as the King should not be the
sole merchant in this peace. Upon these airs of peace, the King
was content that the Bishop of Exeter and the Lord Daubigny
(Governor of Calais) should give a meeting unto the Lord Cordes,
for the treaty of a peace. But himself nevertheless and his army,
the fifteenth of October, removed from Calais, and in four days'
march sat him down before Bulloigne.

During this siege of Bulloigne (which continued near a
month) there passed no memorable action nor accident of war:
only Sir John Savage, a valiant captain, was slain, riding about the
walls of the town to take a view. The town was both well fortified
and well manned; yet it was distressed, and ready for an assault;
which if it had been given (as was thought) would have cost much
blood; but yet the town would have been carried in the end.
Meanwhile a peace was concluded by the commissioners, to continue for both the Kings' lives. Where there was no article of importance; being in effect rather a bargain than a treaty. For all
things remained as they were, save that there should be paid to
the King seven hundred forty-five thousand ducats in present, for
his charges in that journey; and five and twenty thousand crowns
yearly, for his charges sustained in the aids of the Britons. For

which annual, though he had Maximilian bound before for those charges, yet he counted the alteration of the hand as much as the principal debt; and besides it was left somewhat indefinitely when it should determine or expire; which made the English esteem it as a tribute carried under fair terms. And the truth is, it was paid both to the King and to his son Henry the Eighth, longer than it could continue upon any computation of charges. There was also assigned by the French King unto all the King's principal councillors great pensions, besides rich gifts for the present. Which whether the King did permit, to save his own purse from rewards, or to communicate the envy of a business that was displeasing to his people, was diversely interpreted. For certainly the King had no great fancy to own this peace. And therefore a little before it was concluded, he had under-hand procured some of his best captains and men of war to advise him to a peace under their hands, in an earnest manner, in the nature of a supplication. But the truth is, this peace was welcome to both Kings. To Charles, for that it assured unto him the possession of Brittaine, and freed the enterprise of Naples. To Henry, for that it filled his coffers; and that he foresaw at that time a storm of inward troubles coming upon him, which presently after brake forth. But it gave no less discontent to the nobility and principal persons of the army, who had many of them sold or engaged their estates upon the hopes of the war. They stuck not to say, *That the King cared not to plume his nobility and people, to feather himself.* And some made themselves merry with that the King had said in Parliament: *That after the war was once begun, he doubted not but to make it pay itself;* saying he had kept promise.

Having risen from Bulloigne, he went to Calais, where he stayed some time: from whence also he writ letters (which was a courtesy that he sometimes used) to the Mayor of London and the Aldermen his brethren; half bragging what great sums he had obtained for the peace; knowing well that full coffers of the King is ever good news to London; and better news it would have been, if their benevolence had been but a loan. And upon the seventeenth of December following he returned to Westminster, where he kept his Christmas.

Soon after the King's return, he sent the Order of the Garter to Alphonso Duke of Calabria, eldest son to Ferdinando King of Naples: an honour sought by that Prince to hold him up in the eyes of the Italians; who expecting the arms of Charles, made great account of the amity of England for a bridle to France. It was received by Alphonso with all the ceremony and pomp that could be devised; as things use to be carried that are intended for opinion. It was sent by Urswick; upon whom the King bestowed this ambassage, to help him after many dry employments.

At this time the King began again to be haunted with sprites [spirits], by the magic and curious arts of the Lady Margaret; who raised up the ghost of Richard Duke of York (second son to King Edward the Fourth) to walk and vex the King. This was a finer counterfeit stone than Lambert Symnell; better done, and worn upon greater hands; being graced after with the wearing of a King of France and a King of Scotland, not of a Duchess of Burgundy only. And for Symnell, there was not much in him, more than that he was a handsome boy, and did not shame his robes. But this youth (of whom we are now to speak) was such a mercurial, as the like hath seldom been known; and could make his own part, if any time he chanced to be out. Wherefore this being one of the strangest examples of a personation, that ever was in elder or later times, it deserveth to be discovered and related at the full: although the King's manner of shewing things by pieces, and dark-lights, hath so muffled it, that it hath left it almost as a mystery to this day.

The Lady Margaret, whom the King's friends called Juno, because she was to him as Juno was to Aeneas, stirring both heaven and hell to do him mischief, for a foundation of her particular practices against him did continually by all means possible nourish, maintain, and divulge the flying opinion that Richard Duke of York (second son to Edward the Fourth) was not murdered in the Tower (as was given out) but saved alive; for that those who were employed in that barbarous fact, having destroyed the elder brother, were stricken with remorse and compassion towards the younger, and set him privily at liberty to seek his fortune. This lure she cast abroad, thinking that this fame and belief (together with the fresh example of Lambert Symnell) would draw at one time or other some birds to strike upon it. She used likewise a further diligence, not committing all to chance: for she had some secret espials, (like to the Turks' commissioners for children of tribute,) to look abroad for handsome and graceful youths, to make Plantagenets and Dukes of York. At the last she did light on one, in whom all things met, as one would wish, to serve her turn for a counterfeit of Richard Duke of York.

This was Perkin Warbeck, whose adventures we shall now describe. For first, the years agreed well. Secondly, he was a youth of fine favour and shape. But more than that, he had such a crafty and bewitching fashion both to move pity and to induce belief, as was like a kind of fascination and inchantment to those that saw him or heard him. Thirdly, he had been from his childhood such a wanderer, or (as the King called it) such a landloper, as it was extreme hard to hunt out his nest and parents; neither again could any man, by company or conversing with him, be able to say or detect well what he was; he did so flit from place to place. Lastly, there was a circumstance (which is mentioned by one that writ in the same time) that is very likely to have made somewhat to[29] the matter; which is, that King Edward the Fourth was his godfather. Which, as it is somewhat suspicious for a wanton prince to become gossip in so mean a house, and might make a man think that he might indeed have in him some base blood of the house of York; so at the least (though that were not) it might give the occasion to the boy, in being called King Edward's godson, or perhaps in sport King Edward's son, to entertain such thoughts into his head. For tutor he had none (for ought that appears), as Lambert Symnell had, until he came unto the Lady Margaret who instructed him.

Thus therefore it came to pass. There was a townsman of Tournay that had borne office in that town, whose name was John Osbeck, a converted Jew, married to Katherine de Faro, whose business drew him to live for a time with his wife at London in

---

[29] [likely to have been relevant to, had a bearing on]

King Edward the Fourth's days. During which time he had a son
by her; and being known in court, the King either out of religious
nobleness, because he was a convert, or upon some private acquaintance, did him the honour as to be godfather to his child,
and named him Peter. But afterwards proving a dainty and effeminate youth, he was commonly called by the diminutive of his
name, Peterkin, or Perkin. For as for the name of Warbeck, it was
given him when they did but guess at it, before examinations
had been taken. But yet he had been so much talked on by that
name, as it stuck by him after his true name of Osbeck was
known. While he was a young child, his parents returned with
him to Tournay. Then was he placed in a house of a kinsman of
his, called John Stenbeck, at Antwerp, and so roamed up and
down between Antwerp and Tournay and other towns of Flanders
for a good time; living much in English company, and having the
English tongue perfect. In which time, being grown a comely
youth, he was brought by some of the espials of the Lady Margaret into her presence: who viewing him well, and seeing that he
had a face and personage that would bear a noble fortune; and
finding him otherwise of a fine spirit and winning behaviour;
thought she had now found a curious piece of marble to carve out
an image of a Duke of York. She kept him by her a great while,
but with extreme secrecy. The while she instructed him by many
cabinet conferences. First, in princely behaviour and gesture;
teaching him how he should keep state, and yet with a modest
sense of his misfortunes. Then she informed him of all the circumstances and particulars that concerned the person of Richard
Duke of York, which he was to act; describing unto him the personages, lineaments, and features of the King and Queen his pretended parents, and of his brother and sisters, and divers others
that were nearest him in his childhood, together with all passages,
some secret, some common, that were fit for a child's memory,
until the death of King Edward. Then she added the particulars of
the time from the King's death until he and his brother were committed to the Tower, as well during the time he was abroad as
while he was in sanctuary. As for the times while he was in the
Tower, and the manner of his brother's death, and his own es-

cape; she knew they were things that a very few could control [check up]. And therefore she taught him only to tell a smooth and likely tale of those matters; warning him not to vary from it. It was agreed likewise between them what account he should give of his peregrination abroad; intermixing many things which were true and such as they knew others could testify, for the credit of the rest; but still making them to hang together with the part he was to play. She taught him likewise how to avoid sundry captious and tempting questions, which were like to be asked of him. But in this she found him of himself so nimble and shifting, as she trusted much to his own wit and readiness; and therefore laboured the less in it. Lastly, she raised his thoughts with some present rewards and further promises; setting before him chiefly the glory and fortune of a crown, if things went well; and a sure refuge to her court if the worst should fall. After such time as she thought he was perfect in his lesson, she began to cast with herself from what coast this blazing star should first appear, and at what time. It must be upon the horizon of Ireland; for there had the like meteor strong influence before. The time of the apparition to be, when the King should be engaged into a war with France. But well she knew that whatsoever should come from her would be held suspected. And therefore if he should go out of Flanders immediately into Ireland she might be thought to have some hand in it. And besides, the time was not yet ripe; for that the two Kings were then upon terms of peace. Therefore she wheeled about; and to put all suspicion afar off, and loth to keep him any longer by her (for that she knew secrets are not long-lived), she sent him unknown into Portugal, with the Lady Brampton, an English lady (that embarked for Portugal at that time), with some *privado* of her own to have an eye upon him; and there he was to remain and to expect her further directions. In the mean time she omitted not to prepare things for his better welcome and accepting, not only in the kingdom of Ireland, but in the court of France. He continued in Portugal about a year; and by that time the King of England called his Parliament (as hath been said), and declared open war against France. Now did the sign reign, and the constellation was come, under which Perkin should appear. And

therefore he was straight sent unto by the Duchess to go for Ire
land, according to the first designment. In Ireland he did arrive at
the town of Cork. When he was thither come, his own tale was
(when he made his confession afterwards) that the Irishmen finding him in some good clothes, came flocking about him, and bare
him down that he was the Duke of Clarence that had been there
before: and after, that he was Richard the Third's base son: and
lastly, that he was Richard Duke of York, second son to Edward
the Fourth: but that he for his part renounced all these things,
and offered to swear upon the holy Evangelists that he was no
such man, till at last they forced it upon him, and bad him fear
nothing; and so forth. But the truth is, that immediately upon his
coming into Ireland, he took upon him the said person of the
Duke of York, and drew unto him complices and partakers by all
the means he could devise. Insomuch as he writ his letters unto
the Earls of Desmond and Kildare, to come in to his aid and be of
his party; the originals of which letters are yet extant.

Somewhat before this time, the Duchess had also gained unto
her a near servant of King Henry's own, one Stephen Frion, his
secretary for the French tongue; an active man, but turbulent and
discontented. This Frion had fled over to Charles the French
King, and put himself into his service, at such time as he began
to be in open enmity with the King. Now King Charles, when he
understood of the person and attempts of Perkin (ready of himself to embrace all advantages against the King of England; instigated by Frion, and formerly prepared by the Lady Margaret)
forthwith despatched one Lucas and this Frion in the nature of
ambassadors to Perkin, to advertise him of the King's good inclination to him, and that he was resolved to aid him to recover
his right against King Henry, an usurper of England and an enemy
of France; and wished him to come over unto him at Paris. Perkin
thought himself in heaven now that he was invited by so great a
King in so honourable a manner. And imparting unto his friends
in Ireland for their encouragement how fortune called him, and
what great hopes he had, sailed presently into France. When he
was come to the court of France, the King received him with great
honour; saluted, and stiled [styled] him by the name of the Duke

of York; lodged him and accommodated him in great state; and the better to give him the representation and the countenance of a Prince, assigned him a guard for his person, whereof the Lord Congresall was captain. The courtiers likewise (though it be ill mocking with the French[30]) applied themselves to their King's bent, seeing there was reason of state for it. At the same time there repaired unto Perkin divers Englishmen of quality: Sir George Neville, Sir John Taylor, and about one hundred more; and amongst the rest, this Stephen Frion of whom we spake, who followed his fortune both then and for a long time after, and was indeed his principal counsellor and instrument in all his proceedings. But all this on the French King's part was but a trick, the better to bow King Henry to peace. And therefore upon the first grain of incense that was sacrificed upon the altar of peace at Bulloigne, Perkin was smoked away. Yet would not the French King deliver him up to King Henry (as he was laboured to do), for his honour's sake; but warned him away and dismissed him. And Perkin on his part was as ready to be gone, doubting he might be caught up under-hand. He therefore took his way into Flanders unto the Duchess of Burgundy; pretending that having been variously tossed by fortune he directed his course thither as to a safe harbour; no ways taking knowledge that he had ever been there before, but as if that had been his first address. The Duchess on the other part made it as new and strange to see him; pretending (at the first) that she was taught and made wise by the example of Lambert Symnell, how she did admit of any counterfeit stuff; though even in that (she said) she was not fully satisfied. She pretended at the first (and that was ever in the presence of others) to pose him and sift him, thereby to try whether he were indeed the very Duke of York or no. But seeming to receive full satisfaction by his answers, then she feigned herself to be transported with a kind of astonishment, mixt of joy and wonder, at his miraculous deliverance; receiving him as if he were risen from death to life; and inferring that God, who had in such wonderful manner preserved him from death, did likewise reserve him for

[30] [i.e., though the French play parts badly]

some great and prosperous fortune. As for his dismission out of France, they interpreted it not, as if he were detected or neglected for a counterfeit deceiver; but contrariwise that it did shew manifestly unto the world that he was some great matter; for that it was his abandoning that (in effect) made the peace; being no more but the sacrificing of a poor distressed Prince unto the utility and ambition of two mighty monarchs. Neither was Perkin for his part wanting to himself either in gracious and princely behaviour, or in ready and apposite answers, or in contenting and caressing those that did apply themselves unto him, or in pretty scorn and disdain to those that seemed to doubt of him; but in all things did notably acquit himself: insomuch as it was generally believed (as well amongst great persons as amongst the vulgar) that he was indeed Duke Richard. Nay himself with long and continual counterfeiting and with oft telling a lie, was turned by habit almost into the thing he seemed to be, and from a liar to a believer. The Duchess therefore, as in a case out of doubt, did him all princely honour, calling him always by the name of her nephew, and giving him the delicate title of the White Rose of England; and appointed him a guard of thirty persons, halberdiers, clad in a party-coloured livery of murrey and blue, to attend his person. Her court likewise, and generally the Dutch and strangers, in their usage towards him expressed no less respect.

The news hereof came blazing and thundering over into England, that the Duke of York was sure alive. As for the name of Perkin Warbeck, it was not at that time come to light, but all the news ran upon the Duke of York; that he had been entertained in Ireland, bought and sold in France, and was now plainly avowed and in great honour in Flanders. These fames took hold of divers; in some upon discontent, in some upon ambition, in some upon levity and desire of change, in some few upon conscience and belief, but in most upon simplicity; and in divers out of dependence upon some of the better sort who did in secret favour and nourish these bruits. And it was not long ere these rumours of novelty had begotten others of scandal and murmur against the King and his government, taxing him for a great taxer of his people and discountenancer of his nobility. The loss of

Brittaine and the peace with France were not forgotten. But chiefly
they fell upon the wrong that he did his Queen, and that he did
not reign in her right. Wherefore they said that God had now
brought to light a masculine branch of the House of York that
would not be at his courtesy, howsoever he did depress his poor
lady. And yet (as it fareth in things which are current with the
multitude and which they affect) these fames grew so general, as
the authors were lost in the generality of speakers; they being
like running weeds that have no certain root; or like footings up
and down, impossible to be traced. But after a while these ill
humours drew to a head, and settled secretly in some eminent
persons; which were Sir William Stanley Lord Chamberlain of the
King's household, the Lord Fitzwater, Sir Symon Mountfort, Sir
Thomas Thwaites. These entered into a secret conspiracy to favour Duke Richard's title. Nevertheless none engaged their fortunes in this business openly but two, Sir Robert Clifford and
master William Barley, who sailed over into Flanders, sent indeed
from the party of the conspirators here to understand the truth
of those things that passed there, and not without some help of
moneys from hence; provisionally to be delivered, if they found
and were satisfied that there was truth in these pretences. The
person of Sir Robert Clifford (being a gentleman of fame and
family) was extremely welcome to the Lady Margaret, who after
she had conference with him brought him to the sight of Perkin,
with whom he had often speech and discourse. So that in the end,
won either by the Duchess to affect or by Perkin to believe, he
wrote back into England, that he knew the person of Richard
Duke of York as well as he knew his own, and that this young
man was undoubtedly he. By this means all things grew prepared
to revolt and sedition here, and the conspiracy came to have a
correspondence between Flanders and England.

The King on his part was not asleep. But to arm or levy forces
yet, he thought would but show fear, and do this idol too much
worship. Nevertheless the ports he did shut up, or at least kept a
watch on them, that none should pass to or fro that was suspected.
But for the rest he chose to work by countermine. His purposes
were two; the one to lay open the abuse; the other to break the

knot of the conspirators. To detect the abuse, there were but two ways: the first to make it manifest to the world that the Duke of York was indeed murdered; the other to prove that (were he dead or alive) yet Perkin was a counterfeit. For the first, thus it stood. There were but four persons that could speak upon knowledge to the murder of the Duke of York: Sir James Tirrell (the employed-man from King Richard), John Dighton and Myles Forrest his servants (the two butchers or tormentors), and the priest of the Tower that buried them; of which four, Myles Forrest and the priest were dead, and there remained alive only Sir James Tirrell and John Dighton. These two the King caused to be committed to the Tower and examined touching the manner of the death of the two innocent princes. They agreed both in a tale (as the King gave out) to this effect: That King Richard having directed his warrant for the putting of them to death to Brackenbury, the Lieutenant of the Tower, was by him refused; whereupon the King directed his warrant to Sir James Tirrell to receive the keys of the Tower from the lieutenant (for the space of a night) for the King's special service. That Sir James Tirrell accordingly repaired to the Tower by night, attended by his two servants afore-named, whom he had chosen for the purpose. That himself stood at the stairfoot, and sent these two villains to execute the murder. That they smothered them in their bed; and, that done, called up their master to see their naked dead bodies, which they had laid forth. That they were buried under the stairs, and some stones cast upon them. That when the report was made to King Richard that his will was done, he gave Sir James Tirrell great thanks; but took exception to the place of their burial, being too base for them that were King's children; whereupon another night by the King's warrant renewed, their bodies were removed by the priest of the Tower, and buried by him in some place which (by means of the priest's death soon after) could not be known. Thus much was then delivered abroad, to be the effect of those examinations. But the King nevertheless made no use of them in any of his declarations; whereby, as it seems, those examinations left the business somewhat perplexed. And as for Sir James Tirrell, he was long after beheaded in the Tower-yard for other matters of treason. But John Dighton, who it seemeth spake best for the King, was forthwith set at liberty, and was the principal means of divulging this tradition. Therefore this kind of proof being left so naked, the King used the more diligence in the latter, for the tracing of Perkin. To this purpose he sent abroad into several parts, and especially into Flanders, divers secret and nimble scouts and spies; some feigning themselves to fly over unto Perkin, and to adhere unto him; and some under other pretences to learn, search, and discover all the circumstances and particulars of Perkin's parents, birth, person, travels up and down, and in brief, to have a journal (as it were) of his life and doings. He furnished these his employed-men liberally with money, to draw on and reward intelligences; giving them also in charge, to advertise continually what they found, and nevertheless still to go on. And ever as one advertisement and discovery called up another, he employed other new men, where the business did require it. Others he employed in a more special nature and trust, to be his pioneers in the main countermine. These were directed to insinuate themselves into the familiarity and confidence of the principal persons of the party in Flanders, and so to learn what associates they had and correspondents either here in England or abroad; and how far every one was engaged; and what new ones they meant afterwards to try or board [make advances to]. And as this for the persons, so for the actions themselves, to discover to the bottom (as they could) the utmost of Perkin's and the conspirators their intentions, hopes, and practices. These latter best betrust spies had some of them further instructions, to practise and draw off the best friends and servants of Perkin, by making remonstrance to them how weakly his enterprise and hopes were built, and with how prudent and potent a King they had to deal; and to reconcile them to the King with promise of pardon and good conditions of reward. And (above the rest) to assail, sap, and work into the constancy of Sir Robert Clifford, and to win him (if they could), being the man that knew most of their secrets, and who being won away would most appall and discourage the rest, and in a manner break the knot.

There is a strange tradition, that the King being lost in a

wood of suspicions, and not knowing whom to trust, had both intelligence with the confessors and chaplains of divers great men;
and for the better credit of his espials [spies] abroad with the
contrary side, did use to have them cursed at Paul's (by name)
amongst the bead-roll of the King's enemies, according to the
custom of those times. These spials [spies] plied their charge so
roundly, as the King had an anatomy of Perkin alive; and was
likewise well informed of the particular correspondent conspirators in England, and many other mysteries were revealed; and Sir
Robert Clifford in especial won to be assured to the King, and
industrious and officious for his service. The King therefore (receiving a rich return of his diligence, and great satisfaction touching a number of particulars,) first divulged and spread abroad the
imposture and juggling of Perkin's person and travels, with the
circumstances thereof, throughout the realm; not by proclamation
(because things were yet in examination, and so might receive the
more or the less,) but by court-fames [rumors spread at court],
which commonly print better than printed proclamations. Then
thought he it also time to send an ambassage unto Archduke
Philip into Flanders, for the abandoning and dismissing of Perkin.
Herein he employed Sir Edward Poynings, and Sir William Warham doctor of the canon law. The Archduke was then young and
governed by his council: before whom the ambassadors had audience, and Dr. Warham spake in this manner:

"My lords, the King our master is very sorry, that England
and your country here of Flanders having been counted as man
and wife for so long time, now this country of all others should
be the stage where a base counterfeit should play the part of a
King of England, not only to his Grace's disquiet and dishonour,
but to the scorn and reproach of all sovereign Princes. To counterfeit the dead image of a King in his coin is a high offence by all
laws. But to counterfeit the living image of a King in his person
exceedeth all falsifications, except it should be that of a Mahomet
or an Antichrist, that counterfeit divine honour. The King hath too
great an opinion of this sage council, to think that any of you is
caught with this fable (though way may be given by you to the
passion of some), the thing in itself is so improbable. To set testi-

monies aside of the death of Duke Richard, which the King hath
upon record plain and infallible (because they may be thought to
be in the King's own power), let the thing testify for itself. Sense
and reason no power can command. Is it possible (trow you) that
King Richard should damn his soul and foul his name with so
abominable a murder, and yet not mend his case? Or do you think
that men of blood (that were his instruments) did turn to pity in
the midst of their execution? whereas in cruel and savage beasts,
and men also, the first draught of blood doth yet make them more
fierce and enraged. Do you not know that the bloody executioners
of tyrants do go to such errands with an halter about their neck,
so that if they perform not they are sure to die for it? And do you
think that these men would hazard their own lives for sparing
another's? Admit they should have saved him; what should they
have done with him? Turn him into London streets, that the
watchmen, or any passenger that should light upon him, might
carry him before a justice, and so all come to light? Or should they
have kept him by them secretly? That surely would have required
a great deal of care, charge, and continual fears. But, my lords, I
labour too much in a clear business. The King is so wise, and hath
so good friends abroad, as now he knoweth Duke Perkin from his
cradle. And because he is a great Prince, if you have any good poet
here, he can help him with notes to write his life, and to parallel
him with Lambert Symnell, now the King's falconer. And therefore (to speak plainly to your lordships) it is the strangest thing
in the world, that the Lady Margaret (excuse us if we name her,
whose malice to the King is both causeless and endless), should
now when she is old, at the time when other women give over
child-bearing, bring forth two such monsters, being not the births
of nine or ten months, but of many years. And whereas other
natural mothers bring forth children weak, and not able to help
themselves; she bringeth forth tall striplings, able soon after
their coming into the world to bid battle to mighty Kings. My
lords, we stay unwillingly upon this part. We would to God that
lady would once taste the joys which God Almighty doth serve
up unto her, in beholding her niece to reign in such honour, and
with so much royal issue, which she might be pleased to account

as her own. The King's request unto the Archduke and your lordships might be, that according to the example of King Charles, who hath already discarded him, you would banish this unworthy fellow out of your dominions. But because the King may justly expect more from an ancient confederate than from a new reconciled enemy, he maketh his request unto you to deliver him up into his hands: pirates and imposters of this sort being fit to be accounted the common enemies of mankind, and no ways to be protected by the law of nations."

After some time of deliberation, the ambassadors received this short answer: "That the Archduke, for the love of King Henry, would in no sort aid or assist the pretended Duke, but in all things conserve the amity he had with the King. But for the Duchess Dowager, she was absolute in the lands of her dowry, and that he could not let her to dispose[31] of her own."

The King, upon the return of the ambassadors, was nothing satisfied with this answer: for well he knew that a patrimonial dowry carried no part of sovereignty or command of forces. Besides the ambassadors told him plainly, that they saw the Duchess had a great party in the Archduke's council; and that howsoever it was carried in a course of connivance, yet the Archduke underhand gave aid and furtherance to Perkin. Wherefore (partly out of courage and partly out of policy) the King forthwith banished all Flemings (as well their persons as their wares) out of his kingdom; commanding his subjects likewise (and by name his Merchants Adventurers) which had a resiance [residence] in Antwerp, to return; translating the mart (which commonly followed the English cloth) unto Calais, and embarred also all further trade for the future. This the King did, being sensible in point of honour not to suffer a pretender to the crown of England to affront him so near at hand, and he to keep terms of friendship with the country where he did set up. But he had also a further reach; for that he knew well that the subjects of Flanders drew so great commodity from the trade of England, as by this embargo they would soon wax weary of Perkin; and that the

[31] [could not prevent her from disposing . . .]

tumults of Flanders had been so late and fresh, as it was no time
for the Prince to displease the people. Nevertheless for form's
sake, by way of requital, the Archduke did likewise banish the
English out of Flanders; which in effect was done to his hand.

The King being well advertised that Perkin did more trust
upon friends and partakers within the realm than upon foreign
arms, thought it behoved him to apply the remedy where the disease lay, and to proceed with severity against some of the principal conspirators here within the realm; thereby to purge the ill
humours in England, and to cool the hopes in Flanders. Wherefore he caused to be apprehended, almost at an instant, John
Ratcliffe, Lord Fitzwater, Sir Symon Mountfort, Sir Thomas
Thwaites, William Dawbeny, Robert Ratcliffe, Thomas Chresse-
nor, and Thomas Astwood. All these were arraigned, convicted,
and condemned for high treason, in adhering and promising aid
to Perkin. Of these the Lord Fitzwater was conveyed to Calais,
and there kept in hold and in hope of life, until soon after (either
impatient or betrayed) he dealt with his keeper to have escaped,
and thereupon was beheaded. But Sir Symon Mountfort, Robert
Ratcliffe, and William Dawbeny, were beheaded immediately
after their condemnation. The rest were pardoned, together with
many others, clerks and laics, amongst which were two Domini-
can friars, and William Worseley Dean of Paul's; which latter
sort passed examination, but came not to public trial.

The Lord Chamberlain at that time was not touched; whether
it were that the King would not stir too many humours at once,
but, after the manner of good physicians, purge the head last;
or that Clifford (from whom most of these discoveries came)
reserved that piece for his own coming over; signifying only to
the King in the mean time that he doubted there were some
greater ones in the business, whereof he would give the King
farther account when he came to his presence.

Upon Allhallows-day-even, being now the tenth year of the
King's reign, the King's second son Henry was created Duke of
York; and as well the Duke, as divers others, noblemen, knights-
bachelors, and gentlemen of quality, were made Knights of the
Bath according to the ceremony. Upon the morrow after Twelfth-

day, the King removed from Westminster (where he had kept his Christmas) to the Tower of London. This he did as soon as he had advertisement that Sir Robert Clifford (in whose bosom or budget most of Perkin's secrets were laid up) was come into England. And the place of the Tower was chosen to that end, that if Clifford should accuse any of the great ones, they might without suspicion or noise or sending abroad of warrants be presently attached; the court and prison being within the cincture of one wall. After a day or two the King drew unto him a selected council, and admitted Clifford to his presence; who first fell down at his feet, and in all humble manner craved the King's pardon; which the King then granted, though he were indeed secretly assured of his life before. Then, commanded to tell his knowledge, he did amongst many others (of himself not interrogated) impeach Sir William Stanley, the Lord Chamberlain of the King's household.

The King seemed to be much amazed at the naming of this lord; as if he had heard the news of some strange and fearful prodigy. To hear a man that had done him service of so high a nature as to save his life and set the crown upon his head; a man that enjoyed by his favour and advancement so great a fortune both in honour and riches; a man that was tied unto him in so near a band of alliance, his brother having married the King's mother; and lastly a man to whom he had committed the trust of his person, in making him his chamberlain. That this man, no ways disgraced, no ways discontent, no ways put in fear, should be false unto him. Clifford was required to say over again and again the particulars of his accusation; being warned, that in a matter so unlikely, and that concerned so great a servant of the King's, he should not in any wise go too far. But the King finding that he did sadly [soberly] and constantly (without hesitation or varying, and with those civil protestations that were fit,) stand to that that he had said, offering to justify it upon his soul and life; he caused him to be removed. And after he had not a little bemoaned himself unto his council there present, gave order that Sir William Stanley should be restrained in his own chamber, where he lay before, in the square tower. And the next day he was examined by the lords. Upon his examination he denied little of that wherewith he was charged, nor endeavoured much to excuse or extenuate his fault. So that (not very wisely), thinking to make his offence less by confession, he made it enough for condemnation. It was conceived that he trusted much to his former merits and the interest that his brother had in the King. But those helps were over-weighed by divers things that made against him, and were predominant in the King's nature and mind. First, an over-merit; for convenient merit, unto which reward may easily reach, doth best with Kings: Next, the sense of his power; for the King thought that he that could set him up was the more dangerous to pull him down: Thirdly, the glimmering of a confiscation; for he was the richest subject for value in the kingdom; there being found in his castle of Holte forty thousand marks in ready money and plate, besides jewels, household-stuff, stocks upon his grounds, and other personal estate exceeding great; and for his revenue in land and fee, it was three thousand pounds a year of old rent, a great matter in those times: Lastly, the nature of the time; for if the King had been out of fear of his own estate, it was not unlike he would have spared his life; but the cloud of so great a rebellion hanging over his head made him work sure. Wherefore after some six weeks' distance of time, which the King did honourably interpose, both to give space to his brother's intercession, and to shew to the world that he had a conflict with himself what he should do, he was arraigned of high-treason, and condemned, and presently after beheaded.

Yet is it to this day left but in dark memory, both what the case of this noble person was, for which he suffered; and what likewise was the ground and cause of his defection, and the alienation of his heart from the King. His case was said to be this; that in discourse between Sir Robert Clifford and him he had said, *That if he were sure that that young man were King Edward's son, he would never bear arms against him.* This case seems somewhat a hard case, both in respect of the conditional, and in respect of the other words. But for the conditional, it seemeth the judges of that time (who were learned men, and the three chief of them of the privy council,) thought it was a dangerous thing to admit Ifs and Ands to qualify words of treason; whereby every man might express his malice, and blanch his danger. And it was like to the case (in the following times) of Elizabeth Barton, the holy maid of Kent, who had said, *That if King Henry the Eighth did not take Katherine his wife again, he should be deprived of his crown, and die the death of a dog.* And infinite cases may be put of like nature; which it seemeth the grave judges taking into consideration, would not admit of treasons upon condition. And as for the positive words, *That he would not bear arms against King Edward's son;* though the words seem calm, yet it was a plain and direct over-ruling of the King's title, either by the line of Lancaster or by act of Parliament; which no doubt pierced the King more than if Stanley had charged his lance upon him in the field. For if Stanley would hold that opinion, That a son of King Edward had still the better right, he being so principal a person of authority and favour about the King, it was to teach all England to say as much. And therefore (as those times were) that speech touched the quick. But some writers do put this out of doubt; for they say that Stanley did expressly promise to aid Perkin, and sent him some help of treasure.

Now for the motive of his falling off from the King. It is true that at Bosworth Field the King was beset, and in a manner inclosed round about by the troops of King Richard, and in manifest danger of his life; when this Stanley was sent by his brother with three thousand men to his rescue, which he performed so, that King Richard was slain upon the place. So as the condition of mortal men is not capable of a greater benefit than the King received by the hands of Stanley; being like the benefit of Christ, at once to save and crown. For which service the King gave him great gifts, made him his counsellor and chamberlain; and (somewhat contrary to his nature) had winked at the great spoils of Bosworth Field, which came almost wholly to this man's hands, to his infinite enriching. Yet nevertheless, blown up with the conceit of his merit, he did not think he had received good measure from the King, at least not pressing-down and running over, as he expected. And his ambition was so exorbitant and unbounded, as he became suitor to the King for the Earldom of Chester: which ever being a kind of appanage to the principality

of Wales, and using to go to the King's son, his suit did not only
end in a denial but in a distaste: the King perceiving thereby that
his desires were intemperate, and his cogitations vast and irregu-
lar, and that his former benefits were but cheap and lightly
regarded by him. Wherefore the King began not to brook him
well; and as a little leaven of new distaste doth commonly sour the
whole lump of former merits, the king's wit began now to suggest
unto his passion, that Stanley at Bosworth Field, though he came
time enough to save his life, yet he stayed long enough to en-
danger it. But yet having no matter against him, he continued him
in his places until this his fall.

After him was made Lord Chamberlain, Giles Lord Dawbeny,
a man of great sufficiency and valour, the more because he was
gentle and moderate.

There was a common opinion, that Sir Robert Clifford (who
now was become the state-informer) was from the beginning an
emissary and spy of the King's; and that he fled over into Flanders
with his consent and privity. But this is not probable; both
because he never recovered that degree of grace which he had with
the King before his going over; and chiefly for that the discovery
which he had made touching the Lord Chamberlain (which was
his great service) grew not from anything he learned abroad, for
that he knew it well before he went.

These executions (and specially that of the Lord Chamberlain
which was the chief strength of the party, and by means of Sir
Robert Clifford who was the most inward man of trust amongst
them) did extremely quail the design of Perkin and his complices,
as well through discouragement as distrust. So that they were
now (like sand without lime) ill bound together; especially as
many as were English, who were at a gaze, looking strange one
upon another, not knowing who was faithful to their side; but
thinking that the King (what with his baits and what with his
nets) would draw them all unto him that were any thing worth.
And indeed it came to pass that divers came away by the thread,
sometimes one and sometimes another. Barley, that was joint-
commissioner with Clifford, did hold out one of the longest, till
Perkin was far worn; yet made his peace at length. But the fall of

this great man, being in so high authority and favour (as was thought) with the King, and the manner of carriage of the business, as if there had been secret inquisition upon him for a great time before; and the cause for which he suffered, which was little more than for saying in effect that the title of York was better than the title of Lancaster, which was the case almost of every man, at the least in opinion; was matter of great terror amongst all the King's servants and subjects; insomuch as no man almost thought himself secure, and men durst scarce commune or talk one with another, but there was a general diffidence everywhere. Which nevertheless made the King rather more absolute than more safe. For, *Bleeding inwards and shut vapours strangle soonest and oppress most.*

Hereupon presently came forth swarms and volleys of libels (which are the gusts of liberty of speech restrained, and the females of sedition,) containing bitter invectives and slanders against the King and some of the council: for the contriving and dispersing whereof (after great diligence of enquiry) five mean persons were caught up and executed.

Meanwhile the King did not neglect Ireland, being the soil where these mushrooms and upstart weeds that spring up in a night did chiefly prosper. He sent therefore from hence (for the better settling of his affairs there) commissioners of both robes, the Prior of Lanthony to be his Chancellor in that kingdom, and Sir Edward Poynings, with a power of men, and a marshall [martial?] commission, together with a civil power of his Lieutenant, with a clause, That the Earl of Kildare, then Deputy, should obey him. But the wild Irish, who were the principal offenders, fled into the woods and bogs, after their manner; and those that knew themselves guilty in the Pale fled to them. So that Sir Edward Poynings was enforced to make a wild chase upon the wild Irish; where (in respect of the mountains and fastnesses) he did little good. Which (either out of a suspicious melancholy upon his bad success, or the better to save his service from disgrace,) he would needs impute unto the comfort that the rebels should receive underhand from the Earl of Kildare; every light suspicion growing upon the Earl, in respect of the Kildare that was in the action of

Lambert Symnell, and slain at Stoke-field. Wherefore he caused
the Earl to be apprehended, and sent into England; where upon
examination he cleared himself so well as he was replaced in his
government. But Poynings, the better to make compensation of
the meagreness of his service in the wars by acts of peace, called a
Parliament; where was made that memorable act which at this
day is called Poynings' Law; whereby all the statutes of England
were made to be of force in Ireland. For before they were not;
neither are any now in force in Ireland, which were made in
England since that time; which was the tenth year of the King.

About this time began to be discovered in the King that disposition, which afterwards nourished and whet on by bad counsellors and ministers proved the blot of his times: which was the
course he took to crush treasure out of his subjects' purses, by
forfeitures upon penal laws. At this men did startle the more at
this time, because it appeared plainly to be in the King's nature,
and not out of his necessity, he being now in float for treasure:
for that he had newly received the peace-money from France, the
benevolence-money from his subjects, and great casualties upon
the confiscations of the Lord Chamberlain and divers others. The
first noted case of this kind was that of Sir William Capel, Alderman of London, who upon sundry penal laws was condemned in
the sum of seven and twenty hundred pounds, and compounded
with the King for sixteen hundred; and yet after, Empson would
have cut another chop out of him, if the King had not died in the
instant.

The summer following, the King, to comfort his mother,
whom he did always tenderly love and revere, and to make demonstration to the world that the proceeding against Sir William
Stanley (which was imposed upon him by necessity of state) had
not in any degree diminished the affection he bore to Thomas his
brother, went in progress to Latham, to make merry with his
mother and the Earl, and lay there divers days.

During this progress Perkin Warbeck, finding that time and
temporising, which (while his practices were covert and wrought
well in England) made for him, did now when they were discovered and defeated rather make against him (for that when

matters once go down the hill they stay not without a new force), resolved to try his adventure in some exploit upon England; hoping still upon the affections of the common people towards the House of York. Which body of common people he thought was not to be practised upon as persons of quality are; but that the only practice upon their affections was to set up a standard in the field. The place where he should make his attempt he chose to be the coast of Kent.

The King by this time was grown to such a height of reputation for cunning and policy, that every accident and event that went well was laid and imputed to his foresight, as if he had set it before. As in this particular of Perkin's design upon Kent. For the world would not believe afterwards, but the King, having secret intelligence of Perkin's intention for Kent, the better to draw it on, went of purpose into the north afar off; laying an open side unto Perkin to make him come to the close, and so to trip up his heels, having made sure in Kent beforehand.

But so it was, that Perkin had gathered together a power of all nations, neither in number nor in the hardiness and courage of the persons contemptible; but in their nature and fortunes to be feared as well of friends as enemies; being bankrupts, and many of them felons, and such as lived by rapine. These he put to sea, and arrived upon the coast of Sandwich and Deal in Kent about July.

There he cast anchor, and to prove the affections of the people, sent some of his men to land, making great boasts of the power that was to follow. The Kentish men, perceiving that Perkin was not followed by any English of name or account, and that his forces consisted but of strangers born, and most of them base people and free-booters, fitter to spoil a coast than to recover a kingdom; resorting unto the principal gentlemen of the country, professed their loyalty to the King, and desired to be directed and commanded for the best of the King's service. The gentlemen, entering into consultation, directed some forces in good number to shew themselves upon the coast, and some of them to make signs to entice Perkin's soldiers to land, as if they would join with them; and some others to appear from some other places, and to make semblance as if they fled from them, the better to encourage them to land. But Perkin, who by playing the Prince, or else taught by secretary Frion, had learned thus much, that people under command do use to consult and after to march in order, and rebels contrariwise run upon an head together in confusion; considering the delay of time, and observing their orderly and not tumultuary arming, doubted the worst. And therefore the wily youth would not set one foot out of his ship, till he might see things were sure. Wherefore the King's forces, perceiving that they could draw on no more than those that were formerly landed, set upon them and cut them in pieces ere they could fly back to their ships. In which skirmish (besides those that fled and were slain) there were taken about an hundred and fifty persons. Which, for that the King thought, that to punish a few for example was gentleman's pay, but for rascal people they were to be cut off every man, especially in the beginning of an enterprise; and likewise for that he saw that Perkin's forces would now consist chiefly of such rabble and scum of desperate people; he therefore hanged them all for the greater terror. They were brought to London all railed in ropes, like a team of horses in a cart, and were executed some of them at London and Wapping, and the rest at divers places upon the sea-coast of Kent, Sussex, and Norfolk, for sea-marks or light-houses to teach Perkin's people to avoid the coast. The King being advertised of the landing of the rebels, thought to leave his progress: but being certified the next day that they were partly defeated and partly fled, he continued his progress, and sent Sir Richard Guildford into Kent in message; who calling the country together, did much commend (from the King) their fidelity, manhood, and well handling of that service; and gave them all thanks, and (in private) promised reward to some particulars.

Upon the sixteenth of November (this being the eleventh year of the King) was holden the Serjeants' feast at Ely Place, there being nine serjeants of that call. The King, to honour the feast, was present with his Queen at the dinner; being a Prince that was ever ready to grace and countenance the professors of the law; having a little of that, *That as he governed his subjects by his laws, so he governed his laws by his lawyers.*

This year also the King entered into league with the Italian potentates for the defence of Italy against France. For King Charles had conquered the realm of Naples, and lost it again, in a kind of felicity of a dream. He passed the whole length of Italy without resistance; so that it was true which Pope Alexander was wont to say, *That the Frenchmen came into Italy with chalk in their hands to mark up their lodgings, rather than with swords to fight.* He likewise entered and won in effect the whole kingdom of Naples itself, without striking stroke. But presently thereupon he did commit and multiply so many errors, as was too great a task for the best fortune to overcome. He gave no contentment to the barons of Naples, of the faction of the Angevines; but scattered his rewards according to the mercenary appetites of some about him. He put all Italy upon their guard, by the seizing and holding of Ostia, and the protecting of the liberty of Pisa; which made all men suspect that his purposes looked further than his title of Naples. He fell too soon at difference with Ludovico Sforza, who was the man that carried the keys which brought him in and shut him out. He neglected to extinguish some relicks of the war. And lastly, in regard of his easy passage through Italy without resistance, he entered into an overmuch despising of the arms of the Italians, whereby he left the realm of Naples at his departure so much the less provided. So that not long after his return, the whole kingdom revolted to Ferdinando the younger, and the French were quite driven out. Nevertheless Charles did make both great threats and great preparations to re-enter Italy once again. Wherefore at the instance of divers of the states of Italy (and especially of Pope Alexander) there was a league concluded between the said Pope, Maximilian King of the Romans, Henry King of England, Ferdinando and Isabella King and Queen of Spain (for so they are constantly placed in the original treaty throughout), Augustino Barbadico Duke [Doge] of Venice, and Ludovico Sforza Duke of Milan, for the common defence of their estates. Wherein though Ferdinando of Naples was not named as principal, yet no doubt the kingdom of Naples was tacitly included as a fee of the church.

There died also this year Cecile Duchess of York, mother to

King Edward the Fourth, at her castle of Barkhamsted, being of
extreme years, and who had lived to see three princes of her body
crowned, and four murdered. She was buried at Foderingham, by
her husband.

   This year also the King called his Parliament, where many
laws were made of a more private and vulgar nature than ought
to detain the reader of an history. And it may be justly suspected,
by the proceedings following, that as the King did excell in good
commonwealth laws, so nevertheless he had (in secret) a design
to make use of them as well for collecting of treasure as for cor-
recting of manners; and so, meaning thereby to harrow his people, did accumulate them the rather.

   The principal law that was made this Parliament was a law
of a strange nature, rather just than legal, and more magnani-
mous than provident. This law did ordain, That no person that
did assist in arms or otherwise the King for the time being,
should after be impeached therefore, or attainted, either by the
course of the law or by act of Parliament; but if any such act of
attainder did happen to be made, it should be void and of none
effect; for that it was agreeable to reason of estate that the subject should not inquire of the justness of the King's title or quarrel, and it was agreeable to good conscience that (whatsoever the
fortune of the war were) the subject should not suffer for his
obedience. The spirit of this law was wonderful pious and noble,
being like, in matter of war, unto the spirit of David in matter of
plague, who said, *If I have sinned, strike me; but what have these
sheep done?* Neither wanted this law parts of prudent and deep
foresight. For it did the better take away occasion for the people
to busy themselves to pry into the King's title; for that (howsoever it fell) their safety was already provided for. Besides it could
not but greatly draw unto him the love and hearts of the people,
because he seemed more careful for them than for himself. But
yet nevertheless it did take off from his party that great tie and
spur of necessity to fight and go victors out of the field; considering their lives and fortunes were put in safety and protected
whether they stood to it or ran away. But the force and obligation
of this law was in itself illusory, as to the latter part of it (by a
precedent act of Parliament to bind or frustrate a future). For a

supreme and absolute power cannot conclude itself, neither can that which is in nature revocable be made fixed; no more than if a man should appoint or declare by his will that if he made any later will it should be void. And for the case of the act of Parliament, there is a notable precedent of it in King Henry the Eighth's time; who doubting he might die in the minority of his son, procured an act to pass, *That no statute made during the minority of a King should bind him or his successors, except it were confirmed by the King under his great seal at his full age.* But the first act that passed in King Edward the Sixth's time, was an act of repeal of that former act; at which time nevertheless the King was minor. But things that do not bind may satisfy for the time.

There was also made a shoring [up] or underpropping act for the benevolence: to make the sums which any person had agreed to pay, and nevertheless were not brought in, to be leviable by course of law. Which act did not only bring in the arrears, but did indeed countenance the whole business, and was pretended to be made at the desire of those that had been forward to pay.

This Parliament also was made that good law which gave the attaint upon a false verdict between party and party, which before was a kind of evangile, irremediable.[32] It extends not to causes capital, as well because they are for the most part at the King's suit; as because in them, if they be followed in course of indictment, there passeth a double jury, the indictors and the triers, and so not twelve men but four and twenty. But it seemeth that was not the only reason; for this reason holdeth not in the appeal. But the great reason was, lest it should tend to the discouragement of jurors in cases of life and death, if they should be subject to suit and penalty, where the favour of life maketh against them.[33] It extendeth not also to any suit where the demand

[32] [Parliament made a law enabling a jury to be tried on the charge of giving a false verdict (in cases involving two private parties); hitherto, there had been no recourse in cases where juries had brought in obviously incorrect decisions.]

[33] [Bacon is here describing one of the exceptions to the new law, cases of life and death. Evidently, there was a fear that if jurymen could be tried for being too merciful, they would then become unreasonably harsh.]

is under the value of forty pounds; for that in such cases of petty value it would not quit the charge to go about again.

There was another law made against a branch of ingratitude in women, who having been advanced [given lands] by their husbands, or their husbands' ancestors, should alien and thereby seek to defeat the heirs or those in remainder of the lands whereunto they had been so advanced. The remedy was by giving power to the next to enter for a forfeiture.[34]

There was also enacted that charitable law for the admission of poor suitors *in forma pauperis*, without fee to counsellor [counsel], attorney, or clerk; whereby poor men became rather able to vex than unable to sue. There were divers other good laws made that Parliament, as we said before; but we still observe our manner in selecting out those that are not of a vulgar nature.

The King this while, though he sat in Parliament as in full peace, and seemed to account of the designs of Perkin (who was now returned into Flanders) but as a May-game; yet having the composition of a wise King, stout without and apprehensive within, had given order for the watching of beacons upon the coast, and erecting more where they stood too thin; and had a careful eye where this wandering cloud would break. But Perkin, advised to keep his fire (which hitherto burned as it were upon green wood) alive with continual blowing, sailed again into Ireland; whence he had formerly departed, rather upon the hopes of France than upon any unreadiness or discouragement he found in that people. But in the space of time between, the King's diligence and Poyning's commission had so settled things there, as there was nothing left for Perkin but the blustering affection of the wild and naked people. Wherefore he was advised by his council to seek aid of the King of Scotland; a Prince young and valorous, and in good terms with his nobles and people, and ill affected to King Henry. At this time also both Maximilian and Charles of France began to bear no good will to the King: the one

[34] [If a woman tried to alienate lands which ought to belong to her husband's heirs, those heirs could seek to have the lands handed over to them at once.]

being displeased with the King's prohibition of commerce with Flanders; the other holding the King for suspect, in regard of his late entry into league with the Italians. Wherefore besides the open aids of the Duchess of Burgundy, which did with sails and oars put on and advance Perkin's designs, there wanted not some secret tides from Maximilian and Charles which did further his fortunes. Insomuch as they both by their secret letters and messages recommended him to the King of Scotland.

Perkin therefore coming into Scotland upon those hopes, with a well-appointed company, was by the King of Scots (being formerly well prepared) honourably welcomed, and soon after his arrival admitted to his presence in a solemn manner. For the King received him in state in his chamber of presence, accompanied with divers of his nobles. And Perkin, well attended as well with those that the King had sent before him as with his own train, entered the room where the King was, and coming near to the King, and bowing a little to embrace him, he retired some paces back, and with a loud voice, (that all that were present might hear him) made his declaration in this manner:

"High and mighty King, your Grace and these your nobles here present may be pleased benignly to bow your ears to hear the tragedy of a young man, that by right ought to hold in his hand the ball of a kingdom, but by fortune is made himself a ball, tossed from misery to misery, and from place to place. You see here before you the spectacle of a Plantagenet, who hath been carried from the nursery to the sanctuary, from the sanctuary to the direful prison, from the prison to the hand of the cruel tormentor, and from that hand to the wide wilderness (as I may truly call it), for so the world hath been to me. So that he that is born to a great kingdom, hath not ground to set his foot upon, more than this where he now standeth by your princely favour. Edward the Fourth, late King of England, (as your Grace cannot but have heard,) left two sons, Edward and Richard Duke of York, both very young. Edward the eldest succeeded their father in the crown, by the name of King Edward the Fifth. But Richard Duke of Glocester, their unnatural uncle, first thirsting after the kingdom through ambition, and afterwards thirsting for their

blood out of desire to secure himself, employed an instrument of
his (confident to him as he thought), to murder them both. But
this man that was employed to execute that execrable tragedy,
having cruelly slain King Edward, the eldest of the two, was
moved partly by remorse, and partly by some other mean, to save
Richard his brother; making a report nevertheless to the tyrant
that he had performed his commandment for both brethren. This
report was accordingly believed, and published generally. So that
the world hath been possessed of an opinion that they both were
barbarously made away, though ever truth hath some sparks that
fly abroad until it appear in due time, as this hath had. But Almighty God, that stopped the mouth of the lions, and saved little
Joas from the tyranny of Athaliah when she massacred the King's
children, and did save Isaac when the hand was stretched forth
to sacrifice him, preserved the second brother. For I myself that
stand here in your presence, am that very Richard Duke of York,
brother of that unfortunate Prince King Edward the Fifth, now
the most rightful surviving heir-male to that victorious and most
noble Edward, of that name the Fourth, late King of England.
For the manner of my escape, it is fit it should pass in silence, or
at least in a more secret relation; for that it may concern some
alive, and the memory of some that are dead. Let it suffice to
think, that I had then a mother living, a Queen, and one that expected daily such a commandment from the tyrant for the mur-
dering of her children. Thus in my tender age escaping by God's
mercy out of London, I was secretly conveyed over sea; where
after a time the party that had me in charge (upon what new
fears, change of mind, or practice, God knoweth) suddenly forsook me; whereby I was forced to wander abroad, and to seek
mean conditions for the sustaining of my life. Wherefore distracted between several passions, the one of fear to be known,
lest the tyrant should have a new attempt upon me, the other of
grief and disdain to be unknown, and to live in that base and
servile manner that I did, I resolved with myself to expect the
tyrant's death, and then to put myself into my sister's hands,
who was next heir to the crown. But in this season it happened

one Henry Tidder [Tudor],[35] son to Edmund Tidder Earl of Richmond, to come from France and enter into the realm, and by subtile and foul means to obtain the crown of the same, which to me
rightfully appertained: so that it was but a change from tyrant to
tyrant. This Henry, my extreme and mortal enemy, so soon as he
had knowledge of my being alive, imagined and wrought all the
subtile ways and means he could to procure my final destruction.
For my mortal enemy hath not only falsely surmised me to be a
feigned person, giving me nick-names, so abusing the world; but
also to defer and put me from entry into England, hath offered
large sums of money to corrupt the Princes and their ministers
with whom I have been retained; and made importune labours to
certain servants about my person to murder or poison me, and
others to forsake and leave my righteous quarrel and to depart
from my service; as Sir Robert Clifford and others. So that every
man of reason may well perceive, that Henry, calling himself
King of England, needed not to have bestowed such great sums
of treasure, nor so to have busied himself with importune and in-
cessant labour and industry, to compass my death and ruin, if I
had been such a feigned person. But the truth of my cause being
so manifest, moved the most Christian King Charles, and the
Lady Duchess Dowager of Burgundy, my most dear aunt, not
only to acknowledge the truth thereof, but lovingly to assist me.
But it seemeth that God above, for the good of this whole island,
and the knitting of these two kingdoms of England and Scotland
in a strait concord and amity by so great an obligation, hath reserved the placing of me in the imperial throne of England for
the arms and succours of your Grace. Neither is it the first time
that a King of Scotland hath supported them that were bereft
and spoiled of the kingdom of England, as of late (in fresh memory) it was done in the person of Henry the Sixth. Wherefore for
that your Grace hath given clear signs that you are in no noble

[35] [This spelling comes from Perkin's original proclamation,
which John Speed had seen and partly printed; Bacon has it from
Speed.]

quality inferior to your royal ancestors, I, so distressed a Prince, was hereby moved to come and put myself into your royal hands, desiring your assistance to recover my kingdom of England, promising faithfully to bear myself towards your Grace no otherwise than if I were your own natural brother; and will, upon the recovery of mine inheritance, gratefully do you all the pleasure that is in my utmost power."

After Perkin had told his tale, King James answered bravely and wisely, *That whosoever he were, he should not repent him of putting himself into his hands.* And from that time forth (though there wanted not some about him that would have persuaded him that all was but an illusion) yet notwithstanding, either taken by Perkin's amiable and alluring behaviour, or inclining to the recommendation of the great Princes abroad, or willing to take an occasion of a war against King Henry, he entertained him in all things as became the person of Richard Duke of York, embraced his quarrel, and (the more to put it out of doubt that he took him to be a great Prince and not a representation only) he gave consent that this Duke should take to wife the Lady Katherine Gordon daughter to the Earl Huntley, being a near kinswoman to the King himself, and a young virgin of excellent beauty and virtue.

Not long after, the King of Scots in person, with Perkin in his company, entered with a great army (though it consisted chiefly of borderers being raised somewhat suddenly) into Northumberland. And Perkin, for a perfume before him as he went, caused to be published a proclamation of this tenor following, in the name of Richard Duke of York, true inheritor of the crown of England:

"It hath pleased God, who putteth down the mighty from their seat, and exalteth the humble, and suffereth not the hopes of the just to perish in the end, to give us means at the length to show ourselves armed unto our lieges and people of England. But far be it from us to intend their hurt or damage, or to make war upon them, otherwise than to deliver ourself and them from tyranny and oppression. For our mortal enemy Henry Tidder, a false usurper of the crown of England which to us by natural and

The original of this proclamation remaineth with Sir Robert Cotton, a worthy preserver and treasurer of rare antiquities: from whose manuscripts I have had much light for the furnishing of this work.

lineal right appertaineth, knowing in his own heart our undoubted right, (we being the very Richard Duke of York, younger
son and now surviving heir-male of the noble and victorious Edward the Fourth, late King of England), hath not only deprived
us of our kingdom, but likewise by all foul and wicked means
sought to betray us and bereave us of our life. Yet if his tyranny
only extended itself to our person, (although our royal blood
teacheth us to be sensible of injuries,) it should be less to our
grief. But this Tidder, who boasteth himself to have overthrown
a tyrant, hath ever since his first entrance into his usurped reign,
put little in practice but tyranny and the feats thereof.

"For King Richard, our unnatural uncle, although desire of
rule did blind him, yet in his other actions (like a true Plantagenet) was noble, and loved the honour of the realm and the contentment and comfort of his nobles and people. But this our
mortal enemy, agreeable to the meanness of his birth, hath trod-
den under foot the honour of this nation; selling our best confederates for money, and making merchandise of the blood,
estates, and fortunes of our peers and subjects, by feigned wars
and dishonourable peace, only to enrich his coffers. Nor unlike
hath been his hateful misgovernment and evil deportments here
at home. First he hath (to fortify his false quarrel) caused divers
nobles of this our realm (whom he held suspect and stood in
dread of) to be cruelly murdered; as our cousin Sir William Stanley Lord Chamberlain, Sir Simon Mountfort, Sir Robert Ratcliffe,
William Dawbeney, Humphrey Stafford, and many others, besides such as have dearly bought their lives with intolerable ransoms. Some of which nobles are now in the sanctuary. Also he
hath long kept, and yet keepeth in prison, our right entirely well-
beloved cousin, Edward, son and heir to our uncle Duke of
Clarence, and others; withholding from them their rightful inheritance, to the intent they should never be of might and power
to aid and assist us at our need, after the duty of their legiances.
He also married by compulsion certain of our sisters, and also the
sister of our said cousin the Earl of Warwick, and divers other
ladies of the royal blood, unto certain of his kinsmen and friends
of simple and low degree; and, putting apart all well disposed

nobles, he hath none in favour and trust about his person, but Bishop Foxe, Smith, Bray, Lovel, Oliver King, David Owen, Riseley, Turbervile, Tyler, Cholmeley, Empson, James Hobarte, John Cutte, Garth, Henry Wyate, and such other caitifs and villains of birth, which by subtile inventions and pilling of the people have been the principal finders, occasioners, and counsellors of the misrule and mischief now reigning in England.

"We remembering these premises, with the great and execrable offences daily committed and done by our foresaid great enemy and his adherents, in breaking the liberties and franchises of our mother the holy church, upon pretences of wicked and heathenish policy, to the high displeasure of Almighty God, besides the manifold treasons, abominable murders, manslaughters, robberies, extortions, the daily pilling of the people by dismes, taxes, tallages, benevolences, and other unlawful impositions and grievous exactions, with many other heinous effects, to the likely destruction and desolation of the whole realm: shall by God's grace, and the help and assistance of the great lords of our blood, with the counsel of other sad [sober] persons, see that the commodities of our realm be employed to the most advantage of the same; the intercourse of merchandise betwixt realm and realm to be ministered and handled as shall more be to the common weal and prosperity of our subjects; and all such dismes, taxes, tallages, benevolences, unlawful impositions, and grievous exactions as be above rehearsed, to be foredone and laid apart, and never from henceforth to be called upon, but in such cases as our noble progenitors Kings of England have of old time been accustomed to have the aid, succour, and help of their subjects and true liegemen.

"And farther we do out of our grace and clemency hereby as well publish and promise to all our subjects remission and free pardon of all by-past offences whatsoever against our person or estate, in adhering to our said enemy, by whom we know well they have been misled, if they shall within time convenient submit themselves unto us. And for such as shall come with the foremost to assist our righteous quarrel, we shall make them so far partakers of our princely favour and bounty, as shall be highly for the comfort of them and theirs both during their life and after their death. As also we shall, by all means which God shall put into our hands, demean ourselves to give royal contentment to all degrees and estates of our people, maintaining the liberties of holy church in their entire, preserving the honours, privileges, and preeminences of our nobles from contempt or disparagement, according to the dignity of their blood. We shall also unyoke our people from all heavy burdens and endurances, and confirm our cities, boroughs, and towns in their charters and freedoms, with enlargement where it shall be deserved; and in all points give our subjects cause to think that the blessed and debonaire government of our noble father King Edward (in his last times) is in us revived.

"And forasmuch as the putting to death or taking alive of our said mortal enemy may be a mean to stay much effusion of blood, which otherwise may ensue if by compulsion or fair promises he shall draw after him any number of our subjects to resist us, which we desire to avoid (though we be certainly informed that our said enemy is purposed and prepared to fly the land, having already made over great masses of the treasure of our crown the better to support him in foreign parts). We do hereby declare that whosoever shall take or distress our said enemy, though the party be of never so mean a condition, he shall be by us rewarded with £1000 in money, forthwith to be laid down to him, and an hundred marks by the year of inheritance; besides that he may otherwise merit, both toward God and all good people, for the destruction of such a tyrant.

"Lastly, we do all men to wit, and herein we take also God to witness, that whereas God hath moved the heart of our dearest cousin the King of Scotland to aid us in person in this our righteous quarrel; it is altogether without any pact or promise, or so much as demand, of any thing that may prejudice our crown or subjects; but contrariwise with promise on our said cousin's part, that whensoever he shall find us in sufficient strength to get the upper hand of our enemy (which we hope will be very suddenly), he will forthwith peaceably return into his own kingdom, contenting himself only with the glory of so honourable an enterprise, and our true and faithful love and amity: which we shall ever (by the grace of Almighty God) so order as shall be to the great comfort of both kingdoms."

But Perkin's proclamation did little edify with the people of England; neither was he the better welcome for the company he came in. Wherefore the King of Scotland, seeing none came in to Perkin nor none stirred anywhere in his favour, turned his enterprise into a rode [ride, i.e., raid]; and wasted and destroyed the country of Northumberland with fire and sword. But hearing that there were forces coming against him, and not willing that they should find his men heavy and laden with booty, he returned into Scotland with great spoils, deferring further prosecution till another time. It is said that Perkin, acting the part of a prince handsomely, when he saw the Scottish fell to waste the country, came to the King in a passionate manner, making great lamentation, and desired that that might not be the manner of making the war; for that no crown was so dear to his mind, as that he desired to purchase it with the blood and ruin of his country. Whereunto the King answered half in sport, that he doubted much he was careful for that that was none of his; and that he should be too good a steward for his enemy, to save the country to his use.

By this time, being the eleventh year of the King, the interruption of trade between the English and the Flemish began to pinch the merchants of both nations very sore, which moved them by all means they could devise to affect and dispose their sovereigns respectively to open the intercourse again. Wherein time favoured them. For the Archduke and his council began to see that Perkin would prove but a runagate and citizen of the world; and that it was the part of children to fall out about babies. And the King on his part, after the attempts upon Kent and Northumberland, began to have the business of Perkin in less estimation; so as he did not put it to account in any consultation of state. But that that moved him most was, that being a King that loved wealth and treasure, he could not endure to have trade sick, nor any obstruction to continue in the gate-vein, which disperseth that blood. And yet he kept state so far, as first to be sought unto. Wherein the Merchant Adventurers likewise (being a strong company at that time and well under-set with rich men and good order) did hold out bravely; taking off the commodities of the kingdom, though they lay dead upon their hands for want of vent. At the last, commissioners met at London to treat. On the King's part, Bishop Foxe Lord Privy Seal, Viscount Wells, Kendall Prior of Saint John's, and Warham Master of the Rolls (who began to gain much upon the King's opinion), Urswick, who was almost ever one,[36] and Riseley. On the Archduke's part, the Lord Bevers his Admiral, the Lord Verunsell President of Flanders, and others. These concluded a perfect treaty both of amity and intercourse between the King and the Archduke; containing articles both of state, commerce, and free fishing. This is that treaty which the Flemings call at this day *intercursus magnus;* both because it is more complete than the precedent treaties of the third and fourth year of the King; and chiefly to give it a difference from the treaty that followed in the one and twentieth year of the King, which they call *intercursus malus.* In this treaty there was an express article against the reception of the rebels of either prince by other; purporting, that if any such rebel should be required by the prince whose rebel he was, of the prince confederate, that forthwith the prince confederate should by proclamation command him to avoid his country: which if he did not within fifteen days, the rebel was to stand proscribed, and put out of protection. But nevertheless in this article Perkin was not named, neither perhaps contained, because he was no rebel. But by this means his wings were clipt of his followers that were English. And it was expressly comprised in the treaty, that it should extend to the territories of the Duchess Dowager. After the intercourse thus restored, the English merchants came again to their mansion at Antwerp, where they were received with procession and great joy.

The winter following, being the twelfth year of his reign, the King called again his Parliament; where he did much exaggerate

[36] [Urswick was almost always one of the king's commissioners in situations such as this one]

both the malice and cruel predatory war lately made by the King of Scotland: That that King, being in amity with him, and no ways provoked, should so burn in hatred towards him, as to drink of the lees and dregs of Perkin's intoxication, who was every where else detected and discarded: and that when he perceived it was out of his reach to do the King any hurt, he had turned his arms upon unarmed and unprovided people, to spoil only and depopulate, contrary to the laws both of war and peace: concluding, that he could neither with honour nor with the safety of his people to whom he did owe protection, let pass these wrongs unrevenged. The Parliament understood him well, and gave him a subsidy limited to the sum of one hundred and twenty thousand pounds, besides two fifteens[37]. For his wars were always to him as a mine of treasure, of a strange kind of ore; iron at the top, and gold and silver at the bottom. At this Parliament (for that there had been so much time spent in making laws the year before, and for that it was called purposely in respect of the Scottish war) there were no laws made to be remembered. Only there passed a law, at the suit of the Merchant Adventurers of England, against the Merchant Adventurers of London, for monopolising and exacting upon the trade; which it seemeth they did a little to save themselves, after the hard time they had sustained by want of trade. But those innovations were taken away by Parliament.

But it was fatal [fated] to the King to fight for his money. And though he avoided to fight with enemies abroad, yet he was still enforced to fight for it with rebels at home. For no sooner began the subsidy to be levied in Cornwall, but the people there began to grudge and murmur; the Cornish being a race of men stout of stomach, mighty of body and limb, and that lived hardly in a barren country, and many of them could (for a need) live

[37] [Taxes were granted by Parliament by one of two methods: the older, the tenth and fifteenth, was a tax on moveable property, originally of a tenth on urban and a fifteenth on rural. By Henry's time, this had been fixed at around £30,000 for each tenth and fifteenth. The subsidy was a newer tax, levied on property and goods, worth at this time around £100,000.]

under-ground, that were tinners. They muttered extremely, that it was a thing not to be suffered that for a little stir of the Scots, soon blown over, they should be thus grinded to powder with payments: and said it was for them to pay that had too much, and lived idly; but they would eat their bread that they got with the sweat of their brows, and no man should take it from them. And as in the tides of people once up there want not commonly stirring winds to make them more rough; so this people did light upon two ringleaders or captains of the rout. The one was Michael Joseph, a blacksmith or farrier of Bodmin, a notable talking fellow, and no less desirous to be talked of. The other was Thomas Flammock, a lawyer, who by telling his neighbours commonly upon any occasion that the law was on their side, had gotten great sway amongst them. This man talked learnedly, and as if he could tell how to make a rebellion and never break the peace. He told the people that subsidies were not to be granted nor levied in this case; that is, for wars of Scotland (for that the law had provided another course by service of escuage, for those journeys), much less when all was quiet, and war was made but a pretence to poll and pill [pillage] the people. And therefore that it was good they should not stand now like sheep before the shearers, but put on harness and take weapons in their hands; yet to do no creature hurt, but go and deliver the King a strong petition for the laying down of those grievous payments, and for the punishment of those that had given him that counsel, to make others beware how they did the like in time to come. And said for his part he did not see how they could do the duty of true Englishmen and good liege-men, except they did deliver the King from such wicked ones that would destroy both him and the country. Their aim was at Archbishop Morton and Sir Reginold Bray, who were the King's screens in this envy.

After that these two, Flammock and the blacksmith, had by joint and several pratings found tokens of consent in the multitude, they offered themselves to lead them, until they should hear of better men to be their leaders, which they said would be ere long: telling them further, that they would be but their servants, and first in every danger; but doubted not but to make

both the west-end and the east-end of England to meet in so good
a quarrel; and that all (rightly understood) was but for the King's
service.

The people upon these seditious instigations did arm, most
of them with bows and arrows, and bills, and such other weapons
of rude and country people; and forthwith under the command of
their leaders (which in such cases is ever at pleasure) marched
out of Cornwall through Devonshire unto Taunton in Somerset-
shire, without any slaughter, violence, or spoil of the country. At
Taunton they killed in fury an officious and eager commissioner
for the subsidy, whom they called the Provost of Perin. Thence
they marched to Wells, where the Lord Audley (with whom their
leaders had before some secret intelligence), a nobleman of an ancient family, but unquiet and popular and aspiring to ruin, came
in to them, and was by them with great gladness and cries of joy
accepted as their general; they being now proud that they were
led by a nobleman. The Lord Audley led them on from Wells to
Salisbury, and from Salisbury to Winchester. Thence the foolish
people who (in effect) led their leaders had a mind to be led into
Kent; fancying that the people there would join with them, contrary to all reason or judgment; considering the Kentish men had
shewed great loyalty and affection to the King so lately before.
But the rude people had heard Flammock say that Kent was never
conquered, and that they were the freest people of England. And
upon these vain noises, they looked for great matters at their
hands, in a cause which they conceited to be for the liberty of the
subject. But when they were come into Kent, the country was so
well settled, both by the King's late kind usage towards them,
and by the credit and power of the Earl of Kent, the Lord Abergavenny, and the Lord Cobham, as neither gentleman nor yeo-
man came in to their aid; which did much damp and dismay many
of the simpler sort; insomuch as divers of them did secretly fly
from the army and went home; but the sturdier sort, and those
that were most engaged, stood by it, and rather waxed proud
than failed in hopes and courage. For as it did somewhat appall
them, that the people came not in to them; so it did no less encourage them, that the King's forces had not set upon them, hav-

ing marched from the west unto the east of England. Wherefore
they kept on their way, and encamped upon Blackheath, between
Greenwich and Eltham; threatening either to bid battle to the
King (for now the seas went higher than to Morton and Bray),
or to take London within his view; imagining with themselves
there to find no less fear than wealth.

But to return to the King. When first he heard of this commotion of the Cornishmen occasioned by the subsidy, he was
much troubled therewith; not for itself, but in regard of the concurrence of other dangers that did hang over him at that time.
For he doubted lest a war from Scotland, a rebellion from Cornwall, and the practices and conspiracies of Perkin and his partakers, would come upon him at once: knowing well that it was a
dangerous triplicity to a monarchy, to have the arms of a foreigner, the discontents of subjects, and the title of a pretender to
meet. Nevertheless the occasion took him in some part well provided. For as soon as the Parliament had broken up, the King had
presently raised a puissant army to war upon Scotland. And King
James of Scotland likewise on his part had made great preparations, either for defence or for new assailing of England. But as
for the King's forces, they were not only in preparation, but in
readiness presently to set forth, under the conduct of Dawbeney
the Lord Chamberlain. But as soon as the King understood of the
rebellion of Cornwall, he stayed those forces, retaining them for
his own service and safety. But therewithal he dispatched the
Earl of Surrey into the north, for the defence and strength of
those parts, in case the Scots should stir. But for the course he
held towards the rebels, it was utterly differing from his former
custom and practice; which was ever full of forwardness and
celerity to make head against them, or to set upon them as soon
as ever they were in action. This he was wont to do. But now,
besides that he was attempered by years, and less in love with
dangers by the continued fruition of a crown, it was a time when
the various appearance to his thoughts of perils of several natures
and from divers parts did make him judge it his best and surest
way to keep his strength together in the seat and centre of his
kingdom. According to the ancient Indian emblem—in such a

swelling season, to hold the hand upon the middle of the bladder, that no side might rise. Besides, there was no necessity put upon him to alter this counsel. For neither did the rebels spoil the country, in which case it had been dishonour to abandon his people; neither on the other side did their forces gather or increase, which might hasten him to precipitate, and assail them before they grew too strong. And lastly, both reason of estate and war seemed to agree with this course: for that insurrections of base people are commonly more furious in their beginnings. And by this means also he had them the more at vantage, being tired and harassed with a long march; and more at mercy, being cut off far from their country, and therefore not able by any sudden flight to get to retreat, and to renew the troubles.

When therefore the rebels were encamped on Blackheath, upon the hill, whence they might behold the city of London, and the fair valley about it; the King, knowing well that it stood him upon, by how much the more he had hitherto protracted the time in not encountering them, by so much the sooner to dispatch with them; that it might appear to have been no coldness in foreslowing but wisdom in choosing his time; resolved with all speed to assail them; and yet with that providence and surety as should leave little to venture or fortune. And having very great and puissant forces about him, the better to master all events and accidents, he divided them into three parts. The first was led by the Earl of Oxford in chief, assisted by the Earls of Essex and Suffolk. These noblemen were appointed, with some cornets of horse and bands of foot, and good store of artillery wheeling about, to put themselves beyond the hill where the rebels were encamped, and to beset all the skirts and descents thereof, except those that lay towards London; thereby to have these wild beasts as it were in a toil. The second part of his forces (which were those that were to be most in action, and upon which he relied most for the fortune of the day) he did assign to be led by the Lord Chamberlain, who was appointed to set upon the rebels in front, from that side which is towards London. The third part of his forces (being likewise great and brave forces) he retained about himself, to be ready upon all events, to restore the fight or consummate the

victory; and meanwhile to secure the city. And for that purpose
he encamped in person in Saint George's Fields, putting himself
between the city and the rebels.

But the City of London (especially at the first) upon the near
encamping of the rebels, was in great tumult; as it useth to be with
wealthy and populous cities, especially those which, being for
greatness and fortune queens of their regions, do seldom see out
of their windows or from their towers an army of enemies. But
that which troubled them most was the conceit that they dealt
with a rout of people, with whom there was no composition or
condition, or orderly treating, if need were; but likely to be bent
altogether upon rapine and spoil. And although they had heard
that the rebels had behaved themselves quietly and modestly by
the way as they went; yet they doubted much,[38] That would not
last, but rather make them more hungry, and more in appetite to
fall upon spoil in the end. Wherefore there was great running to
and fro of people, some to the gates, some to the walls, some to
the water-side; giving themselves alarms and panic fears continually. Nevertheless both Tate the Lord Mayor and Shaw and
Haddon the Sheriffs did their parts stoutly and well, in arming and
ordering the people; and the King likewise did adjoin some captains of experience in the wars to advise and assist the citizens.
But soon after, when they understood that the King had so ordered
the matter, that the rebels must win three battles before they
could approach the city, and that he had put his own person between the rebels and them, and that the great care was rather how
to impound the rebels that none of them might escape, than that
any doubt was made to vanquish them; they grew to be quiet and
out of fear; the rather for the confidence they reposed (which was
not small) in the three leaders, Oxford, Essex, and Dawbeney; all
men well famed and loved amongst the people. As for Jasper Duke
of Bedford, whom the King used to employ with the first in his
wars, he was then sick, and died soon after.

It was the two and twentieth of June, and a Saturday (which
was the day of the week the King fancied), when the battle was

---

[38] [The statement following is in indirect discourse.]

fought; though the King had, by all the art he could devise, given out a false day, as if he prepared to give the rebels battle on the Monday following, the better to find them unprovided and in disarray. The lords that were appointed to circle the hill, had some days before planted themselves (as at the receipt) in places convenient. In the afternoon towards the decline of the day, (which was done the better to keep the rebels in opinion that they should not fight that day,) the Lord Dawbeney marched on towards them, and first beat some troops of them from Deptford-bridge; where they fought manfully; but being in no great number were soon driven back, and fled up to their main army upon the hill. The army at that time hearing of the approach of the King's forces, were putting themselves in array, not without much confusion. But neither had they placed upon the first high ground towards the bridge any forces to second the troops below that kept the bridge; neither had they brought forwards their main battle (which stood in array far into the heath) near to the ascent of the hill; so that the Earl with his forces mounted the hill and recovered [gained] the plain without resistance. The Lord Dawbeney charged them with great fury; insomuch as it had like by accident to have brandled [endangered] the fortune of the day. For by inconsiderate forwardness in fighting in the head of his troops, he was taken by the rebels, but immediately rescued and delivered. The rebels maintained the fight for a small time, and for their persons shewed no want of courage; but being ill armed and ill led and without horse or artillery, they were with no great difficulty cut in pieces and put to flight. And for their three leaders, the Lord Audley, the blacksmith, and Flammock, (as commonly the captains of commotions are but half-couraged men,) suffered themselves to be taken alive. The number slain on the rebels' part were some two thousand men; their army amounting (as it is said) unto the number sixteen thousand. The rest were (in effect) all taken; for that the hill (as was said) was encompassed with the King's forces round about. On the King's part there died about three hundred, most of them shot with arrows, which were reported to be of the length of a taylor's yard; so strong and mighty a bow the Cornishmen were said to draw.

The victory thus obtained, the King created divers bannerets, as well upon Blackheath, where his lieutenant had won the field, (whither he rode in person to perform the said creation) as in St. George's Fields, where his own person had been encamped. And for matter of liberality, he did by open edict give the goods of all the prisoners unto those that had taken them; either to take them in kind or compound for them as they could. After matter of honour and liberality, followed matter of severity and execution. The Lord Audley was led from Newgate to Tower Hill, in a paper coat painted with his own arms; the arms reversed, the coat torn; and at Tower Hill beheaded. Flammock and the blacksmith were hanged, drawn and quartered at Tyburn: the blacksmith taking pleasure upon the hurdle (as it seemeth by words that he uttered) to think that he should be famous in after-times. The King was once in mind to have sent down Flammock and the blacksmith to have been executed in Cornwall, for the more terror. But being advertised that the country was yet unquiet and boiling, he thought better not to irritate the people further. All the rest were pardoned by proclamation, and to take out their pardons under seal as many as would. So that more than the blood drawn in the field, the King did satisfy himself with the lives of only three offenders for the expiation of this great rebellion.

It was a strange thing to observe the variety and inequality of the King's executions and pardons: and a man would think it at the first a kind of lottery or chance. But looking into it more nearly, one shall find there was reason for it; much more perhaps, than after so long a distance of time we can now discern. In the Kentish commotion (which was but an handful of men) there were executed to the number of one hundred and fifty; and in this so mighty a rebellion but three. Whether it were that the King put to account the men that were slain in the field; or that he was not willing to be severe in a popular cause; or that the harmless behaviour of this people (that came from the west of England to the east without mischief, almost, or spoil of the country) did somewhat mollify him and move him to compassion; or lastly, that he made a great difference between people that did rebel upon wantonness, and them that did rebel upon want.

After the Cornishmen were defeated, there came from Calais to the King an honourable ambassage from the French King, which had arrived at Calais a month before, and was there stayed in respect of the troubles; but honourably entertained and defrayed. The King at their first coming sent unto them, and prayed them to have patience, till a little smoke that was raised in his country, were over; which would soon be: slighting (as his manner was) that openly, which nevertheless he intended seriously. This ambassage concerned no great affair, but only the prolongation of days for payment of money, and some other particulars of the frontiers. And it was indeed but a wooing ambassage, with good respects to entertain the King in good affection: but nothing was done or handled to the derogation of the King's late treaty with the Italians.

But during the time that the Cornishmen were in their march towards London, the King of Scotland (well advertised of all that passed and knowing himself sure of a war from England whensoever those stirs were appeased) neglected not his opportunity; but thinking the King had his hands full, entered the frontiers of England again with an army, and besieged the castle of Norham in person with part of his forces, sending the rest to forage the country. But Foxe Bishop of Duresme [Durham] (a wise man, and one that could see through the present to the future) doubting as much before, had caused his castle of Norham to be strongly fortified, and furnished with all kind of munition; and had manned it likewise with a very great number of tall soldiers, more than for the proportion of the castle, reckoning rather upon a sharp assault than a long siege. And for the country likewise, he had caused the people to withdraw their cattle and goods into fast places, that were not of easy approach; and sent in post to the Earl of Surrey (who was not far off in Yorkshire) to come in diligence to the succour. So as the Scottish King both failed of doing good upon the castle, and his men had but a catching harvest of their spoils. And when he understood that the Earl of Surrey was coming on with great forces, he returned back into Scotland. The Earl finding the castle freed, and the enemy retired, pursued with all celerity into Scotland; hoping to have overtaken the Scottish King, and to have given him battle. But not attaining him in time, sat down before the castle of Aton, one of the strongest places (then esteemed) between Berwick and Edinburgh, which in a small time he took. And soon after the Scottish King retiring further into his country, and the weather being extraordinary foul and stormy, the Earl returned into England. So that the expeditions on both parts were (in effect) but a castle taken and a castle distressed; not answerable to the puissance of the forces, nor to the heat of the quarrel, nor to the greatness of the expectation.

Amongst these troubles both civil and external, came into England from Spain, Peter Hialas, some call him Elias (surely he was the forerunner of the good hap that we enjoy at this day: for his ambassage set the truce between England and Scotland; the truce drew on the peace; the peace the marriage; and the marriage the union of the kingdoms); a man of great wisdom, and (as those times were) not unlearned; sent from Ferdinando and Isabella, Kings of Spain, unto the King, to treat a marriage between Katherine, their second daughter, and Prince Arthur. This treaty was by him set in a very good way, and almost brought to perfection. But it so fell out by the way, that upon some conference which he had with the King touching this business, the King (who had a great dexterity in getting suddenly into the bosom of ambassadors of foreign Princes, if he liked the men; insomuch as he would many times communicate with them of his own affairs, yea and employ them in his service,) fell into speech and discourse incidently, concerning the ending of the debates and differences with Scotland. For the King naturally did not love the barren wars with Scotland, though he made his profit of the noise of them: and he wanted not in the council of Scotland those that would advise their King to meet him at the half way, and to give over the war with England; pretending to be good patriots, but indeed favouring the affairs of the King. Only his heart was too great to begin with Scotland for the motion of peace. On the other side, he had met with an ally of Ferdinando of Arragon, as fit for his turn as could be. For after that King Ferdinando had, upon assured confidence of the marriage to succeed, taken upon him the person of a fraternal ally to the King, he would not let, in a Spanish gravity, to counsel the King in his own affairs. And the King on his part not being wanting to himself, but making use of every man's humours, made his advantage of this in such things as he thought either not decent or not pleasant to proceed from himself; putting them off as done by the counsel of Ferdinando: wherefore he was content that Hialas (as in a matter moved and advised from Hialas himself) should go into Scotland, to treat of a concord between the two Kings. Hialas took it upon him: and coming to the Scottish King, after he had with much art brought King James to hearken to the more safe and quiet counsels, writ unto the King that he hoped that peace would with no great difficulty cement and close, if he would send some wise and temperate councillor of his own, that might treat of the conditions. Whereupon the King directed Bishop Foxe (who at that time was at his castle of Norham) to confer with Hialas, and they both to treat with some commissioners deputed from the Scottish King. The commissioners on both sides met. But after much dispute upon the articles and conditions of peace propounded upon either part, they could not conclude a peace. The chief impediment thereof was the demand of the King to have Perkin delivered into his hands; as a reproach to all Kings, and a person not protected by the law of nations. The King of Scotland on the other side peremptorily denied so to do; saying that he for his part was no competent judge of Perkin's title: but that he had received him as a suppliant, protected him as a person fled for refuge, espoused him with his kinswoman, and aided him with his arms, upon the belief that he was a Prince; and therefore that he could not now with his honour so unrip and in a sort put a lie upon all that he had said and done before, as to deliver him up to his enemies. The Bishop likewise (who had certain proud instructions from the King, at the least in the front, though there were a pliant clause at the foot, that remitted all to the Bishop's discretion, and required him by no means to break off in ill terms,) after that he had failed to obtain the delivery of Perkin, did move a second point of his instructions; which was, that the Scottish King would give the King an interview in person at Newcastle. But this being reported to the Scottish King, his answer was, *That he meant to treat a peace, and not*

to go a begging for it. The Bishop also (according to another article of his instructions) demanded restitution of the spoils taken
by the Scottish, or damages for the same. But the Scottish commissioners answered, *That that was but as water spilt upon the
ground, which could not be gotten up again; and that the King's
people were better able to bear the loss than their master to repair
it.* But in the end (as persons capable of reason on both sides) they
made rather a kind of recess than a breach of treaty, and concluded upon a truce for some months following. But the King of
Scotland, though he would not formally retract his judgment of
Perkin, wherein he had engaged himself so far; yet in his private
opinion, upon often speech with the Englishmen and divers other
advertisements, began to suspect him for a counterfeit; wherefore
in a noble fashion he called him unto him, and recounted the
benefits and favours that he had done him in making him his ally,
and in provoking a mighty and opulent King by an offensive war
in his quarrel, for the space of two years together; nay more, that
he had refused an honourable peace, whereof he had a fair offer if
he would have delivered him; and that to keep his promise with
him, he had deeply offended both his nobles and people, whom he
might not hold in any long discontent. And therefore required
him to think of his own fortunes, and to choose out some fitter
place for his exile: telling him withal that he could not say but the
English had forsaken him before the Scottish; for that upon two
several trials, none had declared themselves on his side. But nevertheless he would make good what he said to him at his first receiving, which was *That he should not repent him for putting
himself into his hands;* for that he would not cast him off, but
help him with shipping and means to transport him where he
should desire. Perkin, not descending at all from his stage-like
greatness, answered the King in few words; *That he saw his time
was not yet come; but whatsoever his Fortunes were, he should
both think and speak Honour of the King.* Taking his leave, he
would not think on Flanders, doubting it was but hollow ground
for him since the treaty of the Archduke concluded the year before; but took his lady, and such followers as would not leave
him, and sailed over into Ireland.

This twelfth year of the King a little before this time, Pope
Alexander (who loved best those Princes that were furthest off
and with whom he had least to do) taking very thankfully the
King's late entrance into league for the defence of Italy, did remunerate him with an hallowed sword and cap of maintenance,
sent by his Nuncio. Pope Innocent had done the like, but it was
not received in that glory. For the King appointed the Mayor and
his brethren to meet the Pope's orator at London Bridge, and all
the streets between the bridge-foot and the palace of Paul's (where
the King then lay) were garnished with the citizens, standing in
their liveries. And the morrow after (being Allhallown-day) the
King, attended with many of his prelates, nobles, and principal
courtiers, went in procession to Paul's, and the cap and sword
were borne before him. And after the procession, the King himself
remaining seated in the quire, the Lord Archbishop upon the
greese of the quire[39] made a long oration, setting forth the greatness and eminency of that honour which the Pope (in these ornaments and ensigns of benediction) had done the King; and how
rarely and upon what high deserts they used to be bestowed: and
then recited the King's principal acts and merits, which had made
him appear worthy in the eyes of his Holiness of this great honour.

All this while the rebellion of Cornwall (whereof we have
spoken) seemed to have no relation to Perkin; save that perhaps
Perkin's proclamation had stricken upon the right vein, in promising to lay down exactions and payments; and so had made them
now and then have a kind thought on Perkin. But now these bub-
bles by much stirring began to meet, as they use to do upon the
top of water. The King's lenity (by that time the Cornish rebels,
who were taken and pardoned, and as it was said, many of them
sold by them that had taken them for twelve pence and two shillings apiece, were come down into their country) had rather em-
boldened them than reclaimed them. Insomuch as they stuck not
to say to their neighbours and countrymen that *The King did well
to pardon them; for that he knew he should leave few subjects in
England, if he hanged all that were of their mind:* and began whet-

[39] [steps of the choir]

ting and inciting one another to renew the commotion. Some of the
subtlest of them, hearing of Perkin's being in Ireland, found
means to send to him to let him know that if he would come over
to them they would serve him.

When Perkin heard this news, he began to take heart again,
and advised upon it with his council, which were principally three:
Herne a mercer that had fled for debt; Skelton a taylor, and Astley
a scrivener; for secretary Frion was gone. These told him that he
was mightily overseen both when he went into Kent and when he
went into Scotland: the one being a place so near London, and
under the King's nose; and the other a nation so distasted with
the people of England, that if they had loved him never so well,
yet they would never have taken his part in that company. But if
he had been so happy as to have been in Cornwall at the first,
when the people began to take arms there, he had been crowned
at Westminster before this time. For these Kings (as he had now
experience) would sell poor princes for shoes: but he must rely
wholly upon people; and therefore advised him to sail over with
all possible speed into Cornwall. Which accordingly he did; having in his company four small barks, with some sixscore or seven-
score fighting-men. He arrived in September at Whitsand-Bay,
and forthwith came to Bodmin, the blacksmith's town; where
there assembled unto him to the number of three thousand men of
the rude people. There he set forth a new proclamation, stroking
the people with fair promises, and humouring them with invectives against the King and his government. And as it fareth with
smoke that never looseth itself till it be at the highest, he did now
before his end raise his stile [style], intitling himself no more
Richard Duke of York, but Richard the Fourth, King of England.
His council advised him by all means to make himself master of
some good walled town; as well to make his men find the sweetness of rich spoils, and to allure to him all loose and lost people
by like hopes of booty; as to be a sure retreat to his forces, in case
they should have any ill day or unlucky chance in the field.
Wherefore they took heart to them, and went on and besieged the
city of Exeter, the principal town for strength and wealth in those
parts.

When they were come before Exeter, they forbore to use any force at the first, but made continual shouts and outcries to terrify the inhabitants. They did likewise in divers places call and talk to them from under the walls, to join with them, and be of their party; telling them that the King [Richard] would make them another London, if they would be the first town that should acknowledge him. But they had not the wit to send to them, in any orderly fashion, agents or chosen men to tempt them and to treat with them. The citizens on their part shewed themselves stout and loyal subjects. Neither was there so much as any tumult or division amongst them, but all prepared themselves for a valiant defence, and making good the town. For well they saw that the rebels were of no such number or power that they needed to fear them as yet: and well they hoped that before their numbers increased the King's succours would come in. And howsoever, they thought it the extremest of evils to put themselves at the mercy of those hungry and disorderly people. Wherefore setting all things in good order within the town, they nevertheless let down with cords from several parts of the walls privily, several messengers (that if one came to mischance another might pass on), which should advertise the King of the state of the town, and implore his aid. Perkin also doubted that succours would come ere long, and therefore resolved to use his utmost force to assault the town. And for that purpose having mounted scaling-ladders in divers places upon the walls, made at the same instant an attempt to force one of the gates. But having no artillery nor engines, and finding that he could do no good by ramming with logs of timber, nor by the use of iron bars and iron crows and such other means at hand, he had no way left him but to set one of the gates on fire; which he did. But the citizens well perceiving the danger, before the gate could be fully consumed, blocked up the gate and some space about it on the inside with faggots and other fuel, which they likewise set on fire, and so repulsed fire with fire; and in the mean time raised up rampiers of earth, and cast up deep trenches, to serve instead of wall and gate. And for the escaladaes, they had so bad success, as the rebels were driven from the walls with the loss of two hundred men.

The King when he heard of Perkin's siege of Exeter, made sport with it, and said to them that were about him, *That the King of rake-hells was landed in the west, and that he hoped now to have the honour to see him, which he could never yet do.* And it appeared plainly to those that were about the King, that he was indeed much joyed with the news of Perkin's being in English ground, where he could have no retreat by land; thinking now, that he should be cured of those privy stitches, which he had long had about his heart, and had sometimes broken his sleeps in the midst of all his felicity. And to set all men's hearts on fire, he did by all possible means let it appear, that those that should now do him service to make an end of these troubles, should be no less accepted of him than he that came upon the eleventh hour and had the whole wages of the day. Therefore now (like the end of a play) a great number came upon the stage at once. He sent the Lord Chamberlain, and the Lord Brooke, and Sir Rice ap Thomas, with expedite forces to speed to Exeter to the rescue of the town, and to spread the fame of his own following in person with a royal army. The Earl of Devonshire and his son, with the Carews and the Fulfordes and other principal persons of Devonshire (uncalled from the court, but hearing that the King's heart was so much bent upon this service), made haste with troops that they had raised to be the first that should succour the city of Exeter, and prevent the King's succours. The Duke of Buckingham likewise, with many brave gentlemen, put themselves in arms, not staying either the King's or Lord Chamberlain's coming on, but making a body of forces of themselves, the more to endear their merit; signifying to the King their readiness, and desiring to know his pleasure. So that according to the proverb, In the coming down every Saint did help.

Perkin hearing this thunder of arms and preparations against him from so many parts, raised his siege and marched to Taunton, beginning already to squint one eye upon the crown and another upon the sanctuary; though the Cornishmen were become like metal often fired and quenched, churlish, and that would sooner break than bow; swearing and vowing not to leave him till the uttermost drop of their blood were spilt. He was at his rising from

Exeter between six and seven thousand strong, many having come
unto him after he was set before Exeter, upon fame of so great an
enterprise, and to partake of the spoil; though upon the raising of
the siege some did slip away. When he was come near Taunton, he
dissembled all fear, and seemed all the day to use diligence in
preparing all things ready to fight. But about midnight he fled
with threescore horse to Bewley in the New Forest, where he and
divers of his company registered themselves sanctuary-men, leaving his Cornishmen to the four winds; but yet thereby easing them
of their vow; and using his wonted compassion, not to be by
when his subjects' blood should be spilt. The King, as soon as he
heard of Perkin's flight, sent presently five hundred horse to pursue and apprehend him, before he should get either to the sea or
to that same little island called a sanctuary. But they came too late
for the latter of these. Therefore all they could do was to beset the
sanctuary, and to maintain a strong watch about it, till the King's
pleasure were further known. As for the rest of the rebels, they
(being destituted of their head) without stroke stricken submitted
themselves unto the King's mercy. And the King who commonly
drew blood (as physicians do) rather to save life than to spill it,
and was never cruel when he was secure; now he saw the danger
was past, pardoned them all in the end, except some few desperate
persons, which he reserved to be executed, the better to set off his
mercy towards the rest. There were also sent with all speed some
horse to Saint Michael's Mount in Cornwall, where the Lady
Katherine Gordon was left by her husband, whom in all fortunes
she entirely loved; adding the virtues of a wife to the virtues of her
sex. The King sent in the greater diligence, not knowing whether
she might be with child, whereby the business would not have
ended in Perkin's person. When she was brought to the King, it
was commonly said that the King received her not only with compassion but with affection; pity giving more impression to her
excellent beauty. Wherefore comforting her, to serve as well his
eye as his fame, he sent her to his Queen, to remain with her;
giving her very honourable allowance for the support of her estate, which she enjoyed both during the King's life and many
years after. The name of the White Rose, which had been given

to her husband's false title, was continued in common speech to her true beauty.

The King went forwards on his journey, and made a joyful entrance into Exeter, where he gave the citizens great commendations and thanks; and taking the sword he wore from his side, he gave it to the Mayor, and commanded it should be ever after carried before him. There also he caused to be executed some of the ringleaders of the Cornishmen, in sacrifice to the citizens; whom they had put in fear and trouble. At Exeter the King consulted with his council, whether he should offer life to Perkin if he would quit the sanctuary and voluntarily submit himself. The council were divided in opinion. Some advised the King to take him out of sanctuary perforce, and to put him to death, as in a case of necessity, which in itself dispenseth with consecrated places and things; wherein they doubted not also but the King should find the Pope tractable to ratify his deed, either by declaration or at least by indulgence. Others were of opinion, since all was now safe and no further hurt could be done, that it was not worth the exposing of the King to new scandal and envy. A third sort fell upon the opinion that it was not possible for the King ever either to satisfy the world well touching the imposture or to learn out the bottom of the conspiracy, except by promise of life and pardon and other fair means he should get Perkin into his hands. But they did all in their preambles much bemoan the King's case, with a kind of indignation at his fortune; that a Prince of his high wisdom and virtue should have been so long and so oft exercised and vexed with idols. But the King said that it was the vexation of God Almighty himself to be vexed with idols, and therefore that that was not to trouble any of his friends: and that for himself he always despised them, but was grieved that they had put his people to such trouble and misery. But (in conclusion) he leaned to the third opinion, and so sent some to deal with Perkin; who seeing himself a prisoner and destitute of all hopes, having tried princes and people, great and small, and found all either false, faint, or unfortunate, did gladly accept of the condition. The King did also while he was at Exeter appoint the Lord Darcy and others commissioners for the fining of all such as were of any value, and had any hand or partaking in the aid or comfort of Perkin or the Cornishmen, either in the field or in the flight.

These commissioners proceeded with such strictness and severity, as did much obscure the King's mercy in sparing of blood, with the bleeding of so much treasure. Perkin was brought unto the King's court, but not to the King's presence; though the King to satisfy his curiosity saw him sometimes out of a window or in passage. He was in shew at liberty, but guarded with all care and watch that was possible, and willed to follow the King to London. But from his first appearance upon the stage in his new person of a sycophant or juggler, instead of his former person of a Prince, all men may think how he was exposed to the derision not only of the courtiers but also of the common people, who flocked about him as he went along (that one might know afar off where the owl was, by the flight of birds), some mocking, some wondering, some cursing, some prying and picking matter out of his countenance and gesture to talk of. So that the false honour and respects which he had so long enjoyed was plentifully repaid in scorn and contempt. As soon as he was come to London, the King gave also the City the solace of this May-game. For he was conveyed leisurely on horseback, but not in any ignominious fashion, through Cheapside and Cornhill to the Tower, and from thence back again unto Westminster, with the churmne [babble] of a thousand taunts and reproaches. But to amend the show, there followed a little distance off Perkin, an inward counsellor of his, one that had been serjeant farrier to the King. This fellow, when Perkin took sanctuary, chose rather to take a holy habit than a holy place, and clad himself like an hermit, and in that weed wandered about the country, till he was discovered and taken. But this man was bound hand and foot upon the horse, and came not back with Perkin, but was left at the Tower, and within few days after executed. Soon after, now that Perkin could tell better what himself was, he was diligently examined; and after his confession taken, an extract was made of such parts of them as were thought fit to be divulged; which was printed and dispersed abroad. Wherein the King did himself no right: for as there was a laboured tale of particulars of Perkin's father and mother and grandsire and grandmother and uncles and cousins, by names and surnames, and from what places he travelled up and down; so there was little or nothing to purpose of any thing concerning his designs, or any practices that had been held with him; nor the Duchess of Burgundy herself (that all the world did take knowledge of as the person that had put life and being into the whole business) so much as named or pointed at; so that men missing of that they looked for, looked about for they knew not what, and were in more doubt than before. But the King chose rather not to satisfy than to kindle coals. At that time also it did not appear by any new examinations or commitments that any other person of quality was discovered or appeached, though the King's closeness made that a doubt dormant.

About this time a great fire in the night-time suddenly began at the King's palace of Shyne, near unto the King's own lodgings, whereby a great part of the building was consumed, with much costly household-stuff; which gave the King occasion of building from the ground that fine pile of Richmond, which is now standing.

Somewhat before this time also, there fell out a memorable accident. There was one Sebastian Gabato [Cabot], a Venetian, dwelling in Bristow, a man seen and expert in cosmography and navigation. This man seeing the success and emulating perhaps the enterprise of Christopherus Columbus in that fortunate discovery towards the south-west, which had been by him made some six years before, conceited with himself that lands might likewise be discovered towards the north-west. And surely it may be he had more firm and pregnant conjectures of it than Columbus had of his at the first. For the two great islands of the old and new world, being (in the shape and making of them) broad towards the north and pointed towards the south, it is likely that the discovery first began where the lands did nearest meet. And there had been before that time a discovery of some lands, which they took to be islands, and were indeed the continent of America, towards the north-west. And it may be, that some relation of this nature coming afterwards to the knowledge of Columbus, and by him suppressed (desirous rather to make his enterprise the child

of his science and fortune than the follower of a former discovery), did give him better assurance that all was not sea from the
west of Europe and Africke unto Asia, than either Seneca's prophecy, or Plato's antiquities, or the nature of the tides and land-
winds and the like, which were the conjectures that were given
out, whereupon he should have relied; though I am not ignorant
that it was likewise laid unto the casual and wind-beaten discovery (a little before) of a Spanish pilot who died in the house of
Columbus. But this Gabato bearing the King in hand that he
would find out an island endued with rich commodities, procured
him to man and victual a ship at Bristow for the discovery of that
island: with whom ventured also three small ships of London merchants, fraught with some gross and slight wares, fit for commerce
with barbarous people. He sailed (as he affirmed at his return and
made a card thereof), very far westwards, with a quarter of the
north, on the north side of Terra de Labrador, until he came to the
latitude of sixty-seven degrees and a half, finding the seas still
open. It is certain also that the King's fortune had a tender of that
great empire of the West-Indies. Neither was it a refusal on the
King's part, but a delay by accident, that put by so great an ac-
quest. For Christopherus Columbus, refused by the King of Portugal (who would not embrace at once both east and west), employed his brother Bartholomeus Columbus unto King Henry to
negotiate for his discovery. And it so fortuned that he was taken
by pirates at sea, by which accidental impediment he was long ere
he came to the King; so long, that before he had obtained a capitu-
lation with the King for his brother the enterprise by him was
achieved, and so the West-Indies by providence were then reserved for the crown of Castilia. Yet this sharpened the King so,
that not only in this voyage, but again in the sixteenth year of his
reign, and likewise in the eighteenth thereof, he granted forth
new commissions for the discovery and investing of unknown
lands.

In this fourteenth year also (by God's wonderful providence,
that boweth things unto his will, and hangeth great weights upon
small wires) there fell out a trifling and untoward accident, that
drew on great and happy effects. During the truce with Scotland,

there were certain Scottish young gentlemen that came into
Norham town, and there made merry with some of the English of
the town; and having little to do, went sometimes forth, and
would stand looking upon the castle. Some of the garrison of the
castle, observing this their doing twice or thrice, and having not
their minds purged of the late ill blood of hostility, either suspected them or quarrelled [accused] them for spies. Whereupon
they fell at ill words, and from words to blows, so that many were
wounded of either side, and the Scottishmen, being strangers in
the town, had the worst; insomuch that some of them were slain,
and the rest made haste home. The matter being complained on,
and often debated before the Wardens of Marches of both sides,
and no good order taken, the King of Scotland took it to himself,
and being much kindled, sent a herald to the King to make protestation that if reparation were not done, according to the conditions of the truce, his King did denounce war. The King (who
had often tried fortune and was inclined to peace) made answer
that what had been done was utterly against his will and without
his privity; but if the garrison soldiers had been in fault, he would
see them punished, and the truce in all points to be preserved.
But this answer seemed to the Scottish King but a delay, to make
the complaint breathe out with time; and therefore it did rather
exasperate him than satisfy him. Bishop Foxe, understanding from
the King that the Scottish King was still discontent and impatient,
being troubled that the occasion of breaking the truce should
grow from his men, sent many humble and deprecatory letters to
the Scottish King to appease him. Whereupon King James, mollified by the Bishop's submiss and eloquent letters, writ back unto
him, that though he were in part moved by his letters, yet he
should not be fully satisfied except he spake with him; as well
about the compounding of the present differences, as about other
matters that might concern the good of both kingdoms. The
Bishop, advising first with the King, took his journey for Scotland. The meeting was at Melrosse, an abbey of the Cistercians,
where the King then abode. The King first roundly uttered unto
the Bishop his offence conceived for the insolent breach of truce
by his men of Norham Castle: whereunto Bishop Foxe made such

an humble and smooth answer, as it was like oil into the wound, whereby it began to heal. And this was done in the presence of the King and his council. After the King spake with the bishop apart, and opened himself unto him, saying that these temporary truces and peaces were soon made and soon broken; but that he desired a straiter amity with the King of England; discovering his mind, that if the King would give him in marriage the Lady Margaret, his eldest daughter, that indeed might be a knot indissoluble. That he knew well what place and authority the Bishop deservedly had with his master. Therefore if he would take the business to heart and deal in it effectually, he doubted not but it would succeed well. The Bishop answered soberly, that he thought himself rather happy than worthy to be an instrument in such a matter, but would do his best endeavour. Wherefore the Bishop returning to the King and giving him account of what had passed and finding the King more than well disposed in it, gave the King advice, first to proceed to a conclusion of peace, and then to go on with the treaty of marriage by degrees. Hereupon a peace was concluded, which was published a little before Christmas, in the fourteenth year of the King's reign, to continue for both the Kings' lives and the over-liver of them and a year after. In this peace there was an article contained, That no Englishman should enter into Scotland, and no Scottishman into England, without letters commendatory from the Kings of either nation. This at the first sight might seem a means to continue a strangeness between the nations; but it was done to lock in the borderers.

This year there was also born to the King a third son, who was christened by the name of Edmond, and shortly after died. And much about the same time came news of the death of Charles the French King: for whom there were celebrated solemn and princely obsequies.

It was not long but Perkin (who was made of quicksilver, which is hard to hold or imprison), began to stir. For deceiving his keepers, he took him to his heels, and made speed to the sea-coast. But presently all corners were laid for him, and such diligent pursuit and search made, as he was fain to turn back and get him to the house of Bethleem, called the Priory of Shyne (which had the privilege of sanctuary), and put himself into the hands of the Prior of that monastery. The Prior was thought an holy man, and much reverenced in those days. He came to the King and besought the King for Perkin's life only, leaving him otherwise to the King's discretion. Many about the King were again more hot than ever to have the King to take him forth and hang him. But the King (that had an high stomach and could not hate any that he despised) bid, *Take him forth and set the knave in the stocks*. And so promising the Prior his life, he caused him to be brought forth. And within two or three days after, upon a scaffold set up in the palace-court at Westminster, he was fettered and set in the stocks for the whole day. And the next day after, the like was done by him at the cross in Cheapside, in both places he read his confession of which we made mention before; and was from Cheapside conveyed and laid up in the Tower. Notwithstanding all this the King was (as was partly touched before) grown to be such a partner with fortune, as no body could tell what actions the one and what the other owned. For it was believed generally that Perkin was betrayed; and that this escape was not without the King's privity, who had him all the time of his flight in a line; and that the King did this to pick a quarrel to him, to put him to death, and to be rid of him at once. But this is not probable. For that the same instruments who observed him in his flight might have kept him from getting into sanctuary.

But it was ordained that this winding-ivy of a Plantagenet should kill the true tree itself. For Perkin after he had been a while in the Tower, began to insinuate himself into the favour and kindness of his keepers, servants to the Lieutenant of the Tower Sir John Digby, being four in number: Strangeways, Blewet, Astwood, and Long-Roger. These varlets with mountains of promises he sought to corrupt, to obtain his escape. But knowing well that his own fortunes were made so contemptible as he could feed no man's hopes (and by hopes he must work, for rewards he had none), he had contrived with himself a vast and tragical plot; which was, to draw into his company Edward Plantagenet Earl of

Warwick, then prisoner in the Tower, whom the weary life of a
long imprisonment, and the often and renewing fears of being
put to death, had softened to take any impression of counsel for
his liberty. This young Prince he thought these servants would
look upon, though not upon himself. And therefore after that by
some message by one or two of them he had tasted of the Earl's
consent, it was agreed that these four should murder their master
the Lieutenant secretly in the night, and make their best of such
money and portable goods of his as they should find ready at
hand; and get the keys of the Tower, and presently to let forth
Perkin and the Earl. But this conspiracy was revealed in time before it could be executed. And in this again the opinion of the
King's great wisdom did surcharge him with a sinister fame, that
Perkin was but his bait to entrap the Earl of Warwick. And in the
very instant while this conspiracy was in working (as if that also
had been the King's industry) it was fatal that there should break
forth a counterfeit Earl of Warwick, a cordwainer's son, whose
name was Ralph Wilford, a young man taught and set on by an
Augustin Friar called Patrick. They both from the parts of Suffolk
came forwards into Kent, where they did not only privily and
underhand give out that this Wilford was the true Earl of Warwick; but also the friar, finding some light credence in the people,
took the boldness in the pulpit to declare as much, and to incite
the people to come in to his aid. Whereupon they were both presently apprehended, and the young fellow executed, and the friar
condemned to perpetual imprisonment. This also happening so
opportunely to represent the danger to the King's estate from the
Earl of Warwick, and thereby to colour the King's severity that
followed; together with the madness of the friar, so vainly and
desperately to divulge a treason before it had gotten any manner
of strength; and the saving of the friar's life, which nevertheless
was indeed but the privilege of his order; and the pity in the common people (which if it run in a strong stream doth ever cast up
scandal and envy), made it generally rather talked than believed
that all was but the King's device. But howsoever it were, hereupon Perkin (that had offended against grace now the third time)
was at the last proceeded with, and by commissioners of Oyer

and Determiner[10] arraigned at Westminster, upon divers treasons committed and perpetrated after his coming on land within this kingdom (for so the judges advised, for that he was a foreigner), and condemned, and a few days after executed at Tyburn; where he did again openly read his confession, and take it upon his death to be true. This was the end of this little cockatrice of a King, that was able to destroy those that did not espy [see through] him first. It was one of the longest plays of that kind that hath been in memory, and might perhaps have had another end, if he had not met with a King both wise, stout, and fortunate.

As for Perkin's three councillors, they had registered themselves sanctuary-men, when their master did; and whether upon pardon obtained or continuance within the privilege, they came not to be proceeded with.

There was executed with Perkin the Mayor of Cork and his son, who had been principal abettors of his treasons. And soon after were likewise condemned eight other persons about the Tower-conspiracy, whereof four were the Lieutenant's men. But of those eight but two were executed. And immediately after was arraigned before the Earl of Oxford (then for the time High Steward of England) the poor Prince the Earl of Warwick; not for the attempt to escape simply (for that was not acted; and besides the imprisonment not being for treason, the escape by law could not be treason), but for conspiring with Perkin to raise sedition, and to destroy the King. And the Earl confessing the indictment had judgment, and was shortly after beheaded on Tower-hill.

This was also the end not only of this noble and commiserable person Edward the Earl of Warwick, eldest son to the Duke of Clarence, but likewise of the line-male of the Plantagenets, which had flourished in great royalty and renown from the time of the famous King of England, King Henry the Second. Howbeit it was a race often dipped in their own blood. It hath remained since only transplanted into other names, as well of the imperial line as

[40] [Such a commission examined prisoners, to hear and determine their cases; it decided whether suspected men should be brought to trial or not.]

of other noble houses. But it was neither guilt of crime, nor reason of state, that could quench the envy that was upon the King for this execution. So that he thought good to export it out of the land, and to lay it upon his new ally Ferdinando King of Spain. For these two Kings understanding one another at half a word, so it was that there were letters shewed out of Spain, whereby in the passages concerning the treaty of the marriage, Ferdinando had written to the King in plain terms that he saw no assurance of his succession as long as the Earl of Warwick lived; and that he was loth to send his daughter to troubles and dangers. But hereby as the King did in some part remove the envy from himself, so he did not observe that he did withal bring a kind of malediction and infausting [ill-luck] upon the marriage, as an ill prognostic. Which in event so far proved true, as both Prince Arthur enjoyed a very small time after the marriage, and the Lady Katherine herself (a sad and a religious woman) long after, when King Henry the Eighth his resolution of a divorce from her was first made known to her, used some words, *That she had not offended, but it was a judgment of God, for that her former marriage was made in blood;* meaning that of the Earl of Warwick.

This fifteenth year of the King, there was a great plague both in London and in divers parts of the kingdom. Wherefore the King after often change of places, whether to avoid the danger of the sickness, or to give occasion of an interview with the Archduke, or both, sailed over with his Queen to Calais. Upon his coming thither the Archduke sent an honourable ambassage unto him, as well to welcome him into those parts, as to let him know that if it pleased him he would come and do him reverence. But it was said withal, that the King might be pleased to appoint some place that were out of any walled town or fortress, for that he had denied the same upon like occasion to the French King. And though he said he made a great difference between the two Kings, yet he would be loth to give a precedent, that might make it after to be expected at his hands by another whom he trusted less. The King accepted of the courtesy, and admitted of his excuse, and appointed the place to be at Saint Peter's Church without Calais. But withal he did visit the Archduke with ambassadors sent from

himself, which were the Lord St. John and the secretary, unto
whom the Archduke did the honour as (going to mass at St.
Omer's) to set the Lord Saint John on his right hand and the
secretary on his left, and so to ride between them to church. The
day appointed for the interview the King went on horseback
some distance from Saint Peter's Church to receive the Archduke.
And upon their approaching, the Archduke made haste to light,
and offered to hold the King's stirrup at his alighting, which the
King would not permit, but descending from horseback, they embraced with great affection. And withdrawing into the church to a
place prepared, they had long conference, not only upon the confirmation of former treaties, and the freeing of commerce, but
upon cross-marriages to be had between the Duke of York the
King's second son, and the Archduke's daughter; and again between Charles the Archduke's son and heir, and Mary the King's
second daughter. But these blossoms of unripe marriages were but
friendly wishes, and the airs of loving entertainment; though one
of them came afterwards to conclusion in treaty, though not in
effect. But during the time that the two Princes conversed and
communed together in the suburbs of Calais, the demonstrations
on both sides were passing hearty and affectionate, especially on
the part of the Archduke; who (besides that he was a Prince of an
excellent good nature) being conscious to himself how drily the
King had been used by his council in the matter of Perkin, did
strive by all means to recover it in the King's affection. And having also his ears continually beaten with the counsels of his father
and father-in-law, who (in respect of their jealous hatred against
the French King) did always advise the Archduke to anchor himself upon the amity of King Henry of England, was glad upon this
occasion to put in ure [use] and practice their precepts, calling the
King patron, and father, and protector, (these very words the
King repeats, when he certified of the loving behaviour of the
Archduke to the city) and what else he could devise to express
his love and observance to the King. There came also to the King
the Governor of Picardy and the Bailiff of Amiens, sent from
Lewis the French King to do him honour, and to give him knowledge of his victory and winning of the duchy of Milan. It seemeth

the King was well pleased with the honours he received from those parts, while he was at Calais; for he did himself certify all the news and occurents of them in every particular from Calais to the Mayor and Aldermen of London, which no doubt made no small talk in the City. For the King, though he could not entertain the good will of the citizens as Edward the Fourth did, yet by affability and other princely graces did ever make very much of them, and apply himself to them.

This year also died John Morton, Archbishop of Canterbury, Chancellor of England, and Cardinal. He was a wise man and an eloquent, but in his nature harsh and haughty, much accepted by the King, but envied by the nobility and hated of the people. Neither was his name left out of Perkin's proclamation for any good will; but they would not bring him in amongst the King's casting counters, because he had the image and superscription upon him of the Pope, in his honour of Cardinal. He wanne [won] the King with secrecy and diligence, but chiefly because he was his old servant in his less fortunes, and also for that (in his affections) he was not without an inveterate malice against the house of York, under whom he had been in trouble. He was willing also to take envy from the King more than the King was willing to put upon him. For the King cared not for subterfuges, but would stand envy, and appear in any thing that was to his mind; which made envy still grow upon him more universal, but less daring. But in the matter of exactions, time did after shew that the Bishop in feeding the King's humour did rather temper it. He had been by Richard the Third committed as in custody to the Duke of Buckingham, whom he did secretly incite to revolt from King Richard. But after the Duke was engaged, and thought the Bishop should have been his chief pilot in the tempest, the Bishop was gotten into the cock-boat, and fled over beyond seas. But whatsoever else was in the man, he deserveth a most happy memory, in that he was the principal means of joining the two Roses. He died of great years, but of strong health and powers.

The next year, which was the sixteenth year of the King and the year of our Lord one thousand five hundred, was the year of jubilee at Rome. But Pope Alexander, to save the hazard and charges of men's journeys to Rome, thought good to make over those graces by exchange to such as would pay a convenient rate, seeing they could not come to fetch them. For which purpose was sent into England Jasper Pons a Spaniard, the Pope's commissioner, better chosen than were the commissioners of Pope Leo afterwards employed for Germany; for he carried the business with great wisdom and semblance of holiness: insomuch as he levied great sums of money within this land to the Pope's use, with little or no scandal. It was thought the King shared in the money. But it appeareth by a letter which Cardinal Adrian, the King's pensioner, writ to the King from Rome some few years after, that this was not so. For this Cardinal, being to persuade Pope Julius on the King's behalf to expedite the bull of dispensation for the marriage between Prince Henry and the Lady Katherine, finding the Pope difficile [reluctant] in granting thereof, doth use it as a principal argument concerning the King's merit towards that see, that he had touched none of those deniers which had been levied by Pons in England. But that it might the better appear (for the satisfaction of the common people) that this was consecrate money, the same nuncio brought unto the King a brief from the Pope, wherein the King was exhorted and summoned to come in person against the Turk. For that the Pope, out of the care of an universal father, seeing almost under his eyes the successes and progresses of that great enemy of the faith, had had in the conclave, and with the assistance of the ambassadors of foreign Princes, divers consultations about a holy war and general expedition of Christian Princes against the Turk. Wherein it was agreed and thought fit, that the Hungarians, Polonians, and Bohemians, should make a war upon Thracia: the French and Spaniards upon Graecia; and that the Pope (willing to sacrifice himself in so good a cause) in person, and in company of the King of England, the Venetians, and such other states as were great in maritime power, would sail with a puissant navy through the Mediterrane unto Constantinople. And that to this end his Holiness had sent nuncios to all Christian Princes, as well for a cessation of all quarrels and differences amongst themselves, as for speedy preparations and contributions of forces and treasure for this sacred enterprise. To this the King (who understood well the court of Rome) made an answer rather solemn than serious. Signifying, "That no Prince on earth should be more forward and obedient both by his person and by all his possible forces and fortunes to enter into this sacred war than himself. But that the distance of place was such, as no forces that he should raise for the seas could be levied or prepared but with double the charge and double the time (at the least) that they might be from the other Princes that had their territories nearer adjoining. Besides, that neither the manner of his ships (having no galleys) nor the experience of his pilots and mariners could be so apt for those seas as theirs. And therefore that his Holiness might do well to move one of those other Kings, who lay fitter for the purpose, to accompany him by sea, whereby both all things would be sooner put in readiness, and with less charge; and the emulation and division of command which might grow between those Kings of France and Spain, if they should both join in the war by land upon Graecia, might be wisely avoided. And that for his part he would not be wanting in aids and contribution. Yet notwithstanding if both these Kings should refuse, rather than his Holiness should go alone, he would wait upon him as soon as he could be ready. Always provided that he might first see all differences of the Christian Princes amongst themselves fully laid down and appeased (as for his own part he was in none). And that he might have some good towns upon the coast in Italy put into his hands, for the retreat and safeguard of his men." With this answer Jasper Pons returned, nothing at all discontented. And yet this declaration of the King (as superficial as it was) gave him that reputation abroad, as he was not long after elected by the Knights of the Rhodes protector of their order; all things multiplying to honour in a prince that had gotten such high estimation for his wisdom and sufficiency.

There were these two last years some proceedings against heretics, which was rare in this King's reign; and rather by penances than by fire. The King had (though he were no good schoolman) the honour to convert one of them by dispute at Canterbury.

This year also, though the King were no more haunted with spirits, for that by the sprinkling partly of blood and partly of water he had chased them away; yet nevertheless he had certain apparitions that troubled him, still shewing themselves from one region, which was the house of York. It came so to pass that the Earl of Suffolk, son to Elizabeth eldest sister to King Edward the Fourth by John Duke of Suffolk her second husband, and brother to John Earl of Lincoln, that was slain at Stoke-field, being of a hasty and choleric disposition, had killed a man in his fury. Whereupon the King gave him his pardon, but either willing to leave a cloud upon him or the better to make him feel his grace, produced him openly to plead his pardon. This wrought in the Earl, as in a haughty stomach it useth to do: for the ignominy printed deeper than the grace. Wherefore he being discontent fled secretly into Flanders unto his aunt the Duchess of Burgundy. The King startled at it. But being taught by troubles to use fair and timely remedies, wrought so with him by messages (the Lady Margaret also growing (by often failing in her alchemy) weary of her experiments, and partly being a little sweetened for that the King had not touched her name in the confession of Perkin,) that he came over again upon good terms, and was reconciled to the King.

In the beginning of the next year, being the seventeenth of the King, the Lady Katherine, fourth daughter of Ferdinando and Isabella, King and Queen of Spain, arrived in England at Plymouth the second of October, and was married to Prince Arthur in Paul's the fourteenth of November following: the Prince being then about fifteen years of age, and the lady about eighteen. The manner of her receiving, the manner of her entry into London, and the celebrity of the marriage, were performed with great and true magnificence, in regard of cost, shew, and order. The chief man that took the care was Bishop Foxe, who was not only a grave counsellor for war or peace, but also a good surveyor of works, and a good master of ceremonies, and any thing else that was fit for the active part belonging to the service of court or state of a great King. This marriage was almost seven years in treaty, which was in part caused by the tender years of the marriage-couple, especially of the Prince. But the true reason was that these two Princes, being Princes of great policy and profound judgment, stood a great time looking one upon another's fortunes, how they would go; knowing well that in the mean time the very treaty itself gave abroad in the world a reputation of a strait conjunction and amity between them, which served on both sides to many purposes that their several affairs required, and yet they continued still free. But in the end, when the fortunes of both the Princes did grow every day more and more prosperous and assured, and that looking all about them they saw no better conditions, they shut it up.

The marriage-money the Princess brought (which was turned over to the King by act of renunciation) was two hundred thousand ducats: whereof one hundred thousand were payable ten days after the solemnization, and the other hundred thousand at two payments annual; but part of it to be in jewels and plate, and a due course set down to have them justly and indifferently priced. The jointure or advancement of the lady, was the third part of the principality of Wales, and the dukedom of Cornwall, and of the earldom of Chester, to be after set forth in severalty. And in case she came to be Queen of England her advancement was left indefinite; but thus, that it should be as great as ever any former Queen of England had.

In all the devices and conceits of the triumphs of this marriage, there was a great deal of astronomy. The lady being resembled to Hesperus, and the Prince to Arcturus; and the old King Alphonsus (that was the greatest astronomer of Kings and was ancestor to the lady) was brought in to be the fortune-teller of the match. And whosoever had those toys in compiling, they were not altogether pedantical. But you may be sure that King Arthur the Briton, and the descent of the Lady Katherine from the house of Lancaster, was in no wise forgotten. But (as it should seem) it is not good to fetch fortunes from the stars. For this young Prince (that drew upon him at that time not only the hopes and affections of his country, but the eyes and expectation of foreigners) after a few months, in the beginning of April, deceased at Ludlow Castle, where he was sent to keep his resiance [residence] and court as Prince of Wales. Of this Prince, in respect he died so young, and by reason of his father's manner of education, that did cast no great lustre upon his children, there is little particular memory.

Only thus much remaineth, that he was very studious and learned beyond his years, and beyond the custom of great Princes.

There was a doubt ripped up in the times following, when the divorce of King Henry the Eighth from the Lady Katherine did so much busy the world, whether Arthur was bedded with his lady or no, whereby that matter in fact (of carnal knowledge) might be made part of the case. And it is true that the lady herself denied it, or at least her counsel stood upon it, and would not blanch [pass over] that advantage; although the plenitude of the Pope's power of dispensing was the main question. And this doubt was kept long open in respect of the two Queens that succeeded, Mary and Elizabeth, whose legitimations were incompatible one with another, though their succession was settled by act of Parliament. And the times that favoured Queen Mary's legitimation would have it believed that there was no carnal knowledge between Arthur and Katherine; not that they would seem to derogate from the Pope's absolute power to dispense even in that case; but only in point of honour, and to make the case more favourable and smooth. And the times that favoured Queen Elizabeth's legitimation (which were the longer and the later) maintained the contrary. So much there remaineth in memory: that it was half a year's time between the creation of Henry Prince of Wales and Prince Arthur's death; which was construed to be, for to expect a full time whereby it might appear whether the Lady Katherine were with child by Prince Arthur or no. Again the lady herself procured a bull for the better corroboration of the marriage, with a clause of (*vel forsan cognitam*) which was not in the first bull. There was given in evidence also when the cause of the divorce was handled, a pleasant passage, which was; that in a morning Prince Arthur upon his up-rising from bed with her called for drink, which he was not accustomed to do, and finding the gentleman of his chamber that brought him the drink to smile at it and to note it, he said merrily to him that he had been in the midst of Spain which was a hot region, and his journey had made him dry; and that if the other had been in so hot a clime he would have been drier than he. Besides the Prince was upon the point of sixteen years of age when he died, and forward, and able in body.

The February following, Henry Duke of York was created
Prince of Wales, and Earl of Chester and Flint. For the dukedom
of Cornwall devolved to him by statute. The King also being fast-
handed and loth to part with a second dowry, but chiefly being
affectionate both by his nature and out of politic considerations to
continue the alliance with Spain, prevailed with the Prince (though
not without some reluctation, such as could be in those years, for
he was not twelve years of age) to be contracted with the Princess
Katherine. The secret providence of God ordaining that marriage
to be the occasion of great events and changes.

The same year were the espousals of James King of Scotland
with the Lady Margaret the King's eldest daughter; which was
done by proxy, and published at Paul's Cross, the five and twentieth of January, and Te Deum solemnly sung. But certain it is,
that the joy of the City thereupon shewed, by ringing of bells and
bonfires and such other incense of the people, was more than could
be expected in a case of so great and fresh enmity between the
nations; especially in London, which was far enough off from feeling any of the former calamities of the war. And therefore might
truly be attributed to a secret instinct and inspiring (which many
times runneth not only in the hearts of Princes but in the pulse
and veins of people) touching the happiness thereby to ensue in
time to come. This marriage was in August following consummate at Edinburgh: the King bringing his daughter as far as Colly-
weston on the way; and then consigning her to the attendance of
the Earl of Northumberland; who with a great troop of lords and
ladies of honour brought her into Scotland to the King her husband.

This marriage had been in treaty by the space of almost three
years, from the time that the King of Scotland did first open his
mind to Bishop Foxe. The sum given in marriage by the King was
ten thousand pounds: and the jointure and advancement assured
by the King of Scotland was two thousand pounds a year after
King James his death, and one thousand pounds a year in present
for the lady's allowance or maintenance, this to be set forth in
lands, of the best and most certain revenue. During the treaty it is

reported that the King remitted the matter to his council, and that some of the table in the freedom of councillors (the King being present) did put the case,—that if God should take the King's two sons without issue, that then the kingdom of England would fall to the King of Scotland, which might prejudice the monarchy of England. Whereunto the King himself replied; That if that should be, Scotland would be but an accession to England, and not England to Scotland, for that the greater would draw the less. And that it was a safer union for England than that of France. This passed as an oracle, and silenced those that moved the question.

The same year was fatal as well for deaths as marriages; and that with equal temper. For the joys and feasts of the two marriages were compensed with the mournings and funerals of Prince Arthur (of whom we have spoken), and of Queen Elizabeth, who died in child-bed in the Tower, and the child lived not long after. There died also that year Sir Reginold Bray, who was noted to have had with the King the greatest freedom of any councillor; but it was but a freedom the better to set off flattery; yet he bare more than his just part of envy for the exactions.

At this time the King's estate was very prosperous: secured by the amity of Scotland; strengthened by that of Spain; cherished by that of Burgundy; all domestic troubles quenched; and all noise of war (like a thunder afar off) going upon Italy. Wherefore nature, which many times is happily contained and refrained by some bands of fortune, began to take place in the King; carrying (as with a strong tide) his affections and thoughts unto the gathering and heaping up of treasure. And as Kings do more easily find instruments for their will and humour than for their service and honour, he had gotten for his purpose, or beyond his purpose, two instruments, Empson and Dudley (whom the people esteemed as his horse-leeches and shearers) bold men and careless of fame, and that took toll of their master's grist. Dudley was of a good family, eloquent, and one that could put hateful business into good language. But Empson, that was the son of a sieve-maker, triumphed always upon the deed done; putting off all other respects whatsoever. These two persons being lawyers in science and privy councillors in authority, (as the corruption of the best things is the worst) turned law and justice into wormwood and rapine. For first their manner was to cause divers subjects to be indicted of sundry crimes, and so far forth to proceed in form of law; but when the bills were found, then presently to commit them; and nevertheless not to produce them in any reasonable time to their answer, but to suffer them to languish long in prison, and by sundry artificial devices and terrors to extort from them great fines and ransoms, which they termed compositions and mitigations.

Neither did they, towards the end, observe so much as the half-face of justice, in proceeding by indictment; but sent forth their precepts to attach men and convent them before themselves and some others at their private houses, in a court of commission; and there used to shuffle up a summary proceeding by examination, without trial of jury; assuming to themselves there to deal both in pleas of the crown and controversies civil.

Then did they also use to inthral and charge the subjects' lands with tenures *in capite,* by finding false offices, and thereby to work upon them for wardships, liveries, premier seisins, and alienations, (being the fruits of those tenures); refusing (upon divers pretexts and delays) to admit men to traverse those false offices, according to the law.[41] Nay the King's wards after they had accomplished their full age could not be suffered to have livery of their lands without paying excessive fines, far exceeding

[41] [Empson and Dudley pretended to find that a man held an office—for example, that he had been granted the right to hold a court —which evidenced his holding his land *in capite.* This meant that the man held directly of the Crown, and royal tenants *in capite* were liable to certain feudal exactions such as wardship (the Crown takes over the land while the heir is under age), livery [relief] (a fee any ward must pay his overlord to gain possession of his lands at the time of his inheritance, amounting to half the first year's profits), premier seisin (the King's right to the first year's profits of newly inherited lands) and alienations (fees [fines] if the land is transferred). It was thus worth a good deal to the Crown to prove that a man held his land *in capite*—which explains why Empson and Dudley also refused to allow the victims to traverse (deny) the claim.]

all reasonable rates. They did also vex men with information of intrusion, upon scarce colourable titles.[42]

When men were outlawed in personal actions, they would not permit them to purchase their charters of pardon, except they paid great and intolerable sums; standing upon the strict point of law, which upon outlawries giveth forfeiture of goods. Nay contrary to all law and colour, they maintained the King ought to have the half of men's lands and rents, during the space of full two years, for a pain in case of outlawry. They would also ruffle with jurors and inforce them to find as they would direct, and (if they did not) convent them, imprison them, and fine them.

These and many other courses, fitter to be buried than repeated, they had of preying upon the people; both like tame hawks for their master, and like wild hawks for themselves; insomuch as they grew to great riches and substance. But their principal working was upon penal laws, wherein they spared none great nor small; nor considered whether the law were possible or impossible, in use or obsolete, but raked over all old and new statutes, though many of them were made with intention rather of terror than of rigour; having ever a rabble of promoters, questmongers, and leading jurors at their command, so as they could have any thing found, either for fact or valuation.

There remaineth to this day a report, that the King was on a time entertained by the Earl of Oxford (that was his principal servant both for war and peace) nobly and sumptuously, at his castle at Henningham. And at the King's going away, the Earl's servants stood in a seemly manner in their livery coats, with cognizances, ranged on both sides, and made the King a lane. The King called the Earl to him, and said, *My lord, I have heard much*

[42] [An information of intrusion is a proceeding to evict a man from property that is claimed by the man instituting the proceeding. Here Empson and Dudley invented royal titles to lands on little evidence, and then tried to force out the "intruders"—who might have been there for generations. Since a case could be expensive to fight, many men would "compound", or pay a fine. So an information of intrusion would certainly vex people; it could also be used to profit the royal treasury (at the price of considerable unpopularity).]

of your hospitality, but I see it is greater than the speech. These
handsome gentlemen and yeomen which I see on both sides of me
are sure your menial servants. The Earl smiled and said, *It may*
please your Grace, that were not for mine ease. They are most of
them my retainers, that are come to do me service at such a time as
this, and chiefly to see your Grace. The King started a little, and
said, *By my faith, (my lord) I thank you for my good cheer, but I*
may not endure to have my laws broken in my sight. My attorney
must speak with you.[43] And it is part of the report, that the Earl
compounded for no less than fifteen thousand marks. And to shew
further the King's extreme diligence; I do remember to have seen
long since a book of accompt of Empson's, that had the King's
hand almost to every leaf by way of signing, and was in some
places postilled in the margent with the King's hand likewise,
where was this remembrance.

Item, Received, of such a one, five marks, for a pardon to be
procured; and if the pardon do not pass, the money to be repaid;
except the party be some other ways satisfied.

And over against this memorandum (of the King's own hand),
    Otherwise satisfied.

Which I do the rather mention because it shews in the King a
nearness, but yet with a kind of justness. So these little sands and
grains of gold and silver (as it seemeth) holp [helped] not a little
to make up the great heap and bank.

But meanwhile to keep the King awake, the Earl of Suffolk,
having been too gay at Prince Arthur's marriage, and sunk himself
deep in debt, had yet once more a mind to be a knight-errant, and

---

[43] [Henry had made a point of enforcing the laws against livery,
that is against dressing men in a private uniform. In the fifteenth
century, livery had been used to build up the private armies which had
been responsible for much of the civil warfare which so disturbed the
country. So Henry was none too pleased to find himself confronted
with Oxford's liveried retainers, despite Oxford's avowal that the
display was mounted in the king's honor.]

to seek adventures in foreign parts; and taking his brother with him fled again into Flanders. That (no doubt) which gave him confidence, was the great murmur of the people against the King's government. And being a man of a light and rash spirit, he thought every vapour would be a tempest. Neither wanted he some party within the kingdom. For the murmur of people awakes the discontents of nobles, and again that calleth up commonly some head of sedition. The King resorting to his wonted and tried arts, caused Sir Robert Curson, captain of the castle at Hammes, (being at that time beyond sea, and therefore less likely to be wrought upon by the King) to fly from his charge and to feign himself a servant of the Earl's. This knight having insinuated himself into the secrets of the Earl, and finding by him upon whom chiefly he had either hope or hold, advertised the King thereof in great secrecy; but nevertheless maintained his own credit and inward trust with the Earl. Upon whose advertisements, the King attached William Courtney Earl of Devonshire, his brother-in-law, married to the Lady Katherine, daughter to King Edward the Fourth; William Delapole, brother to the Earl of Suffolk; Sir James Tirrell and Sir John Windham, and some other meaner persons, and committed them to custody. George Lord Abergavenny and Sir Thomas Green were at the same time apprehended; but as upon less suspicion, so in a freer restraint, and were soon after delivered. The Earl of Devonshire being interessed in the blood of York, (that was rather feared than nocent [dangerous]), yet as one that might be the object of others' plots and designs, remained prisoner in the Tower during the King's life. William Delapole was also long restrained, though not so straitly. But for Sir James Tirrell (against whom the blood of the innocent Princes, Edward the Fifth and his brother, did still cry from under the altar), and Sir John Windham, and the other meaner ones, they were attainted and executed; the two knights beheaded. Nevertheless to confirm the credit of Curson (who belike had not yet done all his feats of activity), there was published at Paul's Cross about the time of the said executions the Pope's bull of excommunication and curse against the Earl of Suffolk and Sir Robert Curson and some others by name, and likewise in general against all the abettors of the said Earl: wherein it must be confessed, that heaven was made too much to bow to earth, and religion to policy. But soon after, Curson (when he saw time) returned into England, and withal into wonted favour with the King, but worse fame with the people. Upon whose return the Earl was much dismayed, and seeing himself destitute of hopes (the Lady Margaret also by tract of time and bad success being now become cool in those attempts), after some wandering in France and Germany, and certain little projects, no better than squibs of an exiled man, being tired out, retired again into the protection of the Archduke Philip in Flanders, who by the death of Isabella was at that time King of Castile, in the right of Joan his wife.

This year, being the nineteenth of his reign, the King called his Parliament; wherein a man may easily guess how absolute the King took himself to be with his Parliament, when Dudley, that was so hateful, was made Speaker of the House of Commons. In this Parliament there were not made many statutes memorable touching public government. But those that were, had still the stamp of the King's wisdom and policy.

There was a statute made for the disannulling of all patents of lease or grant to such as came not upon lawful summons to serve the King in his wars, against the enemies or rebels, or that should depart without the King's licence; with an exception of certain persons of the long-robe [lawyers]. Providing nevertheless that they should have the King's wages from their house, till their return home again. There had been the like made before for offices, and by this statute it was extended to lands. But a man may easily see by many statutes made in this King's time, that the King thought it safest to assist martial law by law of Parliament.

Another statute was made, prohibiting the bringing in of manufactures of silk wrought by itself or mixt with any other thread. But it was not of stuffs of whole-piece (for that the realm had of them no manufacture in use at that time), but of knit silk or texture of silk; as ribbands, laces, cauls, points, and girdles, &c. which the people of England could then well skill to make. This law pointed at a true principle: That where foreign materials are but superfluities, foreign manufactures should be prohibited. For that will either banish the superfluity, or gain the manufacture.

There was a law also of resumption of patents of gaols, and the reannexing of them to the sheriffwicks; privileged officers being no less an interruption of justice than privileged places.[44]

There was likewise a law to restrain the by-laws or ordinances of corporations, which many times were against the prerogative of the King, the common law of the realm, and the liberty of the subject, being fraternities in evil. It was therefore provided that they should not be put in execution, without the allowance of the chancellor, treasurer, and the two chief justices, or three of them; or of the two justices of circuit where the corporation was.

Another law was (in effect) to bring in the silver of the realm to the mint, in making all clipped, minished [diminished] or impaired coins of silver not to be current in payments; without giving any remedy of weight, but with an exception only of reasonable wearing, which was as nothing, in respect of the uncertainty, and so upon the matter to set the mint on work, and to give way to new coins of silver which should be then minted.

There likewise was a long statute against vagabonds, wherein two things may be noted; the one, the dislike the Parliament had of gaoling of them, as that which was chargeable, pesterous, and of no open example. The other, that in the statutes of this King's time (for this of the nineteenth year is not the only statute of that kind) there are ever coupled the punishment of vagabonds, and the forbidding of dice and cards and unlawful games unto servants and mean people, and the putting down and suppressing of alehouses, as strings of one root together, and as if the one were unprofitable without the other.

---

[44] [Gaols in private hands were restored to the authority of the sheriffs, Henry being of the opinion that persons with extraordinary privileges (e.g. private persons keeping gaols) were as much an interruption of justice as places endowed with extraordinary privileges (e.g. sanctuaries).]

As for riot and retainers, there passed scarce any Parliament in this time without a law against them: the King ever having an eye to might and multitude.

There was granted also that Parliament a subsidy, both from the temporalty and the clergy. And yet nevertheless ere the year expired there went out commissions for a general benevolence; though there were no wars; no fears. The same year the City gave five thousand marks, for confirmation of their liberties; a thing fitter for the beginnings of kings' reigns than the latter ends. Neither was it a small matter that the mint gained upon the late statute, by the recoinage of groats and half-groats; now twelve-pences and six-pences. As for Empson and Dudley's mills, they did grind more than ever. So that it was a strange thing to see what golden showers poured down upon the King's treasury at once. The last payments of the marriage-money from Spain. The sub-sidy. The benevolence. The recoinage. The redemption of the city's liberties. The casualties. And this is the more to be marvelled at, because the King had then no occasions at all of wars or trou-bles. He had now but one son; and one daughter unbestowed. He was wise. He was of a high mind. He needed not to make riches his glory, he did excel in so many things else; save that certainly avarice doth ever find in itself matter of ambition. Belike he thought to leave his son such a kingdom and such a mass of trea-sure, as he might choose his greatness where he would.

This year was also kept the Serjeants' feast, which was the second call in this King's days.

About this time Isabella Queen of Castile deceased; a right noble lady, and an honour to her sex and times, and the corner-stone of the greatness of Spain that hath followed. This accident the King took not for news at large, but thought it had a great relation to his own affairs; especially in two points: the one for example, the other for consequence. First he conceived that the case of Ferdinando of Arragon after the death of Queen Isabella, was his own case after the death of his own Queen; and the case of Joan the heir unto Castile, was the case of his own son Prince Henry. For if both of the Kings had their kingdoms in the right of their wives, they descended to the heirs and did not accrue to the husbands. And although his own case had both steel and parchment more than the other (that is to say, a conquest in the field and an act of Parliament) yet notwithstanding that natural title of descent in blood did (in the imagination even of a wise man) breed a doubt that the other two were not safe nor sufficient. Wherefore he was wonderful diligent to inquire and observe what became of the King of Arragon in holding and continuing the kingdom of Castile; and whether he did hold it in his own right, or as administrator to his daughter; and whether he were like to hold it in fact, or to be put out by his son-in-law. Secondly, he did revolve in his mind, that the state of Christendom might by this late accident have a turn. For whereas before time himself with the conjunction of Arragon and Castile (which then was one), and the amity of Maximilian and Philip his son the Archduke, was far too strong a party for France; he began to fear that now the French King (who had great interest in the affections of Philip the young King of Castile), and Philip himself now King of Castile (who was in ill terms with his father-in-law about the present government of Castile), and thirdly Maximilian, Philip's father, (who was ever variable, and upon whom the surest aim that could be taken was that he would not be long as he had been last before) would, all three being potent Princes, enter into some strait league and confederation amongst themselves. Whereby though he should not be endangered, yet he should be left to the poor amity of Arragon. And whereas he had been heretofore a kind of arbiter of Europe, he should now go less, and be over-topped by so great a conjunction. He had also (as it seems) an inclination to marry, and bethought himself of some fit conditions abroad. And amongst others he had heard of the beauty and virtuous behaviour of the young Queen of Naples, the widow of Ferdinando the younger, being then of matronal years of seven and twenty: by whose marriage he thought that the kingdom of Naples, having been a goal [object of contention] for a time between the King of Arragon and the French King, and being but newly settled, might in some part be deposited in his hands, who was so able to keep the stakes. Therefore he sent in ambassage or message three confident persons, Francis Marsin, James Braybrooke, and John Stile, upon two several inquisitions, rather than negotiations: the one touching the person and condition of the young Queen of Naples, the other touching all particulars of estate that concerned the fortunes and intentions of Ferdinando. And because they may observe best who themselves are observed least, he sent them under colourable pretexts; giving them letters of kindness and compliment from Katherine the Princess to her aunt and niece, the old and young Queen of Naples; and delivering to them also a book of new articles of peace, which notwithstanding it had been delivered unto Doctor de Puebla, the lieger [resident] ambassador of Spain here in England, to be sent, yet for that the King had been long without hearing from Spain, he thought good those messengers, when they had been with the two Queens, should likewise pass on to the court of Ferdinando, and take a copy of the book with them. The instructions touching the Queen of Naples were so curious and exquisite, being as articles whereby to direct a survey or framing a particular of her person, for complexion, favour, feature, stature, health, age, customs, behaviour, conditions, and estate; as, if the King had been young, a man would have judged him to be amorous; but being ancient, it ought to be interpreted that sure he was very chaste, for that he meant to find all things in one woman, and so to settle his affections without ranging. But in this match he was soon cooled, when he heard from his ambassadors that this young Queen had had a goodly jointure in the realm of Naples, well answered during the time of her uncle Frederick, yea and during the time of Lewis the French King, in whose division her revenue fell; but since the time that the kingdom was in Ferdinando's hands, all was assigned to the army and garrisons there, and she received only a pension or exhibition out of his coffers.

The other part of the inquiry had a grave and diligent return, informing the King at full of the present state of King Ferdinando. By this report it appeared to the King that Ferdinando did continue the government of Castile as administrator unto his daughter Joan, by the title of Queen Isabella's will, and partly by the custom of the kingdom (as he pretended); and that all mandates and grants were expedited in the name of Joan his daughter and himself as administrator, without mention of Philip her husband. And that King Ferdinando, howsoever he did dismiss himself of the name of King of Castile, yet meant to hold the kingdom without account and in absolute command.

It appeareth also that he flattered himself with hopes that King Philip would permit unto him the government of Castile during his life; which he had laid his plot to work him unto, both by some councillors of his about him which Ferdinando had at his devotion, and chiefly by promise that in case Philip gave not way unto it he would marry some young lady, whereby to put him by the succession of Arragon and Granada, in case he should have a son; and lastly by representing unto him that the government of the Burgundians, till Philip were by continuance in Spain made as natural of Spain, would not be endured by the Spaniards. But in all those things, though wisely laid down and considered, Ferdinando failed; but that Pluto was better to him than Pallas [death served him better than wisdom].

In the same report also the ambassadors, being mean men and therefore the more free, did strike upon a string which was somewhat dangerous. For they declared plainly that the people of Spain both nobles and commons were better affected unto the part of Philip (so he brought his wife with him) than to Ferdinando; and expressed the reason to be, because he had imposed upon them many taxes and tallages, which was the King's own case between him and his son.

There was also in this report a declaration of an overture of marriage, which Amason the secretary of Ferdinando had made unto the ambassadors in great secret, between Charles Prince of Castile and Mary the King's second daughter; assuring the King that the treaty of marriage then on foot for the said Prince and the daughter of France would break; and that she the said daughter of France should be married to Angolesme, that was the heir apparent of France.

There was a touch also of a speech of marriage between Ferdinando and Madame de Fois, a lady of the blood of France, which afterwards indeed succeeded. But this was reported as learnt in France, and silenced [not spoken of] in Spain.

The King by the return of this ambassage, which gave great light unto his affairs, was well instructed and prepared how to carry himself between Ferdinando King of Arragon and Philip his son-in-law King of Castile; resolving with himself to do all that in him lay to keep them at one within themselves; but howsoever that succeeded, by a moderate carriage and bearing the person of a common friend to lose neither of their friendships; but yet to run a course more entire with the King of Arragon, but more laboured and officious with the King of Castile. But he was much taken with the overture of marriage with his daughter Mary; both because it was the greatest marriage of Christendom, and for that it took hold of both allies.

But to corroborate his alliance with Philip, the winds gave him an interview. For Philip choosing the winter season the better to surprise the King of Arragon, set forth with a great navy out of Flanders for Spain, in the month of January, the one and twentieth year of the King's reign. But himself was surprised with a cruel tempest, that scattered his ships upon the several coasts of England; and the ship wherein the King and Queen were (with two other small barks only) torn, and in great peril to escape the fury of the weather, thrust into Weymouth. King Philip himself, having not been used (as it seems) to sea, all wearied and extreme sick, would needs land to refresh his spirits; though it was against the opinion of his council, doubting it might breed delay, his occasions requiring celerity.

The rumour of the arrival of a puissant navy upon the coast made the country arm. And Sir Thomas Trenchard, with forces suddenly raised, not knowing what the matter might be, came to Weymouth. Where understanding the accident, he did in all humbleness and humanity invite the King and Queen to his house; and forthwith dispatched posts to the court. Soon after came Sir John Caroe likewise, with a great troop of men well armed, using the like humbleness and respects towards the King, when he knew the case. King Philip doubting that they, being but subjects, durst not let him pass away again without the King's notice and leave, yielded to their intreaties to stay till they heard from the court. The King, as soon as he heard the news, com-

manded presently the Earl of Arundel to go to visit the King of
Castile, and let him understand that as he was very sorry for his
mishap, so he was glad that he had escaped the danger of the
seas, and likewise of the occasion himself had to do him honour;
and desiring him to think himself as in his own land; and that the
King made all haste possible to come and embrace him. The Earl
came to him in great magnificence with a brave troop of three
hundred horse; and for more state came by torch-light. After he
had done the King's message, King Philip seeing how the world
went, the sooner to get away, went upon speed to the King at
Windsor, and his Queen followed by easy journeys. The two
Kings at their meeting used all the caresses and loving demonstrations that were possible. And the King of Castile said pleasantly
to the King, *That he was now punished for that he would not
come within his walled town of Calais, when they met last.* But
the King answered, *That walls and seas were nothing where
hearts were open; and that he was here no otherwise but to be
served.* After a day or two's refreshing, the Kings entered into
speech of renewing the treaty; the King saying that though King
Philip's person were the same, yet his fortunes and state were
raised; in which case a renovation of treaty was used amongst
Princes. But while these things were in handling, the King choosing a fit time, and drawing the King of Castile into a room where
they two only were private, and laying his hand civilly upon his
arm, and changing his countenance a little from a countenance of
entertainment, said to him, *Sir, you have been saved upon my
coast, I hope you will not suffer me to wreck upon yours.* The King
of Castile asked him *what he meant by that speech? I mean it*
(saith the King) *by that same harebrain wild fellow my subject the
Earl of Suffolk, who is protected in your country, and begins to
play the fool, when all others are weary of it.* The King of Castile
answered, *I had thought, Sir, your felicity had been above those
thoughts. But if it trouble you, I will banish him.* The King replied,
*those hornets were best in their nest, and worst then when they
did fly abroad; and that his desire was to have him delivered to
him.* The King of Castile herewith a little confused, and in a study,
said, *That can I not do with my honour, and less with yours; for*

you will be thought to have used me as a prisoner. The King presently said, *Then the matter is at an end. For I will take that dishonour upon me, and so your honour is saved.* The King of Castile, who had the King in great estimation, and besides remembered where he was, and knew not what use he might have of the King's amity, for that himself was new in his state of Spain, and unsettled both with his father-in-law and with his people; composing his countenance, said, *Sir, you give law to me; but so will I to you. You shall have him, but upon your honour you shall not take his life.* The King embracing him said, *Agreed.* Saith the King of Castile, *Neither shall it dislike you, if I send to him in such a fashion as he may partly come with his own good will.* The King said, *it was well thought of; and if it pleased him he would join with him in sending to the Earl a message to that purpose.* They both sent severally; and mean while they continued feasting and pastimes; the King being on his part willing to have the Earl sure before the King of Castile went; and the King of Castile being as willing to seem to be enforced. The King also with many wise and excellent persuasions did advise the King of Castile to be ruled by the counsel of his father-in-law Ferdinando; a Prince so prudent, so experienced, so fortunate. The King of Castile (who was in no very good terms with his said father-in-law) answered, *that if his father-in-law would suffer him to govern his kingdoms, he should govern him.*

There were immediately messengers sent from both Kings to recall the Earl of Suffolk; who upon gentle words used to him was soon charmed, and willing enough to return; assured of his life, and hoping of his liberty. He was brought through Flanders to Calais, and thence landed at Dover, and with sufficient guard delivered and received at the Tower of London. Meanwhile King Henry (to draw out the time) continued his feastings and entertainments, and after he had received the King of Castile into the fraternity of the Garter, and for a reciprocal had his son the Prince admitted to the order of the Golden Fleece, he accompanied King Philip and his Queen to the City of London; where they were entertained with the greatest magnificence and triumph that could be upon no greater warning. And as soon as the Earl of Suffolk had been conveyed to the Tower (which was the serious part) the jollities had an end, and the Kings took leave. Nevertheless during their being here, they in substance concluded that treaty which the Flemings term *intercursus malus,* and bears date at Windsor: for there be some things in it more to the advantage of the English than of them; especially for that the free fishing of the Dutch upon the coasts and seas of England, granted in the treaty of *undecimo,* was not by this treaty confirmed; all articles that confirm former treaties being precisely and warily limited and confined to matter of commerce only, and not otherwise.

It was observed that the great tempest which drave [drove] Philip into England blew down the golden eagle from the spire of Paul's, and in the fall it fell upon a sign of the black eagle which was in Paul's church-yard in the place where the school-house now standeth, and battered it and broke it down; which was a strange stooping of a hawk upon a fowl. This the people interpreted to be an ominous prognostic upon the imperial house, which was (by interpretation) also fulfilled upon Philip the Emperor's son, not only in the present disaster of the tempest, but in that that followed. For Philip arriving into Spain and attaining the possession of the kingdom of Castile without resistance (insomuch as Ferdinando, who had spoke so great before, was with difficulty admitted to the speech of his son-in-law) sickened soon after, and deceased.[45] Yet after such time as there was an observation by the wisest of that court, that if he had lived, his father would have gained upon him in that sort, as he would have governed his counsels and designs, if not his affections. By this all Spain returned into the power of Ferdinando in state as it was before; the rather in regard of the infirmity of Joan his daughter, who loving her husband (by whom she had many children) dearly well, and no less beloved of him (howsoever her father to make Philip ill-beloved of the people of Spain gave out that Philip used her not well), was unable in strength of mind to bear the grief of his [Philip's] decease, and fell distracted of her wits: of which malady her father was thought no ways to endeavour the cure,

[45] [i.e. Philip died]

the better to hold his regal power in Castile. So that as the felicity of Charles the Eighth was said to be a dream, so the adversity of Ferdinando was said likewise to be a dream, it passed over so soon.

About this time the King was desirous to bring into the house of Lancaster celestial honour, and became suitor to Pope Julius to canonise King Henry the Sixth for a saint; the rather in respect of that his famous prediction of the King's own assumption to the crown. Julius referred the matter (as the manner is) to certain cardinals to take the verification of his holy acts and miracles: but it died under the reference. The general opinion was, that Pope Julius was too dear, and that the King would not come to his rates. But it is more probable, that that Pope, who was extremely jealous of the dignity of the see of Rome and of the acts thereof, knowing that King Henry Sixth was reputed in the world abroad but for a simple man, was afraid it would but diminish the estimation of that kind of honour, if there were not a distance kept between innocents and saints.

The same year likewise there proceeded a treaty of marriage between the King and the Lady Margaret Duchess Dowager of Savoy, only daughter to Maximilian and sister to the King of Castile; a lady wise and of great good fame. This matter had been in speech between the two Kings at their meeting; but was soon after resumed; and therein was employed for his first piece the King's then chaplain, and after the great prelate, Thomas Wolsey. It was in the end concluded with great and ample conditions for the King, but with promise *de futuro* only. It may be the King was the rather induced unto it, for that he had heard more and more of the marriage to go on between his great friend and ally Ferdinando of Arragon and Madame de Fois; whereby that King began to piece with the French King, from whom he had been always before severed. So fatal a thing it is for the greatest and straitest amities of Kings at one time or other to have a little of the wheel. Nay there is a further tradition (in Spain though not with us) that the King of Arragon, after he knew that the marriage between Charles the young Prince of Castile and Mary the King's second daughter went roundly on (which though it was first moved by the King of Arragon, yet it was afterwards wholly ad-

vanced and brought to perfection by Maximilian and the friends
on that side) entered into a jealousy that the King did aspire to
the government of Castilia, as administrator during the minority
of his son-in-law; as if there should have been a competition of
three for that government: Ferdinando grandfather on the
mother's side; Maximilian grandfather on the father's side; and
King Henry father-in-law to the young Prince. Certainly it is not
unlike but the King's government (carrying the young Prince with
him) would have been perhaps more welcome to the Spaniards
than that of the other two. For the nobility of Castilia, that so
lately put out the King of Arragon in favour of King Philip, and
had discovered themselves so far, could not be but in a secret distrust and distaste of that King. And as for Maximilian, upon
twenty respects he could not have been the man. But this purpose
of the King's seemeth to me (considering the King's safe courses,
never found to be enterprising or adventurous,) not greatly probable, except he should have had a desire to breathe warmer, because he had ill lungs.

This marriage with Margaret was protracted from time to
time, in respect of the infirmity of the King, who now in the two
and twentieth of his reign began to be troubled with the gout:
but the defluxion taking also into his breast, wasted his lungs, so
that thrice in a year (in a kind of return, and especially in the
spring) he had great fits and labours of the tissick [consumption].
Nevertheless he continued to intend business with as great diligence as before in his health: yet so, as upon this warning he did
likewise now more seriously think of the world to come, and of
making himself a saint, as well as King Henry the Sixth, by treasure better employed than to be given to Pope Julius. For this
year he gave greater alms than accustomed, and discharged all
prisoners about the City that lay for fees, or debts under forty
shillings. He did also make haste with religious foundations; and
in the year following, which was the three and twentieth, finished
that of the Savoy. And hearing also of the bitter cries of his people against the oppressions of Dudley and Empson and their
complices; partly by devout persons about him and partly by public sermons (the preachers doing their duty therein), he was

touched with great remorse for the same. Nevertheless Empson and Dudley, though they could not but hear of these scruples in the King's conscience, yet as if the King's soul and his money were in several offices, that the one was not to intermeddle with the other, went on with as great rage as ever. For the same three and twentieth year was there a sharp prosecution against Sir William Capel now the second time, and this was for matters of misgovernment in his mayoralty: the great matter being, that in some payments he had taken knowledge of false moneys, and did not his diligence to examine and beat it out who were the offenders. For this and some other things laid to his charge, he was condemned to pay two thousand pounds; and being a man of stomach, and hardened by his former troubles, refused to pay a mite; and belike used some untoward speeches of the proceedings, for which he was sent to the Tower, and there remained till the King's death. Knesworth likewise, that had been lately Mayor of London, and both his Sheriffs, were for abuses in their offices questioned, and imprisoned, and delivered upon one thousand four hundred pounds paid. Hawis, an Alderman of London, was put in trouble, and died with thought and anguish before his business came to an end. Sir Laurence Ailmer, who had likewise been Mayor of London, and his two Sheriffs, were put to the fine of one thousand pounds. And Sir Laurence for refusing to make payment was committed to prison, where he stayed till Empson himself was committed in his place.

It is no marvel (if the faults were so light and the rates so heavy) that the King's treasure of store that he left at his death, most of it in secret places under his own key and keeping at Richmond, amounted (as by tradition it is reported to have done) unto the sum of near eighteen hundred thousand pounds sterling; a huge mass of money even for these times.

The last act of state that concluded this King's temporal felicity, was the conclusion of a glorious match between his daughter Mary and Charles Prince of Castile, afterwards the great Emperor; both being of tender years: which treaty was perfected by Bishop Foxe and other his commissioners at Calais, the year

before the King's death. In which alliance it seemeth he himself
took so high contentment, as in a letter which he wrote thereupon
to the City of London (commanding all possible demonstrations
of joy to be made for the same) he expresseth himself as if he
thought he had built a wall of brass about his kingdom, when he
had for his sons-in-law a King of Scotland and a Prince of Castile
and Burgundy. So as now there was nothing to be added to this
great King's felicity, being at the top of all worldly bliss, (in regard of the high marriages of his children, his great renown
throughout Europe, and his scarce credible riches, and the perpetual constancy of his prosperous successes) but an opportune
death, to withdraw him from any future blow of fortune. Which
certainly (in regard of the great hatred of his people, and the title
of his son, being then come to eighteen years of age, and being a
bold Prince and liberal, and that gained upon the people by his
very aspect and presence) had not been impossible to have come
upon him.

To crown also the last year of his reign as well as his first,
he did an act of piety, rare and worthy to be taken in imitation.
For he granted forth a general pardon, as expecting a second coronation in a better kingdom. He did also declare in his will, that
his mind was, that restitution should be made of those sums which
had been unjustly taken by his officers.

And thus this Salomon of England (for Salomon also was
too heavy upon his people in exactions) having lived two and
fifty years, and thereof reigned three and twenty years and eight
months, being in perfect memory and in a most blessed mind, in
a great calm of a consuming sickness, passed to a better world, the
two and twentieth of April 1508 [recte: 1509] at his palace of
Richmond which himself had built.

This King (to speak of him in terms equal to his deserving)
was one of the best sort of wonders: a wonder for wise men. He
had parts (both in his virtues and his fortune) not so fit for a
common-place as for observation. Certainly he was religious, both
in his affection and observance. But as he could see clear (for

those times) through superstition, so he would be blinded (now and then) by human policy. He advanced church-men. He was tender in the privilege of sanctuaries, though they wrought him much mischief. He built and endowed many religious foundations, besides his memorable hospital of the Savoy. And yet was he a great alms-giver in secret; which shewed that his works in public were dedicated rather to God's glory than his own. He professed always to love and seek peace; and it was his usual preface in his treaties, that when Christ came into the world peace was sung, and when he went out of the world peace was bequeathed. And this virtue could not proceed out of fear or softness, for he was valiant and active; and therefore no doubt it was truly Christian and moral. Yet he knew the way to peace was not to seem to be desirous to avoid wars. Therefore would he make offers and fames of wars, till he had mended the conditions of peace. It was also much, that one that was so great a lover of peace should be so happy in war. For his arms, either in foreign or civil wars, were never unfortunate; neither did he know what a disaster meant. The war of his coming in, and the rebellions of the Earl of Lincoln and the Lord Audley, were ended by victory. The wars of France and Scotland by peaces sought at his hands. That of Brittaine by accident of the Duke's death. The insurrection of the Lord Lovell, and that of Perkin at Exeter and in Kent, by flight of the rebels before they came to blows. So that his fortune of arms was still inviolate. The rather sure, for that in the quenching of the commotions of his subjects he ever went in person: sometimes reserving himself to back and second his lieutenants, but ever in action. And yet that was not merely forwardness, but partly distrust of others.

He did much maintain and countenance his laws; which (nevertheless) was no impediment to him to work his will. For it was so handled that neither prerogative nor profit went to diminution. And yet as he would sometimes strain up his laws to his prerogative, so would he also let down his prerogative to his Parliament. For mint and wars and martial discipline (things of absolute power) he would nevertheless bring to Parliament. Justice was well administered in his time, save where the King was party; save also that the council-table intermeddled too much with

meum and *tuum*.[46] For it was a very court of justice during his
time, especially in the beginning. But in that part both of justice
and policy which is the durable part, and cut (as it were) in brass
or marble (which is the making of good laws) he did excel. And
with his justice he was also a merciful prince: as in whose time
there were but three of the nobility that suffered: the Earl of Warwick, the Lord Chamberlain, and the Lord Audley; though the
first two were instead of numbers in the dislike and obloquy of
the people. But there were never so great rebellions expiated with
so little blood drawn by the hand of justice, as the two rebellions
of Blackheath and Exeter. As for the severity used upon those
which were taken in Kent, it was but upon a scum of people. His
pardons went ever both before and after his sword. But then he
had withal a strange kind of interchanging of large and inexpected
pardons with severe executions: which (his wisdom considered)
could not be imputed to any inconstancy or inequality, but either
to some reason which we do not now know, or to a principle he
had set unto himself, *That he would vary, and try both ways in
turn.* But the less blood he drew, the more he took of treasure: and
(as some construed it) he was the more sparing in the one that he
might be the more pressing in the other; for both would have
been intolerable. Of nature assuredly he coveted to accumulate
treasure, and was a little poor in admiring riches. The people (into
whom there is infused for the preservation of monarchies a natural
desire to discharge their princes, though it be with the unjust
charge of their councillors and ministers) did impute this unto
Cardinal Morton and Sir Reginold Bray; who (as it after appeared)
as counsellors of ancient authority with him did so second his
humours, as nevertheless they did temper them. Whereas Empson
and Dudley that followed, being persons that had no reputation
with him (otherwise than by the servile following of his bent) did
not give way only (as the first did) but shape him way to those
extremities, for which himself was touched with remorse at his
death; and which his successor renounced, and sought to purge.

[46] [with mine and thine; that is, the Council meddled too much
in law-suits involving private property]

This excess of his had at that time many glosses and interpreta-
tions. Some thought the continual rebellions wherewith he had
been vexed had made him grow to hate his people. Some thought
it was done to pull down their stomachs and to keep them low.
Some, for that he would leave his son a golden fleece. Some suspected he had some high design upon foreign parts. But those
perhaps shall come nearest the truth that fetch not their reasons
so far off; but rather impute it to nature, age, peace, and a mind
fixed upon no other ambition or pursuit. Whereunto I should add,
that having every day occasion to take notice of the necessities
and shifts for money of other great Princes abroad, it did the better (by comparison) set off to him the felicity of full coffers. As to
his expending of treasure, he never spared charge which his affairs required: and in his buildings was magnificent; but his rewards were very limited. So that his liberality was rather upon his
own state and memory than upon the deserts of others.

He was of a high mind, and loved his own will and his own
way; as one that revered himself, and would reign indeed. Had he
been a private man he would have been termed proud: but in a
wise Prince, it was but keeping of distance, which indeed he did
towards all; not admitting any near or full approach neither to
his power or to his secrets. For he was governed by none. His
Queen (notwithstanding she had presented him with divers children, and with a crown also, though he would not acknowledge it)
could do nothing with him. His mother he reverenced much, heard
little. For any person agreeable to him for society (such as was
Hastings to King Edward the Fourth, or Charles Brandon after to
King Henry the Eighth), he had none; except we should account
for such persons Foxe and Bray and Empson, because they were so
much with him. But it was but as the instrument is much with the
workman. He had nothing in him of vain-glory, but yet kept state
and majesty to the height; being sensible that majesty maketh the
people bow, but vain-glory boweth to them.

To his confederates abroad he was constant and just; but
not open. But rather such was his inquiry and such his closeness,
as they stood in the light towards him, and he stood in the dark to
them. Yet without strangeness, but with a semblance of mutual

communication of affairs. As for little envies or emulations upon
foreign princes (which are frequent with many Kings), he had
never any; but went substantially to his own business. Certain it
is, that though his reputation was great at home, yet it was greater
abroad. For foreigners that could not see the passages of affairs,
but made their judgments upon the issues of them, noted that he
was ever in strife and ever aloft. It grew also from the airs which
the princes and states abroad received from their ambassadors and
agents here; which were attending the court in great number;
whom he did not only content with courtesy, reward, and private-
ness; but (upon such conferences as passed with them) put them
in admiration to find his universal insight into the affairs of the
world: which though he did suck chiefly from themselves, yet
that which he had gathered from them all seemed admirable to
every one. So that they did write ever to their superiors in high
terms concerning his wisdom and art of rule. Nay when they were
returned, they did commonly maintain intelligence with him;
such a dexterity he had to impropriate to himself all foreign
instruments.

He was careful and liberal to obtain good intelligence from
all parts abroad. Wherein he did not only use his interest in the
liegers here, and his pensioners which he had both in the court of
Rome and other the courts of Christendom, but the industry and
vigilancy of his own ambassadors in foreign parts. For which purpose his instructions were ever extreme curious and articulate;
and in them more articles touching inquisition than touching negotiation: requiring likewise from his ambassadors an answer, in
particular distinct articles, respectively to his questions.

As for his secret spials which he did employ both at home
and abroad, by them to discover what practices and conspiracies
were against him, surely his case required it: he had such moles
perpetually working and casting to undermine him. Neither can
it be reprehended; for if spials be lawful against lawful enemies,
much more against conspirators and traitors. But indeed to give
them credence by oaths or curses, that cannot be well maintained;
for those are too holy vestments for a disguise. Yet surely there
was this further good in his employing of these flies and familiars;

that as the use of them was cause that many conspiracies were revealed, so the fame and suspicion of them kept (no doubt) many conspiracies from being attempted.

Towards his Queen he was nothing uxorious; nor scarce indulgent; but companiable and respective, and without jealousy. Towards his children he was full of paternal affection, careful of their education, aspiring to their high advancement, regular to see that they should not want of any due honour and respect, but not greatly willing to cast any popular lustre upon them.

To his council he did refer much, and sat oft in person; knowing it to be the way to assist his power and inform his judgment. In which respect also he was fairly patient of liberty both of advice and of vote, till himself were declared.

He kept a strait hand on his nobility, and chose rather to advance clergymen and lawyers, which were more obsequious to him, but had less interest in the people; which made for his absoluteness, but not for his safety. Insomuch as (I am persuaded) it was one of the causes of his troublesome reign; for that his nobles, though they were loyal and obedient, yet did not cooperate with him, but let every man go his own way. He was not afraid of an able man, as Lewis the Eleventh was. But contrariwise he was served by the ablest men that were to be found; without which his affairs could not have prospered as they did. For war, Bedford, Oxford, Surrey, Dawbeny, Brooke, Poynings. For other affairs, Morton, Foxe, Bray, the Prior of Lanthony, Warham, Urswick, Hussey, Frowick, and others. Neither did he care how cunning they were that he did employ: for he thought himself to have the master-reach. And as he chose well, so he held them up well. For it is a strange thing, that though he were a dark prince, and infinitely suspicious, and his times full of secret conspiracies and troubles; yet in twenty-four years reign he never put down or discomposed councillor or near servant, save only Stanley the Lord Chamberlain. As for the disposition of his subjects in general towards him, it stood thus with him; that of the three affections which naturally tie the hearts of the subjects to their sovereign,— love, fear, and reverence,—he had the last in height; the second in good measure; and so little of the first, as he was beholding to the other two.

He was a Prince, sad, serious, and full of thoughts and secret observations; and full of notes and memorials of his own hand, especially touching persons; as whom to employ, whom to reward, whom to inquire of, whom to beware of, what were the dependencies, what were the factions, and the like; keeping (as it were) a journal of his thoughts. There is to this day a merry tale: that his monkey (set on as it was thought by one of his chamber) tore his principal note-book all to pieces, when by chance it lay forth; whereat the court which liked not those pensive accounts was almost tickled with sport.

He was indeed full of apprehensions and suspicions. But as he did easily take them, so he did easily check them and master them; whereby they were not dangerous, but troubled himself more than others. It is true, his thoughts were so many, as they could not well always stand together; but that which did good one way, did hurt another. Neither did he at some times weigh them aright in their proportions. Certainly that rumour which did him so much mischief (that the Duke of York should be saved and alive) was (at the first) of his own nourishing, because he would have more reason not to reign in the right of his wife. He was affable, and both well and fair spoken; and would use strange sweetness and blandishments of words, where he desired to effect or persuade any thing that he took to heart. He was rather studious than learned; reading most books that were of any worth, in the French tongue. Yet he understood the Latin, as appeareth in that Cardinal Hadrian and others, who could very well have written French, did use to write to him in Latin.

For his pleasures, there is no news of them. And yet by his instructions to Marsin and Stile touching the Queen of Naples, it seemeth he could interrogate well touching beauty. He did by pleasures as great Princes do by banquets, come and look a little upon them, and turn way. For never Prince was more wholly given to his affairs, nor in them more of himself. Insomuch as in triumphs of jousts and tourneys and balls and masks (which they then called disguises) he was rather a princely and gentle spectator than seemed much to be delighted.

No doubt, in him as in all men (and most of all in Kings) his fortune wrought upon his nature, and his nature upon his fortune.

He attained to the crown, not only from a private fortune, which might endow him with moderation; but also from the fortune of an exiled man, which had quickened in him all seeds of observation and industry. And his times being rather prosperous than calm, had raised his confidence by success, but almost marred his nature by troubles. His wisdom, by often evading from perils, was turned rather into a dexterity to deliver himself from dangers when they pressed him, than into a providence to prevent and remove them afar off. And even in nature, the sight of his mind was like some sights of eyes; rather strong at hand than to carry afar off. For his wit increased upon the occasion; and so much the more if the occasion were sharpened by danger. Again, whether it were the shortness of his foresight, or the strength of his will, or the dazzling of his suspicions, or what it was; certain it is that the perpetual troubles of his fortunes (there being no more matter out of which they grew) could not have been without some great defects and main errors in his nature, customs, and proceedings, which he had enough to do to save and help with a thousand little industries and watches. But those do best appear in the story itself. Yet take him with all his defects, if a man should compare him with the Kings his concurrents in France and Spain, he shall find him more politic than Lewis the Twelfth of France, and more entire and sincere than Ferdinando of Spain. But if you shall change Lewis the Twelfth for Lewis the Eleventh, who lived a little before, then the consort is more perfect. For that Lewis the Eleventh, Ferdinando, and Henry, may be esteemed for the *tres magi* of kings of those ages. To conclude, if this King did no greater matters, it was long of himself; for what he minded he compassed.

He was a comely personage, a little above just stature, well and straight limbed, but slender. His countenance was reverend, and a little like a churchman: and as it was not strange or dark, so neither was it winning or pleasing, but as the face of one well disposed. But it was to the disadvantage of the painter, for it was best when he spake.

His worth may bear a tale or two, that may put upon him somewhat that may seem divine. When the Lady Margaret his mother had divers great suitors for marriage, she dreamed one night that one in the likeness of a bishop in pontifical habit did tender her Edmund Earl of Richmond (the King's father) for her husband. Neither had she ever any child but the King, though she had three husbands. One day when King Henry the Sixth (whose innocency gave him holiness) was washing his hands at a great feast, and cast his eyes upon King Henry, then a young youth, he said; "This is the lad that shall possess quietly that, that we now strive for." But that that was truly divine in him, was that he had the fortune of a true Christian as well as of a great King, in living exercised and dying repentant. So as he had an happy warfare in both conflicts, both of sin and the cross.

He was born at Pembroke Castle, and lieth buried at Westminster, in one of the stateliest and daintiest monuments of Europe, both for the chapel and for the sepulchre. So that he dwelleth more richly dead, in the monument of his tomb, than he did alive in Richmond or any of his palaces. I could wish he did the like in this monument of his fame.

FINIS

Appendix

Introduction
to the Appendix

The *History of the Reign of King Henry the Seventh* was Bacon's only complete work of history. He did, however, begin others, and he wrote as well a number of pieces that sketch the course of events without really attempting to describe in detail what occurred. Finally, in his philosophical works, he treated historical thinking as one kind among many. Examples of all these writings will be found here.

The "Letter to Lord Chancellor Ellesmere, April 1605" is the earliest example of Bacon's thought concerning the history of the sixteenth century. Typically, his sketch was part of a letter that aimed at promoting government service for the author. The letter was first published by his secretary, Dr. Rawley, in *Resuscitatio* (1657). Our text is from James Spedding, *The Letters and the Life of Francis Bacon* (London: Longman, Green, Longman and Roberts, 1861–1874), III, 249–252. The "History of the reigns of K. Henry the Eighth, K. Edward, Q. Mary, and part of the reign of Q. Elizabeth" appears to have been composed at much the same time as the "Letter to Lord Chancellor Ellesmere," and may have been intended as a prospectus for the work Bacon hoped to be asked to undertake. This view is strengthened by the fact that half the piece is an advertisement for the value of history when written by one such as Bacon; the other half consists of a rapid analysis of Henry VII's reign (the title notwithstanding). Bacon loaned the piece to John Speed, and fragments of it appeared in Speed's *The History of Great Britaine* (London: Iohn Sudbury and Georg Humble, 1611). The text printed here is from James Spedding, R. L. Ellis and D. D. Heath, editors, *The Works of Francis Bacon,* 7 vols. (London: Longman and Co., 1857–1859), VI, 17–22; its first appearance *in toto* was in a miscellaneous collection, *The Cabala* (1663).

The "History of the Reign of King Henry the Eighth" was intended as a continuation of the *History of Henry the Seventh.* Prince Charles, the heir to the throne, had commanded Bacon to keep at his task. But, by 1623, Bacon was no longer in the mood to write history. In the first place, it was becoming clear to him that he would not regain favor in this way; and in the second, he had difficulty in gaining access to the appropriate documents. Thus, he composed no more than a few pages before returning to his philosophical writings. "Henry the Eighth" was first published by Dr. Rawley in *Certaine Miscellany Works* (1629); our text is from Spedding, Ellis, and Heath, *The Works of Francis Bacon,* VI, 269–270.

The eulogy of Queen Elizabeth was written before 1609, apparently as a reply to certain libels on the queen published by Roman Catholics on the Continent. The piece was intended as a partisan apology, and Bacon admitted as much in a letter to his Catholic friend Tobie Matthew. Since Bacon was attempting to influence opinion abroad, he wrote in Latin; the translation used here is Spedding's, published in *The Works of Francis Bacon,* VI, 305–318. The original was circulated in manuscript in 1609, but was not printed until 1658 when Dr. Rawley published it in *Opuscula Philosophica . . .*

Of "The Beginning of the History of Great Britain" almost nothing is known. Spedding argued that it was probably written in 1609–1610. A letter to King James, written to accompany the tract, indicates that it was a part of Bacon's attempt to ingratiate himself with his monarch. Why he did not proceed beyond a few pages is a matter for speculation. Again, the text was first published by Dr. Rawley (*Resuscitatio*, 1657), and our text is from Spedding, Ellis, and Heath, *The Works of Francis Bacon*, VI, 275–279.

Even less is known about the "Character of Julius Caesar." Rawley printed it in 1658, in *Opuscula posthuma*, adding an English translation in the 1661 edition of the *Resuscitatio*. Our text is from Spedding, Ellis, and Heath, *The Works of Francis Bacon*, VI, 341–345. Bacon began a companion essay on Augustus but did not proceed beyond the opening paragraph. It may be found in the *Works*, VI, 347, but is too slight to be included here.

The short Proem (Preface), which Bacon wrote for a treatise entitled "Of the Interpretation of Nature," is included here for the light it sheds on its author's life and method of work. Spedding translated the original Latin in *The Letters and the Life of Francis Bacon*, III, 84–87; this supplies our text. The Proem was first printed in *Scripta in naturali et universali philosophia* (Amsterdam, 1653).

Bacon examined the place of history in the context of human thought twice: first in *The Advancement of Learning*, which he published in 1605, and again in his Latin expansion of that treatise, *De Dignitate et Augmentis Scientiarum* (1623). The selection printed here consists of the first twelve chapters of Book II of the latter. The translation from the Latin was made by R. L. Ellis and was revised by James Spedding; our text (including the notes) is printed from Spedding, Ellis, and Heath, *The Works of Francis Bacon*, IV, 292–314.

Letter
to Lord Chancellor
Ellesmere,
April 1605

It may please your good Lordship,

Some late act of his Majesty, referred to some former speech which I have heard from your Lordship, bred in me a great desire, and by strength of desire a boldness to make an humble proposition to your Lordship, such as in me can be no better than a wish: but if your Lordship should apprehend it, may take some good and worthy effect. The act I speak of, is the order given by his Majesty, as I understand, for the erection of a tomb or monument for our late sovereign Lady Queen Elizabeth: wherein I may note much, but this at this time; That as her Majesty did always right to his Highness' hopes, so his Majesty doth in all things right to her memory; a very just and princely retribution. But from this occasion, by a very easy ascent, I passed furder, being put in mind, by this Representative of her person, of the more true and more firm Representative, which is of her life and government. For as Statuaes and Pictures are dumb histories, so histories are speaking Pictures. Wherein if my affection be not too great, or my reading too small, I am of this opinion, that if Plutarch were alive to write lives by parallels, it would trouble him for virtue and fortune both to find for her a parallel amongst women. And though she was of the passive sex, yet her government was so active, as, in my simple opinion, it made more impression upon the several states of Europe, than it received from thence. But I confess unto your Lordship I could not stay here, but went a little furder into the consideration of the times which have passed since King Henry the 8th; wherein I find the strangest variety that in like number of successions of any hereditary monarchy hath ever been known. The reign of a child; the offer of an usurpation, (though it were but as a Diary [lasting for one day] Ague); the reign of a lady married to a foreign Prince; and the reign of a lady solitary and unmarried. So that as it cometh to pass in massive bodies, that they have certain trepidations and waverings before they fix and settle; so it seemeth that by the providence of God this monarchy, before it was to settle in his Majesty and his generations (in which I hope it is now established for ever), it had these prelusive [preliminary] changes in these barren princes. Neither could I contain myself here (as it is easier to produce than to stay a wish), but calling to remembrance the unworthiness of the history of England (in the main continuance thereof), and the partiality and obliquity of that of Scotland, in the latest and largest author that I have seen: I conceived it would be honour for his Majesty, and a work very memorable, if this island of Great Britain, as it is now joined in Monarchy for the ages to come, so were joined in History for the times past; and that one just and complete History were compiled of both nations. And if any man think it may refresh the memory of former discords, he may satisfy himself with the verse, *olim haec meminisse juvabit:*[1] for the case being now altered, it is matter of comfort and gratulation to remember former troubles.

Thus much, if it may please your Lordship, was in the optative mood.[2] It is true that I did look a little in the potential; wherein the hope which I conceived was grounded upon three ob-

---

[1] [One day, it will delight a man to look back on these things.]

[2] [The form of a verb expressing a wish or desire; found in Greek.]

servations. The first, of the times, which do flourish in learning,
both of art and language; which giveth hope not only that it may
be done, but that it may be well done. For when good things are
undertaken in ill times, it turneth but to loss; as in this very particular we have a fresh example of Polydore Vergile, who being
designed to write the English History by K. Henry the 8th (a
strange choice to chuse a stranger), and for his better instruction
having obtained into his hands many registers and memorials out
of the monasteries, did indeed deface and suppress better things
than those he did collect and reduce. Secondly, I do see that which
all the world seeth in his Majesty, both a wonderful judgment in
learning, and a singular affection towards learning, and the works
of true honour which are of the mind and not of the hand. For
there cannot be the like honour sought in the building of galleries,
or the planting of elms along highways, and the like manufactures, things rather of magnificence than of magnanimity, as there
is in the uniting of states, pacifying of controversies, nourishing
and augmenting of learning and arts, and the particular actions
appertaining unto these; of which kind Cicero judged truly, when
he said to Caesar, *Quantum operibus tuis detrahet vetustas, tan-
tum addet laudibus.*[3] And lastly, I called to mind, that your Lordship at sometimes hath been pleased to express unto me a great
desire, that something of this nature should be performed; an-
swerably indeed to your other noble and worthy courses and actions, wherein your Lordship sheweth yourself not only an
excellent Chancellor and Counsellor, but also an exceeding fa-
vourer and fosterer of all good learning and virtue, both in men
and matters, persons and actions: joining and adding unto the
great services towards his Majesty, which have, in small compass
of time, been accumulated upon your Lordship, many other de-
servings both of the Church and Commonwealth and particulars;
so as the opinion of so great and wise a man doth seem unto me a
good warrant both of the possibility and worth of this matter.
But all this while I assure myself, I cannot be mistaken by your

[3] [As much as the passage of time pulls down your works, so
much will it add to your praises.]

Lordship, as if I sought an office or employment for myself. For no man knoweth better than your Lordship, that (if there were in me any faculty thereunto, as I am most unable), yet neither my fortune nor profession would permit it. But because there be so many good painters both for hand and colours, it needeth but encouragement and instructions to give life and light unto it.

So in all humbleness I conclude my presenting to your good Lordship this wish; which if it perish it is but a loss of that which is not. And thus craving pardon that I have taken so much time from your Lordship, I always remain

Your Lps. very humbly and much bounden

Fr. Bacon.

Gray's Inn this 2d of April, 1605.

The History of the reigns of K. Henry the Eighth, K. Edward, Q. Mary, and part of the reign of Q. Elizabeth

The books which are written do in their kinds represent the faculties of the mind of man: Poesy his imagination; Philosophy his reason; and History his memory. Of which three faculties least exception is commonly taken to memory; because imagination is oftentimes idle, and reason litigious. So likewise History of all writings deserveth least taxation, as that which holdeth least of the author, and most of the things themselves. Again, the use which it holdeth to man's life, if it be not the greatest, yet assuredly is the freest from any ill accident or quality. For those which are conversant much in poets, as they attain to great variety, so withal they become conceited; and those that are brought up in philosophy and sciences do wax (according as their nature is) some of them too stiff and opinionate, and some others too perplexed and confused. Whereas History possesseth the mind of the conceits which are nearest allied unto action, and imprinteth them so, as it doth not alter the complexion of the mind neither to irresolution nor pertinacity. But this is true, that in no sort of writings there is a greater distance between the good and the bad, no not between the most excellent poet and the vainest rhymer, nor between the deepest philosopher and the most frivolous schoolmen, than there is between good histories and those that bear the same or the like title. In which regard, having purposed to write the History of England from the beginning of the reign of K. Henry the eighth of that name near unto the present time wherein Q. Elizabeth reigneth in good felicity, I am delivered of the excuse wherewith the best writers of history are troubled in their proëms [preambles], when they go about without breaking the bounds of modesty to give a reason why they should write that again which others have written well or at least tolerably before. For those which I am to follow are such as I may rather fear the reproach of coming into their number, than the opinion of presumption if I hope to do better than they. But in the mean time it must be considered, that the best of the ancient histories were contrived out of divers particular Commentaries, Relations, and Narrations, which it was not hard to digest with ornament, and thereof to compound one entire Story. And as at the first such writers had the ease of other's labours, so since they have the whole commendation; in regard these former writings are for the most part lost, whereby their borrowings do not appear. But unto me the disadvantage is great, finding no public memories of any consideration or worth, in sort that the supply must be out of the freshness of memory and tradition, and out of the acts, instruments, and negotiations of state themselves, together with the glances of foreign histories; which though I do acknowledge to be the best originals and instructions out of which to write an history, yet the travel must be much greater than if there had been already digested any tolerable chronicle as a simple narration of the actions themselves, which should only have needed out of the former helps to be enriched with the counsels and the speeches and notable particularities. And this was the reason why I mought [might] not attempt to go higher to more ancient times, because those helps and grounds did more and more fail; although if I be not deceived I may truly affirm that there have no times passed over in this nation which have produced greater actions, nor more worthy to be delivered to the ages hereafter. For they be not the great wars and conquests (which many times are the works of fortune and fall out in barbarous times) the rehearsal whereof maketh the profitable and instructing history; but rather times refined in policies and industries, new and rare variety of accidents and alterations, equal and just encounters of state and state in forces and of prince and prince in sufficiency, that bring upon the stage the best parts for observation. Now if you look into the general natures of the times (which I have undertaken) throughout Europe, whereof the times of this nation must needs participate, you shall find more knowledge in the world than was in the ages before, whereby the wits of men (which are the shops wherein all actions are forged) are more furnished and improved. Then if you shall restrain your consideration to the state of this monarchy, first there will occur unto you changes rare, and altogether unknown to antiquity, in matters of religion and the state ecclesiastical. Then to behold the several reigns, of a king that first, or next the first, became absolute in the sovereignty: of a king in minority: of a queen married to a foreigner: and lastly of a queen that hath governed without the help either of a marriage, or of any mighty man of her blood: is no small variety in the affairs of a monarchy, but such as perhaps in four successions in any state at any time is hardly to be found. Besides there have not wanted examples within the compass of the same times neither of an usurpation, nor of rebellions under heads of greatness, nor of commotions merely popular, nor of sundry desperate conspiracies (an unwonted thing in hereditary monarchies), nor of foreign wars of all sorts; invasive, repulsive of invasion, open and declared, covert and underhand, by sea, by land, Scottish, French, Spanish, succors, protections, new and extraordinary kinds of confederacies with subjects. Generally without question the state of this nation never had a larger reach to import the universal affairs of Europe; as that which was in the former part of the time the counterpoise between France and Spain, and in the latter the only encounter and opposition against Spain. Add hereunto the new discoveries and navigations abroad, the new provisions of laws and precedents of state at home, and the accidents memorable both of state and of court; and there will be no doubt but the times which I have chosen are of all former times of this nation the fittest to be registered; if it be not in this respect, that they be of too fresh memory, which point I know very well will be a prejudice, as if this story were written in favour of the time present. But it shall suffice unto me, without betraying mine own name and memory or the liberty of a history, to procure this commendation to the time with posterity, namely, that a private man living in the same time should not doubt to publish an history of the time which should not carry any show or taste at all of flattery; a point noted for an infallible demonstration of a good time.

King Henry, the seventh of that name, after he had lived about fifty-two years, and thereof reigned twenty-three and some months, deceased of a consumption the 22nd day of April, in the palace which he had built at Ritchemount [Richmond], in the year of our Redemption 1509. This king attained unto the crown, not only from a private fortune, which mought [might] endow him with moderation, but also from the fortune of an exiled man, which had quickened in him all seeds of observation and industry. His times were rather prosperous than calm, for he was assailed with many troubles, which he overcame happily; a matter that did no less set forth his wisdom than his fortune; and yet such a wisdom as seemed rather a dexterity to deliver himself from dangers when they pressed him, than any deep foresight to prevent them afar off. Jealous he was over the greatness of his Nobility, as remembering how himself was set up. And much more did this humour increase in him after he had conflicted with such idols and counterfeits as were Lambert Symnell and Perkin Warbeck: the strangeness of which dangers made him think nothing safe. Whereby he was forced to descend to the employment of secret espials [spies] and suborned conspirators, a necessary remedy against so dark and subtle practices; and not to be reprehended, except it were true which some report, that he had intelligence with confessors for the revealing of matters disclosed in confession. And yet if a man compare him with the kings his concurrents in France and Spain, he shall find him more politic than Lewis the

Twelfth of France, and more entire and sincere than Ferdinando of Spain, upon whom notwithstanding he did handsomely bestow the envy of the death of Edward Plantagenet, Earl of Warwick. Great and devout reverence he bare unto religion, as he that employed ecclesiastical men in most of his affairs and negotiations; and as he that was brought hardly and very late to the abolishing of the privilege of sanctuaries in case of treason, and that not before he had obtained it by way of suit from Pope Alexander; which sanctuaries nevertheless had been the forges of most of his troubles. In his government he was led by none, scarcely by his laws, and yet he was a great observer of formality in all his proceedings, which notwithstanding was no impediment to the working of his will; and in the suppressing and punishing of the treasons which during the whole course of his reign were committed against him, he had a very strange kind of interchanging of very large and unexpected pardons with severe executions; which (his wisdom considered) could not be imputed to any inconstancy or inequality, but to a discretion, or at least to a principle that he had apprehended, that it was good not obstinately to pursue one course, but to try both ways. In his wars, he seemed rather confident than enterprising, by which also commonly he was not the poorer; but generally he did seem inclinable to live in peace, and made but offers of war to mend the conditions of peace; and in the quenching of the commotions of his subjects he was ever ready to achieve those wars in person, sometimes reserving himself, but never retiring himself, but as ready to second. Of nature he coveted to accumulate treasure, which the people (into whom there is infused for the preservation of monarchies a natural desire to discharge their princes, though it be with the unjust charge of their counsellors and ministers,) did impute unto Cardinal Morton and Sir Reginold Bray, who (as it after appeared) as counsellors of ancient authority with him, did so second his humour as they tempered and refrained it. Whereas Empson and Dudley that followed (being persons that had no reputation with him, otherwise than the servile following of his own humour) gave him way and shaped him way to those extremities, wherewith himself was touched with remorse at his death, and which his successor disavowed. In expending of treasure he never spared charge that his affairs required, and in his foundations was magnificent enough, but his rewards were very limited; so that his liberality was rather upon his own state and memory than towards the deserts of others. He chose commonly to employ cunning persons, as he that knew himself sufficient to make use of their uttermost reaches, without danger of being abused with them himself.

The History
of the Reign
# of King Henry the Eighth.

After the decease of that wise and fortunate King, King Henry the Seventh, who died in the height of his prosperity, there followed (as useth to do when the sun setteth so exceeding clear) one of the fairest mornings of a kingdom that hath been known in this land or anywhere else. A young King about eighteen years of age, for stature, strength, making, and beauty, one of the goodliest persons of his time. And although he were given to pleasure, yet he was likewise desirous of glory; so that there was a passage open in his mind by glory for virtue. Neither was he unadorned with learning, though therein he came short of his brother Arthur. He had never any the least pique, difference, or jealousy, with the King his father, which might give any occasion of altering court or counsel upon the change; but all things passed in a still. He was the first heir of the White and of the Red Rose; so that there was no discontented party now left in the kingdom, but all men's hearts turned towards him; and not only their hearts, but their eyes also; for he was the only son of the kingdom. He had no brother; which though it be a comfort for Kings to have, yet it draweth the subjects' eyes a little aside. And yet being a married man in those young years, it promised hope of speedy issue to succeed in the Crown. Neither was there any Queen Mother, who might share any way in the government or clash with the counsellors for authority, while the King intended his pleasure. No such thing as any great or mighty subject who might eclipse or overshade the imperial power. And for the people and state in general, they were in such lowness of obedience, as subjects were like to yield who had lived almost four and twenty years under so politic a King as his father; being also one who came partly in by the sword, and had so high a courage in all points of regality, and was ever victorious in rebellions and seditions of the people. The Crown extremely rich and full of treasure; and the kingdom like to be so in short time. For there was no war, no dearth, no stop of trade or commerce; it was only the Crown which sucked too hard; but now being full, and upon the head of a young King, it was like to draw the less. Lastly, he was inheritor of his father's reputation, which was great throughout the world. He had strait alliance with the two neighbour states, an ancient enemy in former times, and an ancient friend, Scotland and Burgundy. He had peace and amity with France, under the assurance not only of treaty and league, but of necessity and inability in the French to do him hurt, in respect the French King's designs were wholly bent upon Italy. So that it may be truly said, there had been scarcely seen or known in many ages such a rare concurrence of signs and promises of a happy and flourishing reign to ensue, as were now met in this young King, called after his father's name, Henry the Eighth.

On the Fortunate Memory
of Elizabeth
Queen of England.

Elizabeth both in her nature and her fortune was a wonderful person among women, a memorable person among princes. But it is not to monks or closet penmen that we are to look for guidance in such a case; for men of that order, being keen in style, poor in judgment, and partial in feeling, are no faithful witnesses as to the real passages of business. It is for ministers and great officers to judge of these things, and those who have handled the helm of government, and been acquainted with the difficulties and mysteries of state business.

The government of a woman has been a rare thing at all times; felicity in such government a rarer thing still; felicity and long continuance together the rarest thing of all. Yet this Queen reigned forty-four years complete, and did not outlive her felicity. Of this felicity I propose to say something; without wandering into praises; for praise is the tribute of men, felicity the gift of God.

First, then, I set it down as part of her felicity that she was raised to sovereignty from a private fortune; not so much because of that feeling so deeply seated in man's nature, whereby benefits which come unexpected and unhoped for are always counted the greater blessings; but because Princes who are brought up in the reigning house with assured expectation of succeeding to the throne, are commonly spoiled by the indulgence and licence of their education, and so turn out both less capable and less temperate. And therefore you will find that the best kings are they who have been trained in both schools of fortune; such as Henry the Seventh with us, and Lewis the Twelfth in France; both of whom, of late years and almost at the same time, came to their kingdoms not only from a private but from an adverse and troubled fortune; and both were eminently prosperous; the one excelling in wisdom, the other in justice. Much like was the case of this Queen, whose early times and opening prospects fortune chequered with uncertainty, that afterwards when she was settled in the throne it might prove to the last constant and equable. For Elizabeth at her birth was destined to the succession, then disinherited, afterwards superseded. Her fortune in her brother's reign was more propitious and serene, in her sister's more troubled and doubtful. And yet she did not pass suddenly from the prison to the throne, with a mind embittered and swelling with the sense of misfortune, but was first restored to liberty and comforted with expectation; and so came to her kingdom at last quietly and prosperously, without tumult or competitor. All which I mention to show how Divine Providence, meaning to produce an excellent Queen, passed her by way of preparation through these several stages of discipline. Nor ought the calamity of her mother to be admitted as an objection to the dignity of her birth: the rather because it is clear that Henry the Eighth had fallen in love with another woman before he fell in anger with Anne, and because he has not escaped the censure of posterity as a man by nature extremely prone both to loves and suspicions, and violent in both even to the shedding of blood. And besides, the criminal charge in which she was involved was in itself, if we consider only the person to whom it related, improbable, and rested upon the slenderest conjectures; as was secretly whispered (as the manner is in such cases) even then, and Anne herself just before her death with a high spirit and in memorable words made protestation. For having procured a messenger whose fidelity and good will she thought she could trust, she sent the King, in the very hour when she was preparing for the scaffold, a message to this effect: "That he kept constant to his course of heaping honours upon her; from a gentlewoman without title he had made her marchioness; he had then raised her to be the partner of his throne and bed; and now at last, because there remained no higher step of earthly honour, he had vouchsafed to crown her innocence with martyrdom." Which words the messenger durst not indeed carry to the King, who was then in the heat of a new love; but fame, the vindicator of truth, transmitted them to posterity.

I account also as no small part of Elizabeth's felicity the period and compass of her administration; not only for its length, but as falling within that portion of her life which was fittest for the control of affairs and the handling of the reins of government. She was twenty-five years old (the age at which guardianship ceases) when she began to reign, and she continued reigning till her seventieth year; so that she never experienced either the disadvantages and subjection to other men's wills incident to a ward, nor the inconveniences of a lingering and impotent old age. Now old age brings with it even to private persons miseries enough; but to kings, besides those evils which are common to all, it brings also decline of greatness and inglorious exits from the stage. For there is hardly any sovereign who reigns till he becomes old and feeble, but suffers some diminution of power and reputation: of which we have a very eminent example in Philip the Second, King of Spain, a most powerful prince and perfect in the art of government; who in his last times when worn out with age became deeply sensible of this which I say, and therefore wisely submitted to the condition of things; voluntarily sacrificed the territories he had won in France, established peace there, attempted the like in other places, that he might leave a settled estate and all things clear and entire to his successor. Elizabeth's fortune on the contrary was so constant and flourishing, that not only did her declining, but though declining still fresh and vigorous years, bring with them no decline at all in the state of her affairs; but it was granted to her for an assured token of her felicity not to die before the fate of the revolt in Ireland had been decided by a victory; lest her glory might seem to be in any part sullied and incomplete.

Nor must it be forgotten withal among what kind of people she reigned; for had she been called to rule over Palmyrenes or in an unwarlike and effeminate country like Asia, the wonder would have been less; a womanish people might well enough be governed by a woman; but that in England, a nation particularly fierce and warlike, all things could be swayed and controlled at the beck of a woman, is a matter for the highest admiration.

Observe too that this same humour of her people, ever eager for war and impatient of peace, did not prevent her from cultivating and maintaining peace during the whole time of her reign. And this her desire of peace, together with the success of it, I count among her greatest praises; as a thing happy for her times, becoming to her sex, and salutary for her conscience. Some little disturbance there was in the northern counties about the tenth year of her reign, but it was immediately quieted and extinguished. The rest of her years flourished in internal peace, secure and profound.

And this peace I regard as more especially flourishing from two circumstances that attended it, and which though they have nothing to do with the merit of peace, add much to the glory of it. The one, that the calamities of her neighbours were as fires to make it more conspicuous and illustrious; the other that the benefits of peace were not unaccompanied with honour of war,—the reputation of England for arms and military prowess being by many noble deeds, not only maintained by her, but increased. For the aids sent to the Low Countries, to France, and to Scotland; the naval expeditions to both the Indies, some of which sailed all round the globe; the fleets despatched to Portugal and to harass the coasts of Spain; the many defeats and overthrows of the rebels in Ireland;—all these had the effect of keeping both the warlike virtues of our nation in full vigour and its fame and honour in full lustre.

Which glory had likewise this merit attached,—that while neighbour kings on the one side owed the preservation of their kingdoms to her timely succours; suppliant peoples on the other, given up by ill-advised princes to the cruelty of their ministers, to the fury of the populace, and to every kind of spoliation and devastation, received relief in their misery; by means of which they stand to this day.

Nor were her counsels less beneficent and salutary than her succours; witness her remonstrances so frequently addressed to the King of Spain that he would moderate his anger against his subjects in the Low Countries, and admit them to return to their allegiance under conditions not intolerable; and her continual warnings and earnest solicitations addressed to the kings of France that they would observe their edicts of pacification. That her counsel was in both cases unsuccessful, I do not deny. The common fate of Europe did not suffer it to succeed in the first; for so the ambition of Spain, being released as it were from prison, would have been free to spend itself (as things then were) upon the ruin of the kingdoms and commonwealths of Christendom. The blood of so many innocent persons, slaughtered with their wives and children at their hearths and in their beds by the vilest rabble, like so many brute beasts animated, armed, and set on by public authority, forbade it in the other; that innocent blood demanding in just revenge that the kingdom which had been guilty of so atrocious a crime should expiate it by mutual slaughters and massacres. But however that might be, she was not the less true to her own part, in performing the office of an ally both wise and benevolent.

Upon another account also this peace so cultivated and maintained by Elizabeth is matter of admiration; namely, that it proceeded not from any inclination of the times to peace, but from her own prudence and good management. For in a kingdom labouring with intestine faction on account of religion, and standing as a shield and stronghold of defence against the then formidable and overbearing ambition of Spain, matter for war was nowise wanting; it was she who by her forces and her counsels combined kept it under; as was proved by an event the most memorable in respect of felicity of all the actions of our time. For when that Spanish fleet, got up with such travail and ferment, waited upon with the

terror and expectation of all Europe, inspired with such confidence
of victory, came ploughing into our channels, it never took so
much as a cockboat at sea, never fired so much as a cottage on the
land, never even touched the shore; but was first beaten in a battle
and then dispersed and wasted in a miserable flight with many
shipwrecks; while on the ground and territories of England peace
remained undisturbed and unshaken.

Nor was she less fortunate in escaping the treacherous attempts of conspirators than in defeating and repelling the forces
of the enemy. For not a few conspiracies aimed at her life were in
the happiest manner both detected and defeated; and yet was not
her life made thereby more alarmed or anxious; there was no increase in the number of her guards; no keeping within her palace
and seldom going abroad; but still secure and confident, and
thinking more of the escape than of the danger, she held her
wonted course, and made no change in her way of life.

Worthy of remark too is the nature of the times in which she
flourished. For there are some times so barbarous and ignorant
that it is as easy a matter to govern men as to drive a flock of
sheep. But the lot of this Queen fell upon times highly instructed
and cultivated, in which it is not possible to be eminent and excellent without the greatest gifts of mind and a singular composition of virtue.

Again, the reigns of women are commonly obscured by
marriage; their praises and actions passing to the credit of their
husbands; whereas those that continue unmarried have their glory
entire and proper to themselves. In her case this was more especially so; inasmuch as she had no helps to lean upon in her government, except such as she had herself provided; no own brother,
no uncle, no kinsman of the royal family, to share her cares and
support her authority. And even those whom she herself raised to
honour she so kept in hand and mingled one with another, that
while she infused into each the greatest solicitude to please her
she was herself ever her own mistress.

Childless she was indeed, and left no issue of her own; a
thing which has happened also to the most fortunate persons, as
Alexander the Great, Julius Caesar, Trajan, and others; and which

has always been a moot-point and argued on both sides; some taking it for a diminution of felicity, for that to be happy both in the individual self and in the propagation of the kind would be a blessing above the condition of humanity; others regarding it as the crown and consummation of felicity, because that happiness only can be accounted perfect over which fortune has no further power; which cannot be where there is posterity.

Nor were outward conditions wanting: a tall stature, a graceful shape, a countenance in the highest degree majestic and yet sweet, a most happy and healthy constitution; to which this also must be added, that retaining her health and vigour to the end, and having experienced neither the vicissitudes of fortune nor the ills of old age, she obtained at last by an easy and gentle death that *euthanasia* which Augustus Caesar was wont so earnestly to pray for; and which is noted in the case of that excellent Emperor Antoninus Pius, whose death wore the appearance of a sweet and placid sleep. So likewise in the last illness of Elizabeth there was nothing miserable, nothing terrible, nothing revolting to human nature. She was not tormented either with desire of life, or impatience of sickness, or pangs of pain: none of the symptoms were frightful or loathsome; but all of that kind which showed rather the frailty than the corruption and dishonour of nature. For a few days before her death, by reason of the exceeding dryness of her body, wasted as it was with the cares of government and never refreshed with wine or a more generous diet, she was struck with paralysis; and yet she retained her powers of speech (a thing not usual in that disease) and of mind and of motion; only somewhat slower and duller. And this state of her body lasted only a few days, as if it were less like the last act of life than the first step to death. For to continue long alive with the faculties impaired is a miserable thing; but to have the sense a little laid asleep and so pass quickly to death, is a placid and merciful period and close of life.

To crown all, as she was most fortunate in all that belonged to herself, so was she in the virtue of her ministers. For she had such men about her as perhaps till that day this island did not produce. But God when he favours kings raises also and accomplishes the spirits of their servants.

Her death was followed by two posthumous felicities, more lofty and august perhaps than those which attended her in life; her successor, and her memory. For successor she has got one who, though in respect of masculine virtue and of issue and of fresh accession of empire he overtop and overshadow her, nevertheless both shows a tender respect for her name and honour, and bestows upon her acts a kind of perpetuity; having made no change of any consequence either in choice of persons or order of proceedings; insomuch that seldom has a son succeeded to a father with such silence and so little change and perturbation. And as for her memory, it is so strong and fresh both in the mouths and minds of men that, now death has extinguished envy and lighted up fame, the felicity of her memory contends in a manner with the felicity of her life. For if any factious rumour (bred of party feeling and religious dissension) still wanders abroad (and yet even this seems now timid and weak and overborne by general consent), sincere it is not, enduring it cannot be. And on this account chiefly it is that I have put together these observations, such as they are, concerning her felicity and the marks she enjoyed of the divine favour, that malevolent men may fear to curse what God has so highly blessed.

And if any man shall say in answer, as was said to Caesar, "Here is much indeed to admire and wonder at, but what is there to praise?" surely I account true wonder and admiration as a kind of excess of praise. Nor can so happy a fortune as I have described fall to the lot of any, but such as besides being singularly sustained and nourished by the divine favour, are also in some measure by their own virtue the makers of such fortune for themselves. And yet I think good to add some few remarks upon her moral character; confining myself however to those points which seem most to give opening and supply fuel to the speeches of traducers.

In religion Elizabeth was pious and moderate, and constant, and adverse to innovation. Of her piety, though the proofs appear most clearly in her actions, yet no slight traces were to be found likewise in her ordinary way of life and conversation. Prayers and divine service, either in her chapel or closet, she seldom failed to attend. Of the Scriptures and the writings of the Fathers, especially those of St. Augustine, she was a great reader. Some prayers upon particular occasions she herself composed. If she chanced even in common talk to speak of God, she almost always both gave him the title of her Maker, and composed her eyes and countenance to an expression of humility and reverence; a thing which I have myself often observed. And as for that which some have given out, that she could not endure the thought of mortality and was impatient of all allusion either to old age or death, that is utterly untrue. For very often, many years before her death, she would pleasantly call herself an old woman, and would talk of the kind of epitaph she would like to have upon her tomb; saying that she had no fancy for glory or splendid titles, but would rather have a line or two of memorial, recording in few words only her name, her virginity, the time of her reign, the reformation of religion, and the preservation of peace. It is true that in the flower of her years, while she was yet able to bear children, being questioned about declaring a successor, she replied that she would not have her winding sheet spread before her eyes while she was alive; and yet not many years before her death, being in a thoughtful mood, meditating probably upon her mortality, and being interrupted by one of her familiars with a complaint that many great offices in the commonwealth were too long vacant, she rose up and said in some displeasure, it was clear that *her* office would not be vacant for an instant.

With regard to her moderation in religion there may seem to be a difficulty, on account of the severity of the laws made against popish subjects. But on this point I have some things to advance which I myself carefully observed and know to be true.

Her intention undoubtedly was, on the one hand not to force consciences, but on the other not to let the state, under pretence of conscience and religion, be brought in danger. Upon this ground she concluded at the first that, in a people courageous and warlike and prompt to pass from strife of minds to strife of hands,

the free allowance and toleration by public authority of two re
ligions would be certain destruction. Some of the more turbulent
and factious bishops also she did, in the newness of her reign
when all things were subject to suspicion,—but not without legal
warrant—restrain and keep in free custody. The rest, both clergy
and laity, far from troubling them with any severe inquisition, she
sheltered by a gracious connivency. This was the condition of
affairs at first. Nor even when provoked by the excommunication
pronounced against her by Pius Quintus (an act sufficient not only
to have roused indignation but to have furnished ground and
matter for a new course of proceeding), did she depart almost at
all from this clemency, but persevered in the course which was
agreeable to her own nature. For being both wise and of a high
spirit, she was little moved with the sound of such terrors; knowing she could depend upon the loyalty and love of her own people,
and upon the small power the popish party within the realm had
to do harm, as long as they were not seconded by a foreign enemy.
About the twenty-third year of her reign however, the case was
changed. And this distinction of time is not artificially devised to
make things fit, but expressed and engraved in public acts.

For up to that year there was no penalty of a grievous kind
imposed by previous laws upon popish subjects. But just then the
ambitious and vast design of Spain for the subjugation of the
kingdom came gradually to light. Of this a principal part was the
raising up within the bowels of the realm of a disaffected and rev-
olutionary party which should join with the invading enemy; and
the hope of effecting this lay in our religious dissensions. To this
object therefore they addressed themselves with all their might;
and, the seminaries beginning then to blossom, priests were sent
over into England for the purpose of kindling and spreading a
zeal for the Romish religion, of teaching and inculcating the power
of Romish excommunication to release subjects from their obedience, and of exciting and preparing men's minds with expectation
of a change. About the same time an attempt was made upon
Ireland with open arms, the name and government of Elizabeth
was assailed with a variety of wicked libels, and there was a
strange ferment and swelling in the world, forerunner of some

greater disturbance. And though I do not say that all the priests
were acquainted with the design, or knew what was doing; for
they may have been only the tools of other men's malice; yet it is
true, and proved by the confessions of many witnesses, that from
the year I have mentioned to the thirtieth of Elizabeth (when the
design of Spain and the Pope was put in execution by that memorable armada of land and sea forces) almost all the priests who
were sent over to this country were charged among the other offices belonging to their function, to insinuate that matters could
not long stay as they were, that a new aspect and turn of things
would be seen shortly, and that the state of England was cared for
both by the Pope and the Catholic princes, if the English would
but be true to themselves. Besides which, some of the priests had
plainly engaged themselves in practices tending directly to the
shaking and subversion of the state; and above all, letters were
intercepted from various quarters by which the plan upon which
they were to proceed was discovered; in which letters it was written, that the vigilance of the Queen and her council in the matter
of the Catholics would be eluded; for that she was only intent
upon preventing the Catholic party from getting a head in the person of any nobleman or great personage, whereas the plan now
was to dispose and prepare everything by the agency of private
persons and men of small mark; and that too without their having
any communication or acquaintance one with another; but all to
be done under the seal of confession. Such were the arts then resorted to—arts with which these men (as we have seen lately in a
case not much unlike) are practised and familiar. This so great
tempest of dangers made it a kind of necessity for Elizabeth to put
some severer constraint upon that party of her subjects which was
estranged from her and by these means poisoned beyond recovery,
and was at the same time growing rich by reason of their immu-
nity from public offices and burdens. And as the mischief increased, the origin of it being traced to the seminary priests, who
were bred in foreign parts, and supported by the purses and
charities of foreign princes, professed enemies of this kingdom,
and whose time had been passed in places where the very name

of Elizabeth was never heard except as that of a heretic excommunicated and accursed, and who (if not themselves stained with treason) were the acknowledged intimates of those that were directly engaged in such crimes, and had by their own arts and poisons depraved and soured with a new leaven of malignity the whole lump of Catholics, which had before been more sweet and harmless; there was no remedy for it but that men of this class should be prohibited upon pain of death from coming into the kingdom at all; which at last, in the twenty-seventh year of her reign, was done. Nor did the event itself which followed not long after, when so great a tempest assailed and fell with all its fury upon the kingdom, tend in any degree to mitigate the envy and hatred of these men; but rather increased it, as if they had utterly cast off all feeling for their country, which they were ready to betray to a foreign servitude. And though it is true that the fear of danger from Spain, which was the spur that goaded her to this severity, did afterwards subside or abate; yet because the memory of the time past remained deeply printed in men's minds and feelings, and the laws once made could not be abrogated without the appearance of inconstancy, or neglected without the appearance of weakness and disorder, the very force of circumstances made it impossible for Elizabeth to return to the former state of things as it was before the twenty-seventh year of her reign. To which must be added the industry of some of her officers to improve the exchequer, and the solicitude of her ministers of justice who saw no hope of salvation for the country but in the laws; all which demanded and pressed the execution of them. And yet what her own natural disposition was appears plainly in this, that she so blunted the law's edge that but a small proportion of the priests were capitally punished. All which I say not by way of apology; for these proceedings need no apology; since the safety of the kingdom turned upon them, and all this severity both in the manner and the measure of it came far short of the bloody examples set by the priesthood,—examples scarcely to be named among Christians, and proceeding moreover some of them rather out of arrogance and malice than out of necessity. But I conceive that I have made good my assertion, and shown that in the cause of religion she was indeed moderate, and that what variation there was was not in her nature but in the times.

Of her constancy in religion and worship the best proof is her dealing with Popery: which though in her sister's reign it had been established by public authority and fostered with great care and labour, and had taken deep root in the land, and was strengthened by the consent and zeal of all who were in authority and power; yet because it was not agreeable either to the word of God or to primitive purity or to her own conscience, she at once with the greatest courage and the fewest helps proceeded to uproot and abolish. And yet she did it not precipitately or upon eager impulse, but prudently and all in due season; as may be gathered from many circumstances, and among the rest from a reply made by her on the following occasion. Not many days after she came to the throne, when prisoners were released (as the custom is to inaugurate and welcome a new reign by the release of prisoners), a certain courtier, who from nature and habit had taken to himself the license of a jester, came to her as she went to chapel, and either of his own motion or set on by wiser men, presented her a petition; adding with a loud voice before all the company, that there were yet four or five prisoners more who deserved liberty, for whom he besought that they might be released likewise; namely, the four Evangelists and the Apostle Paul; who had been long shut up in an unknown tongue, as it were in prison, so that they could not converse with the people. To whom she answered very wisely, that it were good first to inquire further of themselves, whether they would be released or no: thus meeting a sudden question with a doubtful answer, as meaning to keep all clear and whole for her own decision. And yet she did not introduce these changes timidly neither, nor by starts; but proceeding in due order, gravely and maturely, after conference had been first had between the parties, and a Parliament held, she then at last, and yet all within a single year, so ordered and established everything relating to the Church, that to the last day of her life she never allowed a single point to be departed from. Nay at almost every meeting of Parliament she gave a public warning against innovation in the dis-

cipline and rites of the Church. And so much for the point of
religion.

As for those lighter points of character,—as that she allowed
herself to be wooed and courted, and even to have love made to
her; and liked it; and continued it beyond the natural age for such
vanities;—if any of the sadder sort of persons be disposed to make
a great matter of this, it may be observed that there is something
to admire in these very things, which ever way you take them.
For if viewed indulgently, they are much like the accounts we find
in romances, of the Queen in the blessed islands, and her court
and institutions, who allows of amorous admiration but prohibits
desire. But if you take them seriously, they challenge admiration
of another kind and of a very high order; for certain it is that these
dalliances detracted but little from her fame and nothing at all
from her majesty, and neither weakened her power nor sensibly
hindered her business:—whereas such things are not unfrequently
allowed to interfere with the public fortune. But to conclude, she
was no doubt a good and moral Queen; and such too she wished
to appear. Vices she hated, and it was by honest arts that she desired to shine. And speaking of her morality, I remember a circumstance in point. Having ordered a letter to be written to her
ambassador concerning a message which was to be given sepa-
rately to the Queen Mother of the Valois, and finding that her
secretary had inserted a clause directing the ambassador to say to
the Queen Mother by way of compliment, that they were two
Queens from whom though women no less was expected in administration of affairs and in the virtue and arts of government
than from the greatest men,—she would not endure the comparison, but ordered it to be struck out; saying that the arts and principles which she employed in governing were of a far other sort
than those of the Queen Mother. Nor was she spoiled by power
and long reigning: but the praises which pleased her most were
when one so managed the conversation as aptly to insinuate that
even if she had passed her life in a private and mean fortune she
could not have lived without some note of excellency among men;
so little was she disposed to borrow anything of her fortune to the
credit of her virtue. But if I should enter into her praises, whether

moral or political, I should either fall into certain common-place observations and commemorations of virtues, which would be unworthy of so rare a princess; or in order to give them a lustre and beauty peculiar and appropriate, I should have to run into the history of her life,—a task requiring both more leisure and a richer vein. Thus much I have said in few words, according to my ability. But the truth is that the only true commender of this lady is time, which, so long a course as it has run, has produced nothing in this sex like her, for the administration of civil affairs.

The Beginning
of the History
# of Great Britain.

By the decease of Elizabeth, Queen of England, the issues of King
Henry the Eighth failed; being spent in one generation and three
successions. For that King, though he were one of the goodliest
persons of his time, yet he left only by his six wives three children;
who reigning successively and dying childless, made place to the
line of Margaret, his eldest sister, married to James the Fourth
King of Scotland. There succeeded therefore to the kingdom of
England James the Sixth, then King of Scotland, descended of the
same Margaret both by father and mother; so that by a rare event
in the pedigrees of Kings, it seemed as if the Divine Providence, to
extinguish and take away all note of a stranger, had doubled upon
his person, within the circle of one age, the royal blood of England
by both parents. This succession drew towards it the eyes of all
men; being one of the most memorable accidents that had happened a long time in the Christian world. For the kingdom of
France having been reunited in the age before in all the provinces
thereof formerly dismembered; and the kingdom of Spain being
of more fresh memory united and made entire by the annexing of
Portugal in the person of Philip the Second; there remained but

this third and last union, for the counterpoising of the power of these three great monarchies, and the disposing of the affairs of Europe thereby to a more assured and universal peace and concord. And this event did hold men's observations and discourses the more, because the Island of Great Britain, divided from the rest of the world, was never before united in itself under one King; notwithstanding the people be of one language, and not separate by mountains or great waters; and notwithstanding also that the uniting of them has been in former times industriously attempted both by war and treaty. Therefore it seemed a manifest work of Providence and case of reservation for these times; insomuch as the vulgar conceived that there was now an end given and a consummation to superstitious prophecies (the belief of fools, but the talk sometimes of wise men), and to an ancient tacit expectation which had by tradition been infused and inveterated into men's minds. But as the best divinations and predictions are the politic and probable foresight and conjectures of wise men, so in this matter the providence of King Henry the Seventh was in all men's mouths, who, being one of the deepest and most prudent princes of the world, upon the deliberation concerning the marriage of his eldest daughter into Scotland, had by some speech uttered by him showed himself sensible and almost prescient of this event.

Neither did there want a concurrence of divers rare external circumstances (besides the virtues and condition of the person) which gave great reputation to this succession. A king, in the strength of his years, supported with great alliances abroad, established with royal issue at home, at peace with all the world, practised in the regiment of such a kingdom as mought [might] rather enable a king by variety of accidents than corrupt him with affluence or vain glory; and one that besides his universal capacity and judgment, was notably exercised and practised in matters of religion and the church; which in these times by the confused use of both swords are become so intermixed with considerations of estate, as most of the counsels of sovereign princes or republics depend upon them. But nothing did more fill foreign nations with admiration and expectation of his succession, than the wonderful and (by them) unexpected consent of all estates and subjects of

England for the receiving of the King without the least scruple, pause, or question. For it had been generally dispersed by the fugitives beyond the seas (who partly to apply themselves to the ambition of foreigners, and partly to give estimation and value to their own employments, used to represent the state of England in a false light), that after Queen Elizabeth's decease there must follow in England nothing but confusions, interreigns, and perturbations of estate; likely far to exceed the ancient calamities of the civil wars between the houses of Lancaster and York, by how much more the dissensions were like to be more mortal and bloody when foreign competition should be added to domestical, and divisions for religion to matter of title to the crown. And in special, Parsons the Jesuit, under a disguised name, had not long before published an express treatise, wherein whether his malice made him believe his own fancies, or whether he thought it the fittest way to move sedition, like evil spirits which seem to foretell the tempest they mean to move, he laboured to display and give colour to all the vain pretences and dreams of succession which he could imagine; and thereby had possessed many abroad, that knew not the affairs here, with those his vanities. Neither wanted there here within this realm divers persons both wise and well affected, who though they doubted not of the undoubted right, yet setting before themselves the waves of peoples' hearts (guided no less by sudden temporary winds than by the natural course and motion of the waters), were not without fear what mought [might] be the event. For Queen Elizabeth, being a Prince of extreme caution, and yet one that loved admiration above safety, and knowing the declaration of a successor mought in point of safety be disputable, but in point of admiration and respect assuredly to her disadvantage, had from the beginning set it down for a maxim of estate to impose a silence touching succession. Neither was it only reserved as a secret of estate, but restrained by severe laws, that no man should presume to give opinion or maintain argument touching the same; so though the evidence of right drew all the subjects of the land to think one thing, yet the fear of danger of law made no man privy to other's thought. And therefore it rejoiced all men to see so fair a morning of a kingdom, and to be thoroughly secured of former apprehensions; as a man that awaketh out of a fearful dream. But so it was, that not only the consent but the applause and joy was infinite and not be expressed throughout the realm of England upon this succession; whereof the consent (no doubt) may be truly ascribed to the clearness of the right; but the general joy, alacrity, and gratulation were the effects of differing causes. For Queen Elizabeth, though she had the use of many both virtues and demonstrations that mought draw and knit unto her the heart of her people, yet nevertheless carrying a hand restrained in gift and strained in points of prerogative, could not answer the votes either of servants or subjects to a full contentment; especially in her latter days, when the continuance of her reign (which extended to five and forty years) mought discover in people their natural desire and inclination towards change; so that a new court and a new reign were not to many unwelcome. Many were glad, and especially those of settled estate and fortunes, that the fears and incertainties were overblown and that the dye was cast: others that had made their way with the King or offered their service in the time of the former Queen, thought now the time was come for which they had prepared: and generally all such as had any dependance upon the late Earl of Essex (who had mingled the secrecy of his own ends with the popular pretence of advancing the King's title) made account their cause was amended. Again such as mought misdoubt they had given the King any occasion of distaste, did continue by their forwardness and confidence to shew it was but their fastness to the former government, and that those affections ended with the time. The Papists nourished their hopes by collating the case of the Papists in England and under Queen Elizabeth and the case of the Papists in Scotland under the King; interpreting that the condition of them in Scotland was the less grievous, and divining of the King's government here accordingly; besides the comfort they ministered themselves from the memory of the Queen his mother. The ministers, and those which stood for the Presbytery, thought their cause had more sympathy with the discipline of Scotland than the hierarchy of England, and so took themselves to be a degree nearer their desires. Thus had every condition of persons some contemplation of benefit which they promised themselves; overreaching perhaps, according to the nature of hope, but yet not without some probable ground of conjecture. At which time also there came forth in print the King's book, entitled Βασιλικὸν Δῶρον,[1] containing matter of instruction to the Prince his son touching the office of a king; which book falling into every man's hand filled the whole realm as with a good perfume or incense before the King's coming in. For being excellently written, and having nothing of affectation, it did not only satisfy better than particular reports touching the King's disposition; but far exceeded any formal or curious edict or declaration which could have been devised of that nature, wherewith Princes at the beginning of their reigns do use to grace themselves, or at least express themselves gracious, in the eyes of their people. And this was, for the general, the state and constitution of men's minds upon this change. The actions themselves passed in this manner, etc.

[The rest is wanting.]

---

[1] [Basilikon Doron, Kingly Gift: James I's book of instructions for his eldest son.]

Character
of Julius Caesar

Julius Caesar had from the beginning a fortune full of exercise:
which turned to his advantage: for it took away his pride and
braced his sinews. A mind he had, in desires and affections turbulent, but in judgment and intellect very serene; as appears by the
ease with which he delivered himself both in action and speech.
For no man decided quicker, or spoke clearer: there was nothing
embarrassed, nothing involved about him. But in will and appetite he was one who never rested in what he had got, but ever
pressed forward to things beyond. And yet he was not hurried
from one action to another by a humour of weariness, but made
the transitions at the just periods: for he always brought his actions to the most perfect closes. And therefore he that after winning so many victories and making himself so secure did not
despise the relics of civil war in Spain, but went in person to put
an end to them; as soon as ever that last civil war was concluded
and peace established everywhere, immediately set about an expedition against the Parthians. Greatness of mind he undoubtedly
had in a very high degree; yet such as aspired more after personal
aggrandisement than merit towards the public. For he referred

everything to himself, and was himself the true and perfect centre of all his own actions: which was the cause of his singular and almost perpetual felicity. For he allowed neither country, nor religion, nor services, nor kindred, nor friendships, to be any hindrance or bridle to his purposes. Neither was he much bent upon perpetuity; as one who neither established the state of affairs, nor founded or erected anything remarkable either in the way of building or institution; but as it were referred all things to himself. So also he confined his thoughts within the circle of his own times. Only his name he wished to make famous; because he thought he had himself some interest in that. And assuredly in his private wishes he cared more for power than reputation. For he sought reputation and fame not for themselves, but as instruments of power. By natural impulse therefore, not by any moral guiding, he aspired to the supreme authority; and aspired rather to possess it than to be thought worthy of it: a thing which gave him favour with the people, who had no dignity of their own; but with the nobles and great persons, who wished also to preserve their own dignity, procured him the reputation of covetousness and boldness. Wherein assuredly they were not far from the truth: for he was by nature extremely bold, and never showed any bashfulness except when he assumed it on purpose. And yet for all that, this boldness was so fashioned as neither to impeach him of rashness, nor to make him intolerable, nor to bring his nature into suspicion: but was thought to proceed from a simplicity of manners, and confidence, and the nobility of his birth. And the same held good in all things else, that he was taken to be by no means cunning or wily, but frank and veracious. And though he was in fact a consummate master of simulation and dissimulation, and made up entirely of arts, insomuch that nothing was left to his nature except what art had approved, nevertheless there appeared in him nothing of artifice, nothing of dissimulation; and it was thought that his nature and disposition had full play and that he did but follow the bent of them. Yet for the smaller and meaner artifices and precautions, to which men unskilled in affairs and depending not on their own strength but on help from without, are driven for the support of their authority, he was not at all beholden to these;

as being a man exceedingly expert in all human actions, and who managed all business of any consequence for himself, not by others. How to extinguish envy he knew excellently well; and thought it an object worth purchasing even by the sacrifice of dignity; and being in quest of real power, he was content during the whole course of his life to decline and put by all the empty show and pomp and circumstance of it: until at last, whether satiated with power or corrupted by flattery, he aspired likewise to the external emblems thereof, the name of king and the crown; which turned to his destruction. The sovereignty was the mark he aimed at even from his youth; the example of Sylla, the relationship of Marius, the emulation of Pompey, the corruptions and perturbation of the times, readily suggesting it to him. But he made himself a way to the sovereignty in a strange order; first by means of a power popular and seditious, afterwards by a power military and imperatorial. For at first he had to break the force and authority of the senate; during the maintenance of which no man could find a passage to immoderate and extraordinary commands. And after that, he had to overthrow the power of Crassus and Pompey, which could not be done except by arms. And therefore (as a most skilful carpenter of his own fortune) he raised the first structure by means of largesses, corruption of the courts of justice, revival of the memory of Caius Marius and his party (most of the senators and nobles being of the Syllan faction), agrarian laws, putting in of seditious tribunes, secret favouring of the madnesses of Catiline and his conspirators, banishment of Cicero, upon whose cause the authority of the senate turned, and a number of the like arts; but most of all by the conjunction of Crassus and Pompey first with one another and then with himself, which completed it. Which part of his design being accomplished, he immediately addressed himself to the other; obtaining the proconsulship of Gaul for five years, and then again for another five years; and so making himself powerful in arms, legions, and a warlike and opulent province, in a position to threaten Italy. For he saw well that as soon as he had strengthened himself with arms and military power, neither Crassus nor Pompey would be a match for him; seeing that the one trusted to his wealth and the other to his fame and reputation; the one waxed old in years, the other in authority; neither had sound and vigorous safeguards to rest upon. All which things fell out to him according to his desire: the rather because he had the several senators and magistrates, and indeed all persons who had any power, so obliged and bound to himself by private benefits, that there was no danger of any combination being formed to oppose his designs, before he should openly invade the commonwealth. Which though he had always intended to do, and at last did, yet he did not put off his mask; but so carried himself that, what with the reasonableness of his demands, what with the pretence of a desire of peace, what with the moderate use of his successes, he turned the envy on the other party, and made it seem that he was driven for his own safety into a necessary war. The hollowness of which pretence was clearly proved, when the civil wars being ended, and he being in possession of the soverign power, and all the rivals that could cause him any anxiety being removed out of the way, yet he never once thought of restoring the commonwealth, no, nor cared to make so much as a pretence of doing it. Which plainly shows that the desire and purpose of obtaining the sovereignty had always been in him, and at last came out. For he did not merely seize an occasion that offered itself; himself made and shaped the occasions. It was in the business of war that his ability was most conspicuous; and so great it was, that he could not only lead an army but make one. For he was not more skilful in conducting actions than in the management of men's minds: and that not by any ordinary kind of discipline, that inured them to obey commands, or awakened a sense of shame, or enforced by severity; but one that inspired a wonderful ardour and alacrity, and won the battle almost before it began: and endeared him to the soldiery more than was good for a free commonwealth. Versed as he was moreover in every kind of war, and uniting civil arts with military, no accident took him so unexpectedly but he had a remedy prepared for it; nothing fell out so cross, but he drew some advantage from it. For his own person he had a due respect: as one that would sit in his tent during great battles, and manage everything by messages. From which he derived a double advantage; first that he went seldomer into danger, and secondly that if ever the fortune of the day were going against him, his own presence was as good as a fresh reinforcement to restore the battle. And in his warlike arrangements and enterprises he did not conduct things merely according to precedent, but would invent with consummate judgment new devices framed to the occasion. In his friendships he was constant enough, and singularly kind and indulgent. And yet he made choice of such friends that it was easy to see that he meant their friendship to be an instrument and not an impediment. And since his aim both by nature and principle was not to be eminent among great men, but to command among followers, he chose for his friends men that were of mean condition, but industrious and active, to whom he might be all in all. Hence the saying "Let me die, so Caesar live," and the like. With nobles and equals he made friendships according to his occasions; but he admitted no man to intimacy except such whose hopes rested entirely in himself. In letters and learning he was moderately well accomplished, but it was that kind of learning which was of use in the business of life. For he was well versed in history, and had wonderful knowledge of the weight and point of words; and because he attributed much to his felicity, he affected to be learned in the stars. Eloquence he had also, natural and pure. To pleasures he was naturally inclined, and indulged freely in them; which in his early times served the purpose of simulation; for no one feared any danger from such a disposition. But he so governed his pleasures, that they were no hindrance to his interest and main business, and his mind was rather invigorated than made languid by them. At the table he was sober, in his lusts not particular, in public entertainments gay and magnificent. Such being the man, the same thing was his destruction at last which in the beginning was his advancement, I mean the desire of popularity. For there is nothing so popular as the forgiveness of enemies: and this it was which, whether it were virtue or art, cost him his life.

Of the Interpretation
of Nature

Proem[1]

Believing that I was born for the service of mankind, and regarding the care of the commonwealth as a kind of common property which like the air and the water belongs to everybody, I set myself to consider in what way mankind might be best served, and what service I was myself best fitted by nature to perform.

Now among all the benefits that could be conferred upon mankind, I found none so great as the discovery of new arts, endowments, and commodities for the bettering of man's life. For I saw that among the rude people in the primitive times the authors of rude inventions and discoveries were consecrated and numbered among the Gods. And it was plain that the good effects wrought by founders of cities, law-givers, fathers of the people, extirpers of tyrants, and heroes of that class, extend but over narrow spaces and last but for short times; whereas the work of the Inventor, though a thing of less pomp and shew, is felt everywhere and lasts for ever. But above all, if a man could succeed, not in striking out some particular invention, however useful, but in

---

[1] [proem=preface]

kindling a light in nature—a light which should in its very rising touch and illuminate all the border-regions that confine upon the circle of our present knowledge; and so spreading further and further should presently disclose and bring into sight all that is most hidden and secret in the world,—that man (I thought) would be the benefactor indeed of the human race,—the propagator of man's empire over the universe, the champion of liberty, the conqueror and subduer of necessities.

For myself, I found that I was fitted for nothing so well as for the study of Truth; as having a mind nimble and versatile enough to catch the resemblances of things (which is the chief point), and at the same time steady enough to fix and distinguish their subtler differences; as being gifted by nature with desire to seek, patience to doubt, fondness to meditate, slowness to assert, readiness to reconsider, carefulness to dispose and set in order; and as being a man that neither affects what is new nor admires what is old, and that hates every kind of imposture. So I thought my nature had a kind of familiarity and relationship with Truth.

Nevertheless, because my birth and education had seasoned me in business of state; and because opinions (so young as I was) would sometimes stagger me; and because I thought that a man's own country has some special claims upon him more than the rest of the world; and because I hoped that, if I rose to any place of honour in the state, I should have a larger command of industry and ability to help me in my work;—for these reasons I both applied myself to acquire the arts of civil life, and commended my service, so far as in modesty and honesty I might, to the favour of such friends as had any influence. In which also I had another motive: for I felt that those things I have spoken of—be they great or small—reach no further than the condition and culture of this mortal life; and I was not without hope (the condition of Religion being at that time not very prosperous) that if I came to hold office in the state, I might get something done too for the good of men's souls.

When I found however that my zeal was mistaken for ambition, and my life had already reached the turning-point, and my breaking health reminded me how ill I could afford to be so slow, and I reflected moreover that in leaving undone the good that I could do by myself alone, and applying myself to that which could not be done without the help and consent of others, I was by no means discharging the duty that lay upon me,—I put all those thoughts aside, and (in pursuance of my old determination) betook myself wholly to this work. Nor am I discouraged from it because I see signs in the times of the decline and overthrow of that knowledge and erudition which is now in use. Not that I apprehend any more barbarian invasions (unless possibly the Spanish empire should recover its strength, and having crushed other nations by arms should itself sink under its own weight): but the civil wars which may be expected, I think, (judging from certain fashions which have come in of late) to spread through many countries,—together with the malignity of sects, and those compendious artifices and devices which have crept into the place of solid erudition—seem to portend for literature and the sciences a tempest not less fatal, and one against which the Printing-office will be no effectual security. And no doubt but that fair-weather learning which is nursed by leisure, blossoms under reward and praise, which cannot withstand the shock of opinion, and is liable to be abused by tricks and quackery, will sink under such impediments as these. Far otherwise is it with that knowledge, whose dignity is maintained by works of utility and power. For the injuries therefore which should proceed from the times, I am not afraid of them; and for the injuries which proceed from men I am not concerned. For if any one charge me with seeking to be wise overmuch, I answer simply that modesty and civil respect are fit for civil matters; in contemplations nothing is to be respected but Truth. If any one call on me for *works*, and that presently; I tell him frankly, without any imposture at all, that for me—a man not old, of weak health, my hands full of civil business, entering without guide or light upon an argument of all others the most obscure,—I hold it enough to have constructed the machine, though I may not succeed in setting it on work. Nay with the same candour I profess and declare, that the Interpretation of Nature, rightly conducted, ought in the first steps of the ascent, until a certain stage of Generals be reached, to be kept clear of all application to Works. And this has in fact been the error of all those who have heretofore ventured themselves at all upon the waves of experience—that being either too weak of purpose or too eager for display, they have all at the outset sought prematurely for works, as proofs and pledges of their progress, and upon that rock have been wrecked and cast away. If again any one ask me, not indeed for actual works, yet for definite promises and forecasts of the works that are to be, I would have him know that the knowledge which we now possess will not teach a man even what to *wish*. Lastly—though this is a matter of less moment—if any of our politicians, who use to make their calculations and conjectures according to persons and precedents, must needs interpose his judgment in a thing of this nature,—I would but remind him how (according to the ancient fable) the lame man keeping the course won the race of the swift man who left it: and that there is no thought to be taken about precedents, for the thing is without precedent.

Now for my plan of publication—those parts of the work which have it for their object to find out and bring into correspondence such minds as are prepared and disposed for the argument, and to purge the floors of men's understandings, I wish to be published to the world and circulate from mouth to mouth: the rest I would have passed from hand to hand, with selection and judgment. Not but I know that it is an old trick of impostors to keep a few of their follies back from the public which are indeed no better than those they put forward: but in this case it is no imposture at all, but a sober foresight, which tells me that the formula itself of interpretation, and the discoveries made by the same, will thrive better if committed to the charge of some fit and selected minds, and kept private. This however is other people's concern. For myself, my heart is not set upon any of those things which depend upon external accidents. I am not hunting for fame: I have no desire to found a sect, after the fashion of heresiarchs; and to look for any private gain from such an undertaking as this, I count both ridiculous and base. Enough for me the consciousness of well-deserving, and those real and effectual results with which Fortune itself cannot interfere.

De Augmentis scientiarum
Book II, Chapters 1-12

CHAPTER I.

The Division of all Human Learning into History, Poesy, Philosophy;
with reference to the three Intellectual Faculties,—Memory, Imagination, *and* Reason; *and that the same division holds good likewise in*
Theology.

The best division of human learning is that derived from the
three faculties of the rational soul, which is the seat of learning.
History has reference to the Memory, poesy to the Imagination,
and philosophy to the Reason. And by poesy here I mean nothing
else than feigned history or fables; for verse is but a character of
style, and belongs to the arts of speech, whereof I will treat in its
proper place.

History is properly concerned with individuals, which are
circumscribed by place and time. For though Natural History may
seem to deal with species, yet this is only because of the general
resemblance which in most cases natural objects of the same
species bear to one another; so that when you know one, you

know all. And if individuals are found, which are either unique in their species, like the sun and moon; or notable deviations from their species, like monsters; the description of these has as fit a place in Natural History as that of remarkable men has in Civil History. All this relates to the Memory.

Poesy, in the sense in which I have defined the word, is also concerned with individuals; that is, with individuals invented in imitation of those which are the subject of true history; yet with this difference, that it commonly exceeds the measure of nature, joining at pleasure things which in nature would never have come together, and introducing things which in nature would never have come to pass; just as Painting likewise does. This is the work of Imagination.

Philosophy discards individuals; neither does it deal with the impressions immediately received from them, but with abstract notions derived from these impressions; in the composition and division whereof according to the law of nature and fact its business lies. And this is the office and work of Reason.

That these things are so, may be easily seen by observing the commencements of the intellectual process. The sense, which is the door of the intellect, is affected by individuals only. The images of those individuals—that is, the impressions which they make on the sense—fix themselves in the memory, and pass into it in the first instance entire as it were, just as they come. These the human mind proceeds to review and ruminate; and thereupon either simply rehearses them, or makes fanciful imitations of them, or analyses and classifies them. Wherefore from these three fountains, Memory, Imagination, and Reason, flow these three emanations, History, Poesy, and Philosophy; and there can be no others. For I consider history and experience to be the same thing, as also philosophy and the sciences.

Nor do I think that any other division is wanted for Theology. The information derived from revelation and the information derived from the sense differ no doubt both in the matter and in the manner of conveyance; but the human mind is the same, and its repositories and cells the same. It is only like different liquids poured through different funnels into one and the same vessel.

Theology therefore in like manner consists either of Sacred History, or of Parables, which are a divine poesy, or of Doctrines and Precepts, which are a perennial philosophy. For as for that part which seems supernumerary, which is Prophecy, it is but a kind of history: for divine history has this prerogative over human, that the narration may be before the event, as well as after.

CHAPTER II.

The Division of History into Natural *and* Civil; Ecclesiastical *and* Literary *History being included in Civil. Division of Natural History into* History of Generations, Pretergenerations, *and* Arts.

History is either Natural or Civil. Natural History treats of the deeds and works of nature; Civil History of those of men. Matter of Divinity shows itself no doubt in both, but principally in the latter; so much so as to form a species of history proper to itself, which I call Sacred or Ecclesiastical. And a similar distinction is in my opinion also due to Learning and the Arts—their importance being such as to entitle them to a separate history of their own. And this (as well as the Ecclesiastical) I mean to be included in Civil History.

The division which I will make of Natural History is founded upon the state and condition of nature herself. For I find nature in three different states, and subject to three different conditions of existence. She is either free, and follows her ordinary course of development; as in the heavens, in the animal and vegetable creation, and in the general array of the universe; or she is driven out of her ordinary course by the perverseness, insolence, and frowardness of matter, and violence of impediments; as in the case of monsters; or lastly, she is put in constraint, moulded, and made as it were new by art and the hand of man; as in things artificial. Let Natural History therefore be divided into the History of Generations, of Pretergenerations, and of Arts; which last I also call Mechanical and Experimental History. Of these the first treats of the Freedom of Nature, the second of her Errors, the third of her

Bonds. And I am the more induced to set down the History of the Arts as a species of Natural History, because an opinion has long been prevalent, that art is something different from nature, and things artificial different from things natural; whence this evil has arisen,—that most writers of Natural History think they have done enough when they have given an account of animals or plants or minerals, omitting all mention of the experiments of mechanical arts. But there is likewise another and more subtle error which has crept into the human mind; namely, that of considering art as merely an assistant to nature, having the power indeed to finish what nature has begun, to correct her when lapsing into error, or to set her free when in bondage, but by no means to change, transmute, or fundamentally alter nature. And this has bred a premature despair in human enterprises. Whereas men ought on the contrary to be surely persuaded of this; that the artificial does not differ from the natural in form or essence, but only in the efficient; in that man has no power over nature except that of motion; he can put natural bodies together, and he can separate them; and therefore that wherever the case admits of the uniting or disuniting of natural bodies, by joining (as they say) actives with passives, man can do everything; where the case does not admit this, he can do nothing. Nor matters it, provided things are put in the way to produce an effect, whether it be done by human means or otherwise. Gold is sometimes refined in the fire and sometimes found pure in the sands, nature having done the work for herself. So also the rainbow is made in the sky out of a dripping cloud; it is also made here below with a jet of water. Still therefore it is nature which governs everything; but under nature are included these three; the *course* of nature, the *wanderings* of nature, and *art*, or nature with man to help; which three must therefore all be included in Natural History; as indeed they are in great measure by Pliny, the only person who ever undertook a Natural History according to the dignity of it; though he was far from carrying out his undertaking in a manner worthy of the conception.

The first of these, the history of nature in course, is extant, and that in moderate perfection; but the two latter are so weakly and unprofitably handled that they may be set down as deficient. For you will find no sufficient and competent collection of those works of nature which have a digression and deflexion from the ordinary course of generations, productions, and motions; whether they be singularities of place and region, or the strange events of time, or *casuum ingenia* (as they have been called)— devices of chance, or the effects of hidden properties, or productions of nature singular in their kind. It is true, I find books more than enough filled with fabulous experiments, idle secrets, and frivolous impostures, for pleasure and novelty; but a substantial and methodical collection of the Heteroclites or Irregulars of nature well examined and described I find not; especially not with due rejection and as it were public proscription of fables and popular errors. For as things now are, if an untruth in nature once get a footing and be made common, what by reason of men's reverence for antiquity, what by reason of the troublesomeness of putting it to the test anew, and what by reason of the use of the opinion in similitudes and ornaments of speech, it is never overthrown or retracted.

The end of this work, honoured with a precedent in Aristotle, is nothing less than to gratify the appetite of curious and vain wits, as the manner of mirabilaries is to do; but for two reasons, both of great weight; the one to correct the partiality of axioms and opinions, which are framed for the most part upon common and familiar examples; the other, because from the wonders of nature is the most clear and open passage to the wonders of art. For you have but to follow and as it were hound nature in her wanderings, and you will be able, when you like, to lead and drive her afterwards to the same place again. Neither am I of opinion in this history of marvels, that superstitious narratives of sorceries, witchcrafts, charms, dreams, divinations, and the like, where there is an assurance and clear evidence of the fact, should be altogether excluded. For it is not yet known in what cases, and how far, effects attributed to superstition participate of natural causes; and therefore howsoever the use and practice of such arts is to be condemned, yet from the speculation and consideration of them (if they be diligently unravelled) a useful light may be gained, not only for the true judgment of the offences of persons charged with such practices, but likewise for the further disclosing of the secrets of nature. Neither ought a man to make scruple of entering and penetrating into these holes and corners, when the inquisition of truth is his sole object,—as your Majesty has shown in your own example; who, with the two clear and acute eyes of religion and natural philosophy, have looked deeply and wisely into those shadows, and yet proved yourself to be truly of the nature of the sun, which passes through pollutions and is not defiled. I would recommend however that those narrations which are tinctured with superstition be sorted by themselves, and not mingled with those which are purely and sincerely natural. But as for narrations touching the prodigies and miracles of religions, they are either not true or not natural; and therefore impertinent for the story of nature.

For History of Nature Wrought, or Mechanical, as I also call it, I find some collections made of agriculture and likewise of many manual arts; but always (which is a great detriment in this kind of learning) with a neglect and rejection of experiments familiar and vulgar [mean, low, or common]; which yet in the interpretation of nature are of equal, if not of more value than those which are less common. For it is esteemed a kind of dishonour upon learning for learned men to descend to inquiry or meditation upon matters mechanical; except they be such as may be thought secrets of art, or rarities and special subtleties. Which humour of vain and supercilious arrogancy is justly derided in Plato, where he brings in Hippias, a vaunting Sophist, disputing with Socrates, a true and unfeigned inquisitor of truth; where, the discourse being touching beauty, Socrates, after his loose and wandering manner of inductions, put first an example of a fair virgin, then of a fair horse, then of a fair pot well glazed. Whereat Hippias was offended, and said, "Were it not for courtesy's sake, I should be loth to dispute with one that did allege such base and sordid instances." Whereunto Socrates answered, "You have reason, and it becomes you well, being a man so trim in your vestments, and so fairly shod;" and so goes on in irony. But the truth is, that they are not the highest instances, which give the best or securest information; as is expressed not inelegantly in the common story of the philosopher, who, while he gazed upwards to the stars, fell into the water; for if he had looked down he might have seen the stars in the water, but looking aloft he could not see the water in the stars. So it often comes to pass that mean and small things discover great better than great can discover small, and therefore it was well observed by Aristotle "that the nature of everything is best seen in its smallest portions." For which cause he inquires the nature of a commonwealth first in a family and the simplest con-jugations of society—(man and wife, parent and child, master and servant)—which are present in every cottage. Even so likewise the nature of this great city of the world, and the policy thereof, must be first sought in its primary concordances, and smallest portions; as we see that that secret of nature (esteemed one of the great mysteries) of the turning of iron touched with the loadstone towards the north, was found out not in bars of iron but in needles.

But if my judgment be of any weight, the use of History Mechanical is, of all others, the most radical and fundamental towards natural philosophy; such natural philosophy I mean as shall not vanish in the fumes of subtle or sublime speculations, but such as shall be operative to relieve the inconveniences of man's estate. For it will not only be of immediate benefit, by connecting and transferring the observations of one art to the use of others, and thereby discovering new commodities; a result which must needs follow when the experience of different arts shall fall under the observation and consideration of one man's mind; but further, it will give a more true and real illumination concerning the investigation of causes of things and axioms of arts, than has hitherto shone upon mankind. For like as a man's disposition is never well known or proved till he be crossed, nor Proteus ever changed shapes till he was straitened and held fast; so nature exhibits herself more clearly under the trials and vex-ations of art than when left to herself.

Before I dismiss this part of Natural History (which I call mechanical and experimental) I must add that the body of this kind of history should not be made up from the mechanical arts alone, but also from the operative part of the liberal sciences, as well as from many other practices which have not as yet grown up into arts; so as to omit nothing which may tend to inform the intellect. And this is the first division of Natural History.

CHAPTER III.

The Second Division of Natural History, according to its Use and End, into Narrative *and* Inductive; *and that the noblest end of Natural History is to minister and be in order for the Foundation of Philosophy; which is the end aimed at in* Induction. *The Division of the History of Generations into the History of the* Heavenly Bodies, *the History of* Meteors, *the History of the* Globe *of Earth and Sea, the History of the* Masses *or* Greater Colleges, *and the History of the* Species *or* Lesser Colleges.

Natural History, which is threefold (as I said) in subject, is in use twofold. For it is used either for the sake of the knowledge of the things themselves that are committed to the history, or as the primary matter of philosophy. Now the first kind, which aims either to please by the agreeableness of the narrative or to help by the use of experiments, and is pursued for the sake of such pleasure or such profit, I account as far inferior in importance to that which is the stuff and material of a solid and lawful Induction, and may be called the nursing-mother of philosophy. Accordingly I shall now make a second division of Natural History into Narrative and Inductive; the latter whereof I set down as wanting. But let not any one be dazzled either by the great names of ancient philosophers or the great volumes of modern. For I well know that a natural history is extant, large in its bulk, pleasing in its variety, curious often in its diligence; but yet weed it of fables, antiquities, quotations, idle controversies, philology and ornaments (which are more fitted for table talk and the *noctes* of learned men than for the instauration of philosophy), and it will shrink into a small compass. Certainly it is very different from that kind of history which I have in view. For in the first place there are wanting those two parts of natural history which I have just mentioned, Pretergenerations and Arts, of which I make great account; and next, in the third and remaining part, that of Generations, only one out of five parts is sufficiently handled. For the history of Generations is composed of five subordinate parts. First, a history of the *Celestial Bodies*, exhibiting the actual phenomena simply and apart from theories. Second, a history of *Meteors* (including comets), and what they call the *Regions of the Air*; for there is no history of comets, fiery meteors, winds, rains, storms, and the like, which is of any value. Third, a history of the *Earth and Sea* (considered as integral parts of the universe), mountains, rivers, tides, sands, woods, islands, and the shapes of continents as they lie; in all these, inquiring and observing rather the laws of nature than cosmography. Fourth, a history of the *Common Masses of Matter*, which I call the *Greater Colleges* (commonly called the *Elements*); for I find there are no accounts of fire, air, earth, and water, with their natures, motions, operations, and impressions, such as to form a just body of history. Fifth and last, a history of the *Exquisite Collections of Matter*, which I call the *Lesser Colleges*, but which are generally called *Species*. Now it is only in this last that writers have shown any conspicuous industry; and yet in such sort that they have rather filled it with things superfluous (as figures of animals, plants, and the like), than enriched it with sound and careful observations, which should ever be annexed to natural history. And in a word all the natural history we have, whether in the mode of inquiry or in the matter collected, is quite unfit for the end which I have mentioned, namely, the Foundation of Philosophy. Wherefore I set down Inductive History as wanting. And so much for Natural History.

CHAPTER IV.

The Division of Civil History into Ecclesiastical, Literary, *and* Civil *(which retains the name of the Genus) and that the History of* Literature *is wanting. Precepts for the Construction of it.*

Civil History may rightly be divided into three species. First, *Sacred* or *Ecclesiastical*; next, that which we call *Civil History* (using the generic name specially); lastly, the History of *Learning* and *the Arts*. I will begin with the kind last-mentioned; for the two former are extant, while the latter—the History of Learning—(without which the history of the world seems to me as the statue

of Polyphemus without the eye; that very feature being left out
which most marks the spirit and life of the person), I set down as
wanting. Not but I know that in the particular sciences of the
jurisconsults, mathematicians, rhetoricians, philosophers, we have
some slight mention or some barren narrations about the sects,
schools, books, authors, and successions belonging to them; also
that there exist some meagre and unprofitable memoirs of the inventors of arts and usages; but I say that a complete and universal
History of Learning is yet wanting. Of this therefore I will now
proceed to set forth the argument, the method of construction,
and the use.

The *argument* is no other than to inquire and collect out of
the records of all time what particular kinds of learning and arts
have flourished in what ages and regions of the world; their antiquities, their progresses, their migrations (for sciences migrate
like nations) over the different parts of the globe; and again their
decays, disappearances, and revivals. The occasion and origin of
the invention of each art should likewise be observed; the manner
and system of transmission, and the plan and order of study and
practice. To these should be added a history of the sects, and the
principal controversies in which learned men have been engaged,
the calumnies to which they have been exposed, the praises and
honours by which they have been rewarded; an account of the
principal authors, books, schools, successions, academies, socie-
ties, colleges, orders,—in a word, everything which relates to the
state of learning. Above all things (for this is the ornament and
life of Civil History), I wish events to be coupled with their causes.
I mean, that an account should be given of the characters of the
several regions and peoples; their natural disposition, whether apt
and suited for the study of learning, or unfitted and indifferent to
it; the accidents of the times, whether adverse or propitious to
science; the emulations and infusions of different religions; the
enmity or partiality of laws; the eminent virtues and services of
individual persons in the promotion of learning, and the like. Now
all this I would have handled in a historical way, not wasting time,
after the manner of critics, in praise and blame, but simply narra-
ting the fact historically, with but slight intermixture of private
judgment.

For the *manner* of compiling such a history I particularly advise that the matter and provision of it be not drawn from histories and commentaries alone; but that the principal books written in each century, or perhaps in shorter periods, proceeding in regular order from the earliest ages, be themselves taken into consultation; that so (I do not say by a complete perusal, for that would be an endless labour, but) by tasting them here and there, and observing their argument, style, and method, the Literary Spirit of each age may be charmed as it were from the dead.

With regard to the *use* of the work, it is not so much to swell the honour and pomp of learning with a profusion of images; nor because out of my exceeding love for learning I wish the inquiry, knowledge, and preservation of everything that relates thereto to be pursued even to curiosity; but chiefly for a purpose more serious and important; which, in a word, is this: I consider that such a history as I have described, would very greatly assist the wisdom and skill of learned men in the use and administration of learning; that it would exhibit the movements and perturbations, the virtues and vices, which take place no less in intellectual than in civil matters; and that from the observation of these the best system of government might be derived and established. For the works of St. Ambrose or St. Augustine will not make so wise a bishop or divine as a diligent examination and study of Ecclesiastical History; and the History of Learning would be of like service to learned men. For everything is subject to chance and error which is not supported by examples and experience. And so much for the History of Learning.

CHAPTER V.

On the Dignity and Difficulty of Civil History.

I come next to *Civil History,* properly so called, whereof the dignity and authority are pre-eminent among human writings. For to its fidelity are entrusted the examples of our ancestors, the vicissitudes of things, the foundations of civil policy, and the name and reputation of men. But the difficulty is no less than the dignity. For to carry the mind in writing back into the past, and

bring it into sympathy with antiquity; diligently to examine,
freely and faithfully to report, and by the light of words to place
as it were before the eyes, the revolutions of times, the characters
of persons, the fluctuations of counsels, the courses and currents
of actions, the bottoms of pretences, and the secrets of governments; is a task of great labour and judgment—the rather because
in ancient transactions the truth is difficult to ascertain, and in
modern it is dangerous to tell. Hence Civil History is beset on all
sides with faults; some (and these are the greater part) write only
barren and commonplace narratives, a very reproach to history;
others hastily and disorderly string together a few particular relations and trifling memoirs; others merely run over the heads of
events: others, on the contrary, go into all the minutest particularities, and such as have no relation to the main action; some indulge
their imaginations in bold inventions; while others impress on
their works the image not so much of their minds as of their passions, ever thinking of their party, but no good witnesses as to
facts; some are always inculcating their favourite political doctrines, and idly interrupting the narrative by going out of the way
to display them; others are injudiciously prolix in reporting orations and harangues, and even in relating the actions themselves;
so that, among all the writings of men, there is nothing rarer than
a true and perfect Civil History. But my present purpose in this
division of learning is to mark omissions, and not to censure
faults. I will now pursue the divisions of Civil History, and those
of the different kinds; for the species will be exhibited more clearly
under several heads, than under one head curiously traced
through all its members.

CHAPTER VI.

The First Division of Civil History into Memorials, Antiquities, *and*
Perfect History.

Civil History is of three kinds, not unfitly to be compared with
the three kinds of pictures or images. For of pictures and images
we see some are unfinished, and wanting the last touch; some are

perfect; and some are mutilated and defaced by age. So Civil History (which is a kind of image of events and times) may be divided into three kinds, corresponding to these,—*Memorials, Perfect History,* and *Antiquities.* For Memorials are history unfinished, or the first rough draughts of history; and Antiquities are history defaced, or remnants of history which have casually escaped the shipwreck of time.

Memorials, or Preparatory History, are of two sorts, whereof the one may be termed *Commentaries,* the other *Registers.* Commentaries set down a bare continuance and tissue of actions and events without the causes and pretexts, the commencements and occasions, the counsels and orations, and other passages of action. For this is the true nature of a commentary, though Caesar, in modesty mixed with greatness, chose to apply the name of a commentary to the best history extant. But Registers have a twofold character; for they either contain titles of things and persons in order of time, such as are called Annals and Chronologies; or collections of public acts, such as edicts of princes, decrees of councils, judicial proceedings, public speeches, letters of state, and the like, without a perfect continuance or contexture of the thread of the narration.

Antiquities, or remnants of histories, are (as was said) like the spars of a shipwreck; when, though the memory of things be decayed and almost lost, yet acute and industrious persons, by a certain persevering and scrupulous diligence, contrive out of genealogies, annals, titles, monuments, coins, proper names and styles, etymologies of words, proverbs, traditions, archives and instruments as well public as private, fragments of histories scattered about in books not historical,—contrive, I say, from all these things or some of them, to recover somewhat from the deluge of time: a work laborious indeed, but agreeable to men, and joined with a kind of reverence; and well worthy to supersede the fabulous accounts of the origins of nations, and to be substituted for fictions of that kind; entitled however to the less authority, because in things which few people concern themselves about, the few have it their own way.

In these kinds of Imperfect History I think no deficiency is

to be assigned; for they are things, as it were, imperfectly compounded, and therefore any deficiency in them is but their nature.
As for epitomes (which are certainly the corruptions and moths
of histories) I would have them banished, whereto likewise most
men of sound judgment agree, as being things that have fretted
and corroded the bodies of many most excellent histories, and
wrought them into base and unprofitable dregs.

CHAPTER VII.

The Division of Perfect History into Chronicles, Lives, *and* Relations;
and the Explanation thereof.

But *Perfect History* is of three kinds, according to the object which
it propounds for representation. For it either represents a portion
of time, or a person worthy of mention, or an action or exploit of
the nobler sort. The first we call Chronicles or Annals; the second,
Lives; the third, Narrations or Relations. Of these the first excels
in estimation and glory; the second, in profit and examples; and
the third in verity and sincerity. For History of Times represents
the magnitude of public actions, and the public faces and deportments of persons, but omits and covers up in silence the smaller
passages and motions of men and matters. But such being the
workmanship of God, that he hangs the greatest weights upon
the smallest wires, it comes commonly to pass that such a history,
pursuing the greater things alone, rather sets forth the pomp and
solemnity of business than the true and inward springs and re-
sorts thereof. Moreover, when it does add and insert the counsels
and motives, yet from its love of grandeur it introduces into human actions more gravity and prudence than they really have; so
that a truer picture of human life may be found in a satire than in
some histories of this kind. Whereas Lives, if they be well and
carefully written (for I do not speak of elogies and barren commemorations of that sort), propounding to themselves a single
person as their subject, in whom actions both trifling and important, great and small, public and private, must needs be united

and mingled, certainly contain a more lively and faithful representation of things, and one which you may more safely and happily take for example in another case. But special Narrations and Relations of actions (as the Peloponnesian War, the Expedition of Cyrus, the Conspiracy of Catiline, and the like) cannot but be more purely and exactly true than the Perfect Histories of Times; because they may choose a manageable and definite argument, whereof a perfect knowledge and certainty and full information may be had; whereas the story of a time (especially if it be of a period much before the age of the writer) is sure to meet with many gaps in the records, and to contain empty spaces which must be filled up and supplied at pleasure by wit and conjecture. But this which I say touching the sincerity of Relations, must be taken with reservation; for (seeing that everything human is subject to imperfection, and good is almost always associated with evil) it must certainly be confessed that relations of this kind, especially if published near the time of the actions themselves (being commonly written either in favour or in spite), are of all other histories the most to be suspected. But then again the evil carries this remedy along with it; that as these very relations are commonly put forth not by one side only, but by both, according to their several factions and parties, a way may be found to truth between the extremes on either hand; and after party heat has cooled down, a good and prudent historian will obtain from them no bad materials and provision for a more perfect history.

With regard to the deficiencies of these three kinds of history, it is certain that there are many particular histories (I speak of such as may be of some moderate worth and dignity) which have been hitherto neglected, with the greatest detriment to the honour and name of the kings and states to which they belong; though to mention them would take too much time. But leaving the care of foreign stories to foreign states (for I will not be a meddler in other nations' matters), I cannot fail to represent to your Majesty the unworthiness of the history of England as we now have it, in the main continuance thereof, and the partiality and obliquity of that of Scotland, in the latest and largest author that I have seen; supposing that it would be honour for your Majesty, and a work very acceptable to future ages, if this island of Great Britain, as it is now joined in one monarchy for the ages to come, so were joined in one history for the ages past; after the manner of the Sacred History, which draws down the story of the ten tribes and of the two tribes as twins together. And if it shall seem that the greatness of this work (and great and difficult it is) may prevent it from being exactly and worthily performed, there is a memorable period of a much smaller compass of time, as to the history of England; that is to say, from the Union of the Roses to the Union of the Kingdoms; a portion of time wherein to my understanding there has been a greater variety of strange events than in like number of successions of any hereditary monarchy has ever been known. For it begins with the mixed obtaining of a crown, partly by arms, partly by title; an entry by battle, an establishment by marriage; and therefore times corresponding to these beginnings, like waters after a tempest, full of working and swelling, though without extremity of storm; but well passed through by the wisdom of the pilot, who was the most conspicuous for policy of all the kings who preceded him. Then follows the reign of a king whose actions, though conducted more by impulse than policy, exercised no slight influence over the affairs of Europe; balancing and inclining them variably. In whose reign also begun that great alteration in the State Ecclesiastical, an action which seldom comes upon the stage. Then the reign of a minor. Then an attempt at a usurpation, though it was but as a diary [lasting for one day] ague. Then the reign of a queen matched with a foreigner; then of a queen that lived solitary and unmarried. And now, last, this most happy and glorious event, that this island of Britain, divided from all the world, should be united in itself, and that old oracle given to Aeneas (Antiquam exquirite matrem[1]), which fore-showed the rest in store for him, should now be performed and fulfilled upon the most renowned nations of England and Scotland; being now reunited in the ancient mother name of Britain, as a pledge and token of the end and period of all instability and peregrinations; so that as it comes to pass in massive bodies, that they have certain trepidations and waverings before they fix and

[1] Seek out your ancient mother. Virg. Aen. iii. 96.

settle; so it seems to have been ordained by the providence of God that this monarchy, before it settled and was confirmed in your Majesty and your royal generations (in which I hope it is now established for ever), should undergo these prelusive [preliminary] changes and varieties.

For Lives, I find it strange, when I think of it, that these our times have so little esteemed their own virtues, as that the commemoration and writing of the lives of those who have adorned our age should be no more frequent. For although there be but few sovereign kings or absolute commanders, and not many princes in free states (so many free states being now turned into monarchies), yet are there many worthy personages (even living under kings) that deserve better than dispersed report or dry and barren eulogy. For herein the invention of one of the later poets, by which he has enriched the ancient fiction, is not inelegant. He feigns that at the end of the thread or web of every man's life there hangs a little medal or collar, on which his name is stamped; and that Time waits upon the shears of Atropos, and as soon as the thread is cut, snatches the medals, carries them off, and presently throws them into the river Lethe; and about the river there are many birds flying up and down, who catch the medals, and after carrying them round and round in their beak a little while, let them fall into the river; only there are a few swans, which if they get a medal with a name immediately carry it off to a temple consecrated to immortality.[2] Now this kind of swan is for the most part wanting in our age. And although there are many men, more mortal in their cares and desires than in their bodies, who regard the desire of name and memory but as a vanity and ventosity,

Animi nil magnae laudis egentes;[3]

whose philosophy and severity springs no doubt from that root "Non prius laudes contempsimus, quam laudanda facere desivi-

---

[2] Ariosto, *Orlando Furioso*, at the end of the 34th and beginning of the 35th Books.

[3] "Souls that care not for praise."—Virg. Aen. v. 751.

mus"[4]—yet that will not alter Solomon's judgment, "The memory of the just is praised, but the name of the wicked shall rot."[5] The one flourishes for ever; the other either consumes to present oblivion, or turns to an ill odour. And therefore in that style or form of words which is well appropriated to the dead—(of happy memory, of pious memory, of blessed memory),—we seem to acknowledge that which Cicero says (having borrowed it from Demosthenes), "That good fame is the only possession a dead man has;"[6] which possession I cannot but note that in our times it lies in most part waste and neglected.

For *Narrations* and *Relations,* a greater diligence therein is also much to be wished; for there is hardly any great action which is not attended by some good pen that can describe it. And because it is an ability not common to write a perfect history as it ought to be written (as may well appear from the small number even of moderate historians), yet if particular actions were but tolerably reported as they pass, it might be expected that a writer would some time or other arise who by such help and assistance might compile a complete History of Times. For the collection of such Relations would be as a nursery, whereby to plant a fair and stately garden when time should serve.

CHAPTER VIII.

The Division of the History of Times into History Universal *and* Particular—*their Advantages and Disadvantages.*

History of Times is either Universal or Particular; whereof the latter contains the deeds of some kingdom, commonwealth, or people; the former those of the whole world. For there have been those who have affected to write the history of the world from its very beginning; exhibiting by way of history a medley of things and abridgments of narratives. Others have attempted to com-

---

[4] "When we have ceased to do things deserving of praise we find that praise is an idle thing."—Plin. Ep. iii. 91.

[5] Prov. x. 7.

[6] Cf. Cicero, Philipp. ix, and Demos. λογ. επιταφ., 1389, 10.

price, as in a perfect history, the memorable events of their own
age all over the world; with noble enterprise, and no small result.
For the affairs of men are not so far separated by the divisions of
empires or countries, but they have a connexion in many things;
and therefore it is certainly of use to have the fates, acts, and des-
tinies of one age described and contained as it were on one tablet.
It is true also that many writings of no contemptible character
(such as are those Relations of which I previously spoke), which
would otherwise perish and not be reprinted,—that these, or at
all events the principal matters in them, find a place in a general
history of this kind, and in this way are fixed and preserved. But
if due attention be paid to the subject, it will be found that the
laws of regular history are so strict, that they can scarce be observed in such a wide field of matter; so that the dignity of history
is rather diminished than increased by the greatness of the mass
of it. For the writer who has such a variety of things on all sides
to attend to, will become gradually less scrupulous on the point
of information; his diligence, grasping at so many subjects, will
slacken in each; he will take up with rumours and popular reports,
and thus construct his history from relations which are not au-
thentic, or other frivolous materials of the kind. He will be obliged
moreover (lest the work increase beyond measure) purposely to
omit a number of things worthy of record, and often to sink into
abridgments. He is liable likewise to another danger, not small,
and diametrically opposed to the very utility which belongs to
Universal History; for as Universal History preserves some narrations which would perhaps otherwise perish, so on the other hand
it destroys many that are profitable enough in themselves and
would otherwise live, for the sake of that compendious brevity
of which men are so fond.

CHAPTER IX.

Another Division of the History of Times into Annals *and* Journals.

The History of Times is also rightly divided into *Annals* and
Journals; which division, though it takes its name from periods
of time, yet has also reference to the choice of subjects. For it is

well observed by Cornelius Tacitus, after touching upon the magnificence of certain buildings, "That it was found suitable to the
dignity of the Roman people to commit to Annals only matters of
note, but such things as these to the Journals of the City;"[1] thus
referring matters concerning the state to Annals, but the less important kind of actions or accidents to Journals. Certainly, in my
judgment, there ought to be a kind of heraldry in arranging the
precedence of books, no less than of persons. For as nothing
derogates from the dignity of a state more than confusion of ranks
and degrees, so it not a little embases the authority of a history to
intermingle matters of lighter moment, such as triumphs, ceremonies, spectacles, and the like, with matters of state. And surely
it were to be wished that this distinction came into fashion. But
in our times journals are only used in sea-voyages and expeditions
of war; whereas in ancient times it was a matter of honour with
princes to keep journals of what passed day by day in their courts;
as we see in the case of Ahasuerus, King of Persia, who, when he
could not take rest, called for the Chronicles, where he read over
again the account of the conspiracy of the Eunuchs.[2] But the journals of Alexander's house expressed every small particularity, so
that even if he happened to sleep at table it was registered.[3] Not
that, as none but grave matters were included in the Annals, so
none but trifling ones were admitted into Journals; but everything, whether of greater or less concern, was promiscuously
entered in the Journals as it passed.

CHAPTER X.

The Second Division of Civil History into Pure *and* Mixed.

The last division of Civil History is into *Pure* and *Mixed.* Of the
Mixed there are two principal kinds; the one taken from Civil
Science, the other principally from Natural. For some men have

[1] Tac. Ann. xiii. 31.
[2] Esther, vi. 1.
[3] Plut. Symp. i. 6.

introduced a form of writing consisting of certain narratives not woven into a continuous history, but separate and selected according to the pleasure of the author; which he afterwards reviews, and as it were ruminates over, and takes occasion from them to make politic discourse and observation. Now this kind of Ruminated History I greatly approve, provided that the writer keep to it and profess it. But for a man who is professedly writing a Perfect History to be everywhere introducing political reflexions, and thereby interrupting the narrative, is unseasonable and wearisome. For though every wise history is pregnant (as it were) with political precepts and warnings, yet the writer himself should not play the midwife.

Another kind of Mixed History is the History of Cosmography; which is indeed mixed of many things; of Natural History, in respect of the regions themselves, their sites and products; of History Civil, in respect of the habitations, governments, and manners of the people; and of Mathematics, in respect of the climates and configurations of the heavens, beneath which the regions of the world lie. In which kind of history or science we may congratulate our own age. For this great building of the world has in our age been wonderfully opened and thorough-lighted; and though the ancients had knowledge of the zones and the antipodes,

> Nosque ubi primus equis oriens afflavit anhelis,
> Illic sera rubens accendit lumina Vesper,[1]

yet that might be by demonstration rather than by travel. But for a little vessel to emulate the heaven itself, and to circle the whole earth with a course even more oblique and winding than that of the heavenly bodies, is the privilege of our age; so that these times may justly bear in their motto not only *plus ultra*—further yet—in precedence of the ancient *non ultra*—no further;

[1] And while on us the early morning breathes
With panting horses, there the blushing eve
Lights up her tardy signals.

and "Imitable Thunder" in precedence of the ancient "Inimitable Thunder,"

> (Demens qui nimbos, et non imitabile fulmen, &c.)[2]

but likewise, that which exceeds all admiration, "Imitable Heaven," in respect of our sea-voyages, by which the whole globe of earth has, after the manner of the heavenly bodies, been many times compassed and circumnavigated.

And this proficience in navigation and discovery may plant also great expectation of the further proficience and augmentation of the sciences; especially as it may seem that these two are ordained by God to be coevals, that is, to meet in one age. For so the Prophet Daniel, in speaking of the latter times, foretells "That many shall go to and fro on the earth, and knowledge shall be increased,"[3] as if the opening and thorough passage of the world, and the increase of knowledge, were appointed to be in the same age; as we see it is already performed in great part; the learning of these our times, not much giving place to the two former periods or returns of learning (the one of the Grecians, the other of the Romans), but in some respects far exceeding them.

CHAPTER XI.

The Division of Ecclesiastical History into Ecclesiastical History Special, History of Prophecy, *and* History of Providence.

History Ecclesiastical receives nearly the same divisions as History Civil; for there are Ecclesiastical Chronicles, there are Lives of the Fathers, there are Relations of Synods and other things pertaining to the Church. But in itself it is properly divided into *History Ecclesiastical* (using the general name in a special sense),

[2] Virg. Aen. vi. 590.
[3] Daniel, xii. 4.

History of Prophecy, and *History of Divine Judgments or Providence.* The first describes the times of the Church Militant, and its different states; whether fluctuant, as the ark of Noah; or moveable, as the ark in the wilderness; or at rest, as the ark in the Temple; that is, the state of the Church in persecution, in remove, and in peace. In this part I find no deficiency, but rather superfluities; only I would that the virtue and sincerity of the relations were in accordance with the mass and quantity of the matter.

The second, which is History of Prophecy, consists of two relatives, the Prophecy and the Accomplishment; and therefore the plan of such a work ought to be, that every prophecy of Scripture be sorted with the event fulfilling the same, throughout all ages of the world; both for the better confirmation of faith, and for better instruction and skill in the interpretation of those parts of prophecies which are yet unfulfilled; allowing nevertheless that latitude which is agreeable and familiar to divine prophecies, that the fulfilments of them are taking place continually, and not at the particular time only. For they are of the nature of their Author, "to whom a thousand years are but as one day, and one day as a thousand years;"[1] and though the height or fulness of them is commonly referred to some one age or particular period, yet they have at the same time certain gradations and processes of accomplishment through divers ages of the world. This is a work which I find deficient, but it is one that is to be done with great wisdom, sobriety, and reverence, or not at all.

The third part, which is History of Providence, has indeed been handled by the pens of some pious writers, but not without partiality. Its business is to observe that divine correspondence which sometimes exists between God's revealed and secret will. For though the judgments and counsels of God are so obscure that to the natural man they are altogether inscrutable, yea, and many times hidden from the eyes of those that behold them from the tabernacle, yet at some times it pleases the Divine Wisdom, for the better establishment of his people and the confusion of those who are as without God in the world, to write it and report it to

[1] Psalm xc. 4., and 2 Pet. iii. 8.

view in such capital letters that (as the Prophet saith) "He that runneth by may read it;"[2] that is, that mere sensual persons and voluptuaries, who hasten by God's judgments, and never bend or fix their thoughts upon them, are nevertheless, though running fast and busy about other things, forced to discern them. Such are late and unlooked for judgments; deliverances suddenly and unexpectedly vouchsafed; divine counsels, through tortuous labyrinths and by vast circuits, at length manifestly accomplishing themselves; and the like; all which things serve not only to console the minds of the faithful, but to strike and convince the consciences of the wicked.

CHAPTER XII.

Of the Appendices to History; which deal with the Words of Men (as History itself deals with their Actions). The Division thereof into Orations, Letters, *and* Apophthegms.

But not only man's *actions,* but his *words* also should be recorded. And these are no doubt sometimes inserted in history itself, so far as they contribute to the perspicuity and weight of the narrative. But the sayings or words of men are properly preserved in books of *Speeches, Letters,* and *Apophthegms.* Certainly the Speeches of wise men on business and matters of grave and deep importance conduce greatly as well to the knowledge of the things themselves as to eloquence. But for instruction in civil prudence, still greater help is derived from Letters written by great men on weighty subjects. For of all the words of man nothing is more solid and excellent than letters of this kind; for they are more natural than orations, and more advised than conferences on the sudden. And when there is a continued series of them in order of time (as we find in the letters of ambassadors, governors of provinces, and other ministers of state, to kings, senates, and other superior officers; or, again, in the letters of

---

[2] Habakkuk, ii. 2.

rulers to their agents), they are of all others the most valuable materials for history. Neither are Apophthegms themselves only for pleasure and ornament, but also for use and action. For they are (as was said) "words which are as goads," words with an edge or point, that cut and penetrate the knots of business and affairs. Now occasions are continually returning, and what served once will serve again; whether produced as a man's own or cited as an old saying. Nor can there be any question of the utility in civil matters of that which Caesar himself thought worthy of his labour; whose book of Apophthegms I wish were extant; for all the collections which we have of this kind appear to me to have been compiled without much judgment.

And so much concerning History; which is that part of learning which answers to one of the cells, domiciles, or offices of the mind of man, which is that of the Memory.